To Barbara
Jan 28. 1993
Howard F. York

I Can't Forget:

Unusual and Humorous Recollections from the 20's to the 90's

by

Howard F. York

Published by

Howard F. York

Madeleine Bonne McGinnis, Associate Publisher

ISBN 0-9630436-0-9

Designed by Ebert Desktop Publishing

Printed in the United States of America

From an old popular song circa 1926

Memory, Memory
Where Are You Taking Me?
Back Again
Down the Lane
Of Days That Used to Be...

Encouragements

Aleene Sanders - Poplar Bluff, MO
Earl Eberhardt - St. Louis, MO
Ron Edwards - Brentwood, MO
Robert Knickmeyer - Hazelwood, MO
Les Lottman - Affton, MO
Sister Janice Meiners - St. Louis, MO
Norma Eichler - Brentwood, MO
Charles Bemis - Webster Groves, MO
Evelyn Bronner - St. Louis, MO
Shirley Uebel - St. Louis, MO
Marion Meisenbach - St. Louis, MO

A special thanks to Gene Dodel - Brentwood, MO

Contents

For My Wife, Betty

Carolyn and Steve

Noon Adventure

Sometimes, eating out alone at noon, one has an adventure. Mostly pleasant, sometimes dull, but occasionally you get to talk to a near companion and have quite a good time.

This day, I was sitting in a narrow, open, booth, eating a small size chicken dinner; a dinner I enjoyed much more than usual because the meat was dark and juicy, the slaw was sweet and chopped fine, and with mashed potatoes, bun and coffee, all to my taste, I settled down to perhaps a one-half hour before I went back to Brentwood to make some purchases before I went home.

A young father and his son, perhaps three years old, selected a booth in front of me. The father, who wore an all-over beard that was nicely trimmed, and a serious but pleasant manner, seated his son and went over to place his order for lunch. The boy, now on his own, proceeded to pour salt out of the shaker briefly, but seemed to be wary of the pepper shaker. I thought for a moment that some pepper would permeate the air and I'd hear some sneezing. The father had placed his order and came back, not seeming to notice the salt spill, sitting down to wait for his order to be filled.

I thought to myself, "That's me thirty-five or forty years ago, when I'd take Steve, my son, with me so many places and we'd eat lunch together." Steve was about that size when my wife was pregnant and I did occasional sign jobs in the evenings.

It was right after World War II and I was lettering a lot of small planes and I took Steve along with me. He was such a good boy and would sit where you placed him and caused no trouble. Like one time, as he sat under a plane, he quietly gathered all the nuts and bolts and washers and bits of metal from off the floor around him,

1

enough to fill a paper cup. I asked a mechanic about it, and he said Steve could have everything he found. Of course, Steve was overjoyed. We went out quite often, mostly on Saturdays, and at noon Steve loved to eat in the various luncheon places around the airport.

Thinking about this, as I watched the boy in front of me, caused my eyes to moisten slightly and I turned away and tried to look out the window and hold back the lump in my throat. It was hard to do. I remembered how thankful my wife was that I could make the extra money and take Steve off her hands, for now we had Carolyn, and two of them at the house was quite a handful.

The more I reminisced, the harder it got for me. I hoped the father hadn't noticed - I tried to avoid his eyes and looked down at my plate and began to eat more rapidly. My eyes were quite full and I wondered how I could tell this young father how I felt. I didn't think I could do it, but I made up my mind I would try if the opportunity came along.

I dragged out my meal and once I managed a small wave at the boy, who didn't seem to notice. I think the father surmised what I was going through but I wasn't sure. Suddenly, I looked up as the boy broke into crying as if he'd hurt himself somehow, and the father put him on his lap, comforting him just the same as I had done in the past, trying to take his mind off the hurt, and it didn't last long.

I wondered if it was another case of a divorced man taking out his son on his turn to have a weekend with him as part of the family arrangement. I hoped not; on second thought, perhaps the mother had to work on Saturdays so the father was helping out. But as I sat, pondering, trying to think in a positive way, I saw across the way, in another row like ours, another father seating himself across from his young daughter, who was about the same age as the boy. Another case, I thought, of either a divorce or maybe another father whose wife worked on a Saturday, too.

I thought about all the times I had seated Steve in the cockpits of the planes I worked on and how he never abused the privilege by tinkering. I took his picture innumerable times standing along the plane beside the sign or emblem I was painting. His face always showed how pleased he was at my skill. You can believe me, it got harder and harder to keep from breaking down and I had to wipe my nose so frequently with my paper napkin that I knew my father in the next booth had to notice.

I finished my meal and clearing up all my debris, very methodically, so I'd be composed if I had a chance to speak and tell them how wonderful it was to see myself in them, if only forty years ago, and the poignancy of it all, was my sitting there, alone at age seventy-five, with my son a thousand miles away.

I finally got enough nerve to get up and leave. I should have turned away and gone out a different way but I was impelled to go toward them and as I did, I mumbled that I used to take my boy out with me like that, but he was grown up now. Next, I got my wallet out and showed them Steve in his office in Washington, D.C. The father said, "See Steve, his boy is a big man now."

I said, "Did you say his name is Steve?"

He said, "yes" and it was too much for me. I closed my wallet and walked to the door, blindly. It was too much - I had to take out my handkerchief and blow before I got out. What a coincidence! It took a few minutes before I could see clearly enough to drive back to Brentwood.

January 30, 1988

Woodland Drama

On the back edge of our lot is a wild cherry tree. It's about fourteen inches in diameter, but its top has been badly marred by repeated line clearance operations by the various utilities, cable, electric, and telephone companies. So, a large section is dead and through the years has decayed enough to be workable for a wild thing to build a home in; like a flying squirrel or a starling or a woodpecker or a grey squirrel, of which there are quite a few in our area.

Cherry wood is a good, hard, pretty cabinet wood so it took a while for this section of the tree to get rotten enough to be worked. Rotten is not the right word, seasoned would be better.

This spring, quite a drama took place in the tree in front of me as I ate my meals, looking out the back window. A large woodpecker, we always called a flicker, started pecking out a hole in the trunk of the cherry tree, about twenty-four feet up from the ground. I think the hole had already been started a few years ago, but it seemed to be about ready to be settled in. The flicker was there every morning hammering away, making lots of wood chips that fell to the ground. The chips piled up about six inches or so against the base of the tree and every day the pile got bigger. A couple of starlings sat in the tree about three feet away watching, probably thinking, "What a neat place for this winter." Periodically the flicker would try to squeeze in to test the roominess, but it was several days before he could get in and he tried to enlarge even more. Working most of the time was a male bird and very seldom did I see the female. If he did have a mate, I only saw her once or twice. This went on for two weeks or so and occasionally the starlings would go in and out, but never deciding to take over.

One day I noticed some green leaves hanging out of the hole. Guessed the flicker was starting a nest; but using green leaves seemed odd. Of course I'd never seen a flicker build and I guessed he would use twigs or grass or leaves, but never green leafed twigs. But he wasn't around, guarding the hole all the time like I supposed he would.

Then I see what's happening! Mr. Squirrel has taken over the hole and cutting twigs that were sprouting small leaves, carrying them over and stuffing them in the hole. Twig after twig he hauled through the tree tops to the hole and poked them in, sometimes going inside and arranging them to suit himself. Sometimes he'd bring twigs twenty-four inches long, having a hard time bending them in to make them stay in.

But a funny thing happened. Next day I noticed green leafed twigs dangling down on the tree trunk, having caught on the rough bark. When I went out to see, I noticed several on the ground. It puzzled me.

The next day the flicker was back, methodically throwing out all the twigs, one by one. He worked all day doing that, but the next day the squirrel was putting more in. There was never a confrontation or skirmish between the two, or did I observe either bird or squirrel watching each other.

I thought to myself, "I should report this to the Audubon Society or write it up." It was so unusual, but as I watched all summer, the birds never came back and even the squirrel had lost interest, so the hole is waiting there, probably for the starlings to move in for winter. I had hoped to see a family of flickers or a family of young squirrels. Who knows what will happen this winter.

November, 1989

Animals are Interesting

Squirrels

A few years back on an early spring morning, I decided to have a clean up around the front of the house. I started on the front porch, which is an open porch with a concrete floor, open to the elements besides the birds, squirrels, wandering cats, etc. I happened to notice a six-inch-diameter clay flower pot; the kind that has the hole in the bottom, which I have never measured. It could be 1/2- or 3/4-inch in diameter.

After picking up odd things and putting them away, or throwing them away, I picked up the flower pot. It was upside down and lo! about 500 acorns rolled out all over the porch floor. All were the same size. It suddenly dawned on me that some industrious grey squirrel (that's the only kind we have in this neighborhood) had found itself a storehouse in the flower pot and very methodically began saving them up. He must have had a very mechanical eye to have put all the same size through the hole. I wondered, as I stood there, how was he going to get them out? Did he have intelligence to push over the pot? It was probably almost full and wouldn't be too easy to push over. Anyway, I had done it for him, and although winter was over, he probably could still eat them, so I swept them carefully into the bushes along the edge of the porch.

I never checked, as I remember, whether the squirrel came back and retrieved the acorns. I was very busy in my sign business and didn't seem to have the time to pursue nature things like I do now, since I'm retired.

I've repeated this story to friends, infrequently, and just lately thought it worth writing about. ✤

Wrens

Some time ago, in the fall, I decided it was time to clean up my wren house. I've kept one in the front of the house and one in the rear. I always hang them in the same tree on the same limb, or close to it. I'd like to have more wren houses, but somewhere I've heard that wrens are territorial birds and won't tolerate another wren in the same yard.

Anyway, I took the front house down and started to take the screws out of the bottom board, when I noticed the boy next door playing with another boy from up the street. They were about kindergarten age, and I thought they'd like to see me clean out the nest. They came over and we all sat on the porch bench. When I got the board off I took the screwdriver and began removing the twigs. About halfway through I pried out a fliptop metal piece of a soda can; the whole thing, ring and all. The boys were amazed, and me too, especially so. Who would have supposed a wren would pick up an object like that and carry it all the way to his nest. We don't use metal soda cans, so he must have carried it from a neighbor's area.

The funny part was that a year or two later I emptied the same bird house and found a piece of shiny mica, about one-inch wide and three-inches long. It was cardboard thickness and probably fallen from one of my rock bags. I've been a rock and mineral collector for almost 40 years and it probably fell in the grass somehow.

Anyway, I'll never know if it was a chickadee or a wren. If I put out the wren houses too soon in the spring the chickadees build in them first, hatch and brood and leave. The wren doesn't seem to mind adding to the old nest and starting over. ✦

Siskins

Being a retiree, I find new things to occupy my time, and about six years ago started putting bird feeders in the yard. We have placed them opposite our breakfast windows close enough to see what they're doing, but not too close. Tending is not a chore but requires regular attention to keep them filled and to have water, also, nearby. We have a larger two-gallon clear plastic feeder that usually requires filling with sunflower seeds each week. We also have plastic tube feeders with small holes for thistle seeds for the smaller birds like finches, chickadees, and pine siskins.

The siskin is a small bird about the same size as a finch, but he is marked quite different. He has a lot of brown stripes over a grey body and usually shows up when the weather gets colder or stormier or bitter, although this is not always the case. One year we had a dozen or so come for several weeks and suddenly stop.

One morning I was filling up some of the tube feeders, quietly going about my job, because some birds won't fly away if you keep your movements quiet, when I noticed a siskin quite close on a perch, only two feet away. I watched him eat and he didn't seem to be bothered by my presence. I thought to myself, "I'll bet if I move slowly, I might touch him." So I moved, very, very slowly with my arm and hand positioned in one place. I had on brown pants and jacket and a light tan hat. I moved 1/4-inch at a time and soon my hand was only an inch away so I made my move and touched his tail. He then flew away, but I definitely touched him, not even a second, but a real contact. I don't remember if I told anyone in the house, but two or three days later I was in the same area, with maybe the same siskin,

9

so I tried the same maneuver. This time I touched his tail for a full second and then he flew off. That was the end of that. I've never had the experience again, in fact, the siskins haven't been that plentiful, but if they come again, I'll try it.

The whole upshot of this episode was, when I looked up pine siskin in my Audubon bird book, the last line and one word in the book said "tame," so I wasn't so great after all.

At an Audubon Society meeting, I reported this episode to an officer and he said he'd never known anyone who had touched a siskin. Interesting? ✒

Just Ducky!

Part One

by Betty York

We live in Brentwood, and are blessed with a park-like setting for a backyard. A two hundred foot wide strip of ground behind our property extends for several unbroken blocks to either side and has been designated a public nature trail.

Our back boundary adjoins this park, and since there are no fences; visually, the park becomes an extension of our yard. There is a simulated rocky stream and a rustic bridge with a tanbark trail running for about four blocks. Brentwood Forest maintains this strip and has planted it with azaleas, rhododendron, day lilies, pink and white dogwood and red bud, to win several awards for its planning and design. Two blocks to the North is beautiful Jefferson Lake and fountain. This idyllic setting has proved to be a great attraction for wild geese and ducks and the local residents seem happy to keep the wildlife fed.

Last Spring, I noticed a pair of Mallards strolling up and down the trail, almost arm in arm. I saw them two or three days in a row, then one afternoon I saw they were snuggled down in the grass near the bottom of our yard. I was thrilled to think they'd chosen our yard as a quiet retreat, and didn't disturb them. One morning I got up early and there they were again, so I found some bread and quietly opening the door on the porch, I stepped out and began throwing bits of bread in their direction. Without hesitation, they came running and ate all I gave them. I was enchanted!

The next day they brought a friend, another female which I surmised was maybe a daughter. She appeared younger, with brighter plumage and like some kids, definitely nervier, eventually nibbling my fingers with her leatherlike bill. But I'm getting ahead of myself.

These morning feedings soon became routine. I had three ducks! (I also have two cats, but that's another story) they're domesticated Persians and these were wild things that grew more trusting everyday. I christened them Donald and Daisy and Julie.

About the third day I decided they needed some water. Daisy seemed to have trouble swallowing the dry bread. I found a large roasting pan and took it out and filled it with water. My ducks were ecstatic! They drank and drank and then all three tried to climb in and bathe at once. Running back inside I found a large basin and filled that with water too. The addition of water facilities seemed to complete the requirements for a ducky country club and they returned later in their little pans of water. It was a ridiculous sight - to say the least.

By now the loaf of bread was exhausted so I located a feed store in Kirkwood, and hastened out to buy a modest five pounds of duck food, not knowing if they'd eat it at all. Happily, they loved it.

It's surprising how these little wild things can teach you just what they'd like, if you're alert and sensitive to their needs. Daisy still seemed to have difficulty swallowing the dry food, and would take a mouth full of dry feed and then go to the pan of water and get a drink to wash it down. Of course, I thought, ducks are "dabblers" or bottom feeders and that's why you'll see them "bottoms up" while feeding in a lake or pond. Belatedly, I learned to put the dry food in their pan and cover it with an inch or so of water. I imagined I heard a sigh of relief from the three as they guzzled happily.

Twice a day they came, and their visits lasted longer and longer with each duck sitting in his or her little pan for most of the day.

As the days grew warmer, the newspapers were full of ads for kiddie wading pools. The thought did cross my mind...but then I thought, "No, that's silly!"

Two days later I found myself lugging a kiddie pool out of Target's door toward the car! The bright blue object got larger and heavier, the closer I got to the Buick, and it was immediately apparent that it would not fit in the trunk, and when I opened the rear door, it seemed twice the size of the opening. Not easily deterred, and spurred on by the thought of those poor ducks in their little pans, I wrestled the pool into the back seat. I hoped the fold that I had put in the middle was temporary and that the plastic was somehow endowed with a memory of what it was supposed to look like once I got it home. It was hard driving with the pool bent over my head and without the use of a rear view window. Fortunately, Brentwood is not that far from Kirkwood and I made the trip safely. It's hard being a duck Mother!

I hadn't mentioned a pool to Howard, but I told him what I'd done and would he please extricate it from the back seat of the car? This proved to be no small feat and Howard was incredulous as to how I had managed to cram it into the car by myself. I muttered something and pushed while he pulled. Finally it emerged and wonder of wonders, resumed its original round shape. A miracle - and all for seven dollars! We rolled it around to the back yard and filled it with water. This incredible spot of sparkling blue did add something to the landscape and I thought if the ducks decided not to use it - I would! Long suffering Howard may have had some reservations about installing a pool for a couple of ducks but said nothing.

Later that afternoon, here came the procession. Donald led the way, followed by Daisy and Julie. They always walk the two and a half blocks up the hill from the lake, crossing two streets on the way. Occasionally, they will fly off if scared by a dog, but seem to prefer to walk.

We could hardly wait for them to see their "present." They weren't the least bit afraid of it, and drank the fresh water happily for a while. Then Donald decided to take the plunge. Alas, because of his feet being positioned so far to the rear of his body, he was unable to make the eight or nine inch step to the rounded rim of the pool. They all tried valiantly, hopping and scratching at the side, but unable to get in. I was disconsolate! Then I said, "Howard, they need some steps." So the next day Howard heaved two large concrete blocks up on the check-out counter at the hardware store, explaining to all in line that these were steps so our ducks could climb into their pool.

Never mind what everyone thought...it worked, and after circling the pool several times, they learned to hop up on the blocks and then to the pool rim and fall in. You never saw three happier ducks! They swam round and round, wagging their tails in glee. A regular Club Med in Brentwood. ❧

Part Two

With three ducks, the five pounds of duck food were soon exhausted, and after another five pound bag had disappeared, I found myself stepping the order up to ten pounds. The summer wore on and my ducks were waiting for me every morning. At the sound of my voice, I was greeted with loud quacks and tail wagging. Yes, tail wagging, because I've learned when they're happy they shake their tails rapidly from side to side or dip their heads up and down by way of greeting just as if I were another duck. If I sleep a little late they hop up the four steps to the porch screen door and call at the door. Sometimes, when I'm sewing or reading on the porch I look up to see Donald's metallic green head stretched up and looking in the screen door. I know then he's out of food.

Often I can hear them coming up the trail before I see them and if I call out "Come on, Donald, Daisy and Julie," they increase their pace and come waddling in as fast as their little orange legs will carry them. It's a comical sight.

I spend a great deal of time with them and they've become so tame I can't resist wanting to pet them. My efforts are met with hasty retreats and unmistakable dirty looks that say "how could you!" They still will not permit me to touch them and yet it's surprising to see how urbanized these wild creatures have become.

I was feeding Daisy one day, when suddenly a helicopter swooped low over the tree tops, with that thumping roar that you feel, as well as hear, I fully expected Daisy to fly off in panic, but she calmly cocked her head to one side, so that one eye looked skyward and didn't flinch. As much as to say "I'm not afraid of that bird." When

15

the boys come to cut our grass with their two noisy mowers and a trimmer, I'm constantly amazed to see my three Mallards nestled down in the grass around the bird bath, totally unperturbed. The boys almost have to pick them up to move them!

One day I walked out on the porch to find a young couple tiptoeing into the back of our yard. I startled them when I said hello, and they hastily explained that they had been walking down by the lake when they saw three ducks leave the rest and start walking up the sidewalk away from the lake. They were so intrigued, they decided to follow them and were led directly to the York Duck Club. I told them the whole story, as the ducks swam happily, and I was happy to answer all their questions. They were obviously nature lovers too.

Loving all wild things as I do, I love our squirrels too. There always seems to be eight or so in the yard at any given time. We feed the birds all winter and I must admit I could ring the squirrels' little necks when they damage our expensive feeders, but this is summer, and we've four babies as cute as can be. Unfortunately, they've all developed a taste for duck food. I had two nice plastic pans I had been feeding the ducks in this year. Daisy and Julie eat first and not until they're finished does Donald satisfy himself. But they eat a small amount, swim, preen and rest, then eat again. Daisy will chase squirrels who approach while she's eating. She extends her neck and lowers her head and weaving from side to side, advances through the grass like a miniature tank. The squirrels beat a hasty retreat, but are so fond of the cracked corn and whatever else is in the duck food, that they've learned to take desperate measures. For a while the food was safe under the inch or so of water. I did see an older squirrel plunge a little paw into the water and come up with a fist full of food, but he only did it occasionally. One day shortly after I had fed the ducks I looked out, to see two squirrels sitting in the pan gobbling up thick, moist food. Intrigued, I went out to discover one of them had chewed a small hole halfway up the side of the pan, thus draining off all the water and exposing the feed. We use metal pans now, but one has to marvel at their intelligence! Nature is indeed wonderful.

Let me tell you...fifty pounds of duck food weighs a lot! The feed store graciously puts the sack in the car but it's poor Howard who has to divide it up and carry it to the garage, where every available can is pressed into service to hold it.

With the arrival of fifty pounds of feed, the powers-that-be, in Brentwood Forest decided they had too many ducks. After puzzling through a day or two of no ducks, we saw the article in the local paper that because of an over abundance of ducks at the lake, some had been trapped and "moved."

We never saw Donald or Daisy or Julie again and their little pool was such a painful reminder, that Howard emptied it and stored it in the rafters of the garage. I couldn't bear to think I'd never see them again, especially surrounded as we were with about 49 pounds of feed! I tried to console myself with the thought that maybe...just maybe, they'd return next Spring. Would they remember? Would they find the same lake, when there are so many others? Would they remember me? The rest of the summer and all the long winter, I waited, often glancing up at the pool in the rafters, and wondering if we should have just gotten rid of it. Then one day in late March I looked out and there were Donald and Daisy...as ecstatic to see me as I was them. Julie arrived a few days later. I couldn't help wondering how far they'd flown. They looked in good condition, but had they perhaps been shot at on the flyway? I'll never know.

The pool is back in the yard, the feed is all gone and we're into our new batch. They remain as friendly as before and Julie eats from my hand and nibbles my fingers with her leathery bill, but they still refuse to let me pet them. They're usually waiting when I get up and often stay until dark, when they seem to feel a need to be with the others at the lake. Perhaps they think there's safety in numbers.

I'm hoping they won't have a surplus of ducks at the lake this year and wondering how I could trap my three to band them with a conspicuous color. Then I would call the Maintenance division and ask them to please not remove my three, and they could spend the whole summer here. I'm still working on it.

Of course they're a terrible nuisance, noisy, demanding, refusing to swim if the pool's not clean, having to be fed three or four times a day. Our screened porch is raised off the ground and if I haven't noticed their arrival lately they circle round the porch standing on tip toes and stretching their necks while muttering softly that the squirrels have emptied their pan AGAIN, and could we please fill it?

But oh, they're worth it when I hear them calling as they come up the trail and come running when I answer them. I hope they'll keep coming back for many years and I think secretly, Howard does too...now isn't that ducky? ❧

Fish Story

Sometimes it's nice to write about a special person that you've met along the road of experiences. Such a person is Weily, a friend who lives in west St. Louis County.

Weily never liked his name, which is Howard Weilmuenster, so early in life he changed it to "Weily." Weily is a crackerjack sign painter that I met years ago when we both worked for a sign shop in Brentwood. It was there that I discovered a person that could do almost anything; not only well, but very well. He was an artist, singer (we harmonized on many tunes when the boss was not around), played the banjo, ukulele, mandolin, beat everyone he played at table tennis, challenged and almost beat professional billiard players, besides being an expert at chess. How's that for a boy who came from the little town of Middletown, Missouri?

Even when I first met him, Weily had collected all the *National Geographics*, even the earliest ones, and had a sizable collection of old, old phonographs. I remember too, that he had learned to "sign" for the deaf and often displayed how good he was at it, if you pressed him. Once when he wanted some player piano music that was out of print, he got hold of the sheet music from a collector and he and his wife, Alma, hand cut quite a few rolls. Weily, who knew silk screen work and the cutting and precision involved, adapted that knowledge to the cutting of the piano rolls so well that instead of taking days to do it, could do it in a few hours. Amazing!

Weily was drafted into the Korean War. I think his intelligence and all around versatility at doing so many things well kept him in a Headquarters Company. He was assigned to maintenance

19

duties, such as carpenter work, painting and sign painting. One morning, when he was off duty, he had walked away from camp and coming to a rocky stream, or small river, he explored along the banks. Sitting down for a relaxing break and glancing up the river, which was probably 40 or 50 feet wide, he noticed a Korean man, possibly a farmer, wading the river toward him. The rocks stuck up in quite a few places; the depth seemed to be knee-deep to hip deep.

Next, Weily noticed the man was carrying a sledge hammer on his shoulder. He would zig-zag back and forth in the water, and after carefully selecting a rock would go pow! pow!, bashing the rock, not once but twice. Then he would reach under the rock and three times out of four would pull out a good sized fish. His movements in the water had caused the fish to retreat to the shelter under the rock and by his hammer blows he would stun it. He'd hang the fish on a string that was fastened to his belt and move on down the stream. As he passed, Weily could see seven or eight hanging from his belt.

To digress a little, I'd like to relate some other fish experiences I've heard of, especially about men down in the Ozarks, who would go under water, especially in a clear stream, open their eyes and grope among the roots of trees along the bank for large fish that were holed up there. They would seem quite tame and the groper would run his hand and arm in the fish's mouth and out his gill. That way the fish couldn't possibly get away. Down in the country, they called it "hogging" fish. Sometimes if the groper tangled with a large catfish he might have a hard tussle and maybe get "finned." Getting "finned" by a catfish is always quite painful even from a small catfish, for the fin seemed to carry a poison on it. And, sometimes if the water wasn't quite clear a "groper" could grab a snake. What a way to keep from catching fish the conventional way.

Also, I read somewhere that our American Indians would sometimes, during the summer, gather green black walnuts, crush them, and throw them in pools of water, causing the oxygen to get polluted and fish would come to the surface gasping and fall prey to the Indian fishermen. It would be interesting to see if this works.

And, I've also heard of unscrupulous people dynamiting pools to cause fish to be stunned and rise to the surface. Of course this would be illegal, as "hogging" would be, too.

Back to our story. The Korean seemed to have a method of fishing I had never heard of; no bait, no hook or net or pole, etc., only a sledge hammer.

It's been a year or so since I visited Weily. He was studying German so he'd feel at home on a projected trip to that country. Isn't that just like him? ✒

21

Wild Bees

We have a bird bath in our back yard, although I feel it's more for drinking than for bathing; for many of the birds I've watched at it, they drink, but never take a bath. Doves are fun to watch at bathing time. They dip their bills several times and walk in, barely covering their feet, throw a few drops of water over their shoulder and that's it. That's their bath and they fly off.

Many times, during the summer, I observe honey bees around the edge of the water when I'm filling the bird bath and they seem to be wetting their heads or drinking or something. I never have put my head down close to see what, for fear of getting stung. They wouldn't stay too long and wouldn't fly when I added more water, but I noticed one day, they would fly straight up and away. I suddenly remembered I heard that bees always fly in a beeline to their nests or hives so I started watching them very close. One by one, when they seemed to have all the water they wanted, they would fly straight up, quite high, and all went the same direction to a large oak tree, off of our property, a hundred feet or so. I walked as fast as I could, keeping them in sight, as they went towards the tree. It wasn't easy, trailing them through bushes and weeds, etc., but sure enough on the east side, about thirty-five feet up was a hole where I could see dozens of bees going in and out.

It was my third wild bee hive discovery, but it was quite exciting to see, for I had trailed my first bees to their home, from the bird bath to the tree.

Many years ago, at the base of a large oak, in back of the house next door, my children and I found broken pieces of honey comb, in the hollow part near the ground. It was winter and the bees were dormant so I had no fear of poking a stick up in the hollow as far as I could. I knocked down a few more comb fragments but it was a very old hive and nothing came of it.

In later years, we were hiking in the hills of Rockwood Reservation, and one of the girls waved at a bee that had come close to her. I noticed a second and third that came close and discovered she was standing about three feet from a hole in a tree where the bees were coming in and out. We all backed off and watched. The bees were very active, minding their own business, going into a hole about five feet from the ground. I've never been back on that trail to see if the hive was still there. The kids have all grown up now.

I suppose there are many wild bee hives around if we just take time to look for them. I'm told the honey is dark and strong and not pleasant even if you could get some of it.

This year I haven't noticed bees around my bird bath and I don't know why. Maybe I'll watch closer, now that I've written about it.

November, 1989

Another Animal Story

This is a true story that happened a few years ago and recently it popped into my head that it should be recorded. It is really hard to believe, but I had two witnesses.

One summer morning, I went out to my truck parked at the back edge of the parking lot, when I noticed a grey squirrel on the hood acting agitated. I chased him off, got what I wanted out of the truck and went back into the shop.

I owned and operated a commercial sign business in Brentwood and the lot backed up on residential property on the west. Along the back edge was an old-fashioned, heavy, wire fence, the kind that has rounded tops, sort of scalloped with the bottom consisting of points or ends that rested on the ground. It was a durable fence, hard to dent or damage, and exceedingly hard to cut, for the steel was very hard and would no doubt require a bolt cutters to cut, I imagine.

Anyway, a large, silver maple, about two feet in diameter, had grown into the fence at the bottom. In some places the enormous, spread-out root had covered the points of the fence bottom and some were still open and free. It was quite a mixed-up situation.

When I went back to the truck again for something else a few minutes later, there was the squirrel again, acting excited. When I decided to take a look around, he scampered over the fence to the ground and then left.

I bent over, looked closer, and on the ground I saw another squirrel with his tail caught between the points of the fence and the overgrown roots of the tree. I got a yardstick from the truck and poked around, trying to dislodge or untangle the hairs of his tail. But, it looked hopeless, so I finally called to Ed, my helper in the shop, to bring me the tin-snips from the work bench where he was mixing some paint. He came out quickly, sized up the situation, reached down and cut off about two inches of the squirrel's tail, although it was mostly long hair. It didn't seem to faze the squirrel, for he ran quickly up the tree, hopping from limb to limb, keeping his balance as if nothing had happened. But, while I was crouched there, I noticed something else that moved slightly. It was another squirrel that had been lying practically under the first with his tail caught in the wires, also. There was a lot of leaves, ends of wire and matted hair, all in one place.

I poked at this squirrel too, after snipping the hairs from his tail and finally got him loose enough for him to move, when I discovered the long hairs of his tail were hopelessly entangled with hair of a third squirrel. He dragged this squirrel a few inches, and then, seeming to gather his strength, started up the tree, dragging the dead squirrel up behind him. As I was only about three or four feet away, I could tell by the limp and motionless body that he was really dead. I didn't have much time to examine him to see what caused his death because everything happened so quickly. Anyway, I watched the live squirrel go up the tree, over a limb to an electric wire, still carrying the dead one attached to him.

They disappeared down the wire and I couldn't follow because of all the other fences intervening. I wondered how soon he would come down to get shed of his burden. I never did find out although I did watch neighborhood yards and streets for a few days.

Looking around I saw my neighbor lady, Mrs. Chase, and

waved to her hoping she had witnessed the whole scene from her porch. She yelled over to me saying, "I saw that, I really can't believe it." Of course, she and Ed and I were the only witnesses and it all happened so fast that I didn't have time to go to the office for my camera to record the action. It was just one of those things that happens to animals that are never explained. It almost seems that once the first squirrel got entangled, all the others tried to free him by flinging their tails into the troublesome area, and the fact that the first squirrel that attracted my attention had intelligence to know that maybe a human being could help them in some way. The four of them certainly put on an exciting tragic story that day. ✒

Dive Bomber

Each year I put a suet feeder out in the yard not far from our dining room window, maybe twelve to fifteen feet away. It hangs from a light pipe that is fastened to a 10" maple tree. The pipe is bent out at a right angle and the feeder, which is a homemade affair made out of metal 1/4" hardware cloth, is perfect for woodpeckers especially to hang on and eat. The holes, being 1/4" squares, do not give a squirrel nibbling room so they haven't bothered trying to get samples.

However, birds such as the starlings can peck away at the suet with ease. Their beaks, at least 1" long or better, go through the 1/4" holes with no trouble at all. We have four or five that seem to be constantly at the feeder and although it seems that most starlings have dark beaks, there is one whose beak is yellow. I know I should check my bird books to see if it's a female or male but it doesn't make any difference in this story, which is a true one.

It was about nine o'clock and I was eating a late breakfast like a lot of seniors I know do these days, when I noticed a flicker, one of the larger woodpeckers, land on the side of the maple tree clinging on some of the rough bark near the suet feeder. A starling was eating at the top, where I had packed a lot of new suet the day before. The flicker decided he wanted some suet, too, so he swept up onto the feeder with his wings quite spread out, showing the beautiful yellow gold on the underside. He figured the starling would attack and he'd be ready to attack back. And sure enough the starling made a half-hearted attempt to frighten the flicker away, but the almost two-inch beak was too formidable so he flew a short distance away.

The flicker, very unconcerned, began pecking away at the

suet. Every time the starling came close he would pause and make a pass at the starling. He did this several times, and even though the feeder was large enough for them both to eat from opposite sides, the flicker wouldn't have any part of it.

The starling didn't give up but hung around on a twig three or four feet away, acting sort of unconcerned and maybe thinking he'd get some suet when the flicker left. But the flicker didn't leave. He's a bird almost twice the size of a starling and it probably takes a lot more food to fill his stomach.

Next thing I notice is that the starling has made a short pass at the flicker and dropped a dropping that missed the flicker probably by three inches.

I thought to myself, "Wouldn't it be funny if he did hit the flicker?" When thirty seconds later he did, scoring right on top of the flicker's head, sort of above the eye and running down onto the bill. The flicker never paused feeding, acting as though nothing had happened. Was I imagining this, or was this one of nature's little battles going on? I laughed silently to myself and watched another fifteen minutes, but the flicker flew away and the starling came back.

After a short time some little downy woodpeckers flew in, a pair of them, to peck at the suet. They are so small. I know they don't eat much but the starlings don't let them on the feeder while they are there, either. It's what you call the pecking order, I guess.

That was yesterday. Today at about the same time the flicker showed up again and still didn't allow the starlings on the feeder while he was there. One starling flew close but there was no dropping episode, so maybe it was all a coincidence.

December, 1990

28

Dangling On A Rope I

Quite a few years ago, when I was very involved in the sign business, a man, Ed H., came to work for me. He was a crackerjack letterer and had done high-class designing and poster work for many big companies in the St. Louis area. Besides being a big help to me, he was interested in geology (rocks, crystals, minerals, etc.) and we both belonged to the St. Louis Mineral and Gem Society. Naturally, there were many, many discussions about the subject and since he had taken night courses at Washington University, I learned a great deal from him. We would get in many a hot and heavy discourse on geological things of which I was very ignorant. Several times he would mention that he had heard of a large petrified tree in the St. Charles area. It seems like he would only hear rumors and that it was hush hush.

Ed played cards a lot of an evening, in the rear of a filling station not far from his house in Weldon Springs and he'd come in with more information gradually about the tree as the months went by; like the tree was so large that people in the area wanted to display it at the St. Louis World's Fair back in 1904, but it was so large they didn't know how to get it transported. Some said it was twenty feet long, some said it was forty feet long and there was no way it could be moved.

Ed tried to be discreet about his inquiries, but he told his group of card players he didn't believe their stories. Finally, one day he came in the shop and said, "I've found where the petrified tree is and I've got permission to take a group of experts to see it." He meant some of our members of the Society, and over the next few weeks rounded up two others to go on an inspection trip.

It seems the owners of the property, out along the Femme Osage Creek, or river, were in the trucking business and wanted to keep this place secret. But, Ed persuaded them to let him and a group in to explore the area.

Ed picked a professional geologist, a graduate of Missouri University, the president of the St. Louis Mineral and Gem Society, who had a very extensive knowledge of minerals, and me, an eager beaver to be in on the project along with him. We drove out on a Saturday morning in mid-winter. The weather was mild and we enjoyed driving over the narrow gravel roads to the site. We hiked a half a quarter mile across a field to where the ground inclined upward through oaks and hard maples and other typical Ozark trees to a spot about one-third the way up the hill. Ed, the leader, stopped and we all gathered around a hole about six to eight feet in diameter. It was sort of like an abandoned well out in the woods that nobody ever used.

On one side of this hole a shelf of limestone jutted out about three feet. We got down on our knees and tried to see under the shelf. It seemed like there was a roundish piece of rock attached to the underside of the shelf. The visibility was good, it being about 10:30 in the morning, but we could not say if the rock we saw was a petrified tree or not. There was only one way to see and one of us had to volunteer to go down on a rope. I had brought a new one-inch rope from home that belonged to my scout troop. As scout master, I borrowed it from our stock of tents, etc. Still, no one volunteered. The hole only looked about thirty or forty feet deep, so I said, "Tie it around my waist and under my armpits and I'll go down and take samples every so often and put them in my rock sack."

Ed was about a 180 pound man, Joe was over 300 pounds, and Ted was maybe 145 pounds soaking wet. They assured me they could pull me out. I weighed about 160. I didn't have any fear about it, I was anxious to do the research. They lowered me, slowly, and at intervals I'd take chips off the side of this object. It didn't take me long to decide that it was a big stalactite, that somehow many, many years past had grown down from the ledge up near the top. I talked it over with the fellows on top and we couldn't understand why there wasn't a cave around near the stalactite, just a round hole in the ground with a big stalactite attached to the ledge at the top. The whole piece was like a smooth twelve-inch telephone pole, the same diameter all the way down, about forty feet deep and disappearing in the bottom of the hole.

I kept taking pieces off the sides of the object and it flashed through my mind, "You sure are defacing this stalactite!"

I reached the bottom and looked around. It was fairly light and I found a dead rabbit's skeleton and two or three rusty tin cans. Nothing more except maybe a bushel of leaves. The floor had a few loose rocks which made the footing a little slippery as the floor sloped slightly, enough to make you uneasy, so I kept my rope on. I squatted down at one end where the floor seemed to have a dark area, almost a hole. I pushed some leaves aside and found a hole about ten inches by twenty-four inches. I became intensely curious and picked up a rock about lemon-sized and pushed it in the hole. I didn't hear it drop for a few seconds and then I heard a splash. There was water down there a now I knew this was a cave. How big it was, I had no idea.

I didn't come down this hole to squeeze into a smaller hole to explore a cave and I had no flashlight, so I called up that I'd discovered what I thought was possibly a cave and that we'd have to get someone else to do something about it. I threw a couple more rocks in and they all sounded the same, hitting water and making a cavernous sound.

Well, the boys pulled me up and I showed them my samples, which we all agreed were cave onyx, the material most caves are made of. The petrified tree myth was solved, and we all went home.

I knew there was a cave expert in the St. Louis area, a Mr. Dahlgren, who would respond to a rumor of a "wild" cave and would explore it and map it. We learned after quite a few weeks that he had gone out there and explored it with professional cave men. He sent in a report with a map to the owners and also said if the owners wanted to make it into a commercial cave that he would make an intensive, accurate map to show how it could be done, for a fee; how to build walks, bridges, entrances, lighting, etc. The owners, I'm sure, have never done anything about it and I couldn't find the hole again, and if I could I'd be trespassing. It should have a fence around it.

Lately I've thought perhaps the cave could have been named for me since I discovered it. But that is of no consequence. I only know it was quite an adventure, and I've just thought of writing about it lately.

Years later, before Ed stopped working for me, we were talking about the episode and he said, "You were lucky to get out of that hole." I asked why and he said, Joe, although he weighed 300 pounds, was mostly flab and Ted was not strong at all and he (Ed) had to pull me out almost by himself. How about that? ❧

Geode Collecting

I've collected geodes (hollow rocks) that are found all over the middle U.S.A. for the last twenty years. Mostly they are lined with quartz crystals, however, there are quite a few other minerals found in them, such as chalcedony, kaolin, dolomite, sphalerite, marcasite, millerite, etc. Most of these geodes are found in the Warsaw formation, near Keokuk, Iowa, Hamilton, Illinois, etc. Over 200 occurrences are charted on a map of the states of Missouri, Illinois, and Iowa, for those who want to explore them. Quite a few, however, are on private land.

I've collected in these areas in all seasons and all kinds of weather. In fact, the most beautiful geode I've ever found was when I was holding an umbrella over my head in the rain, chipping through the grey shale above a large quarry at Hamilton, Illinois. It (the geode), about three inches in diameter, turned out to be a diamond "dew drop" quartz type. I gasped when I opened it. A description would take a full page to write, but that is not what this letter is primarily about. It is about a peculiar kind of geode found in the west part of St. Louis County, Missouri. The sizes vary from 3/4" by 1 1/4" to 3" by 4 1/2". They are not round, but an occasional round one shows up. They are all kinds of irregular shapes, but none are angular. When opened, they are lined with beautiful, milky quartz crystals.

The geodes themselves are found in loose, light brown, clayey soil and have a rough surface, not like the ones found in the Keokuk, Iowa or Hamilton, Illinois area that are smooth and grey. The various rock outcroppings are sandy limestone. I have specimen geodes that are still attached to the limestone. I feel that these geodes formed elsewhere, at least in the primary stages, finally settling on the flat limestone; then through earth movements, frost, etc., moved about, settling in the clay in irregular veins. These veins are from three inches to eighteen inches below the surface.

A peculiar thing occurs quite frequently with the geodes. Of course they vary in size, but amongst them are clay lumps that seem to be mimicking the same shape as the geodes nearest them. They are quite hard, but easily crack in half, but are not hollow. The particles inside don't seems to be geode-forming minerals. They are quite numerous, and I have begun to wonder if these are geodes in an early forming stage which, after 100 or 1,000 years, could finally become a recognizable geode. I have found a dozen of these in a very crude transitional stage, which I have saved. I would like to have an expert look at them and comment. I have never found any geodes in the Keokuk area similar to these clay nodules (mimics).

There are many more details to tell about these unusual rocks. Perhaps one third of the geodes, when opened, show the milky quartz crystals perfectly formed, covered with a grey or black dust. I've finally decided that the geode is cracked and impurities have seeped in. Scrubbing the interiors with ammonia cleaners generally cleans up the interior and the beautiful, milky quartz crystals gleam in all their glory. Quite a few show dark specks (like pepper) attached to the quartz. I was told they were sphalerite (zinc), but I'm not convinced. I've also theorized that the dust inside could be meteoritic in origin. I made a few poor attempts to test that, but nothing seemed magnetic.

I discovered, about six years ago, and again this past summer

(1988), that many of these geodes, if unopened, would rattle when shook. Most would have to be held up to the ear. Of course, these are loose quartz crystals that have been dislodged by earth movement, frost, etc. They are very intriguing in this aspect. Some are very noisy. Imagine the average layman, or even anyone else's reaction, to this phenomenon! They make good trading material at a mineral show. Of course, ultimately, curiosity may cause the geode to be opened and usually all the crystals fall out. There goes the "rattle rock." Nevertheless, the geode is still a beautiful thing to see, all sparkling and radiant.

During the beginning years I have dug these geodes amongst the grass, tiny shrubs and sprouts, gradually exploring and moving up the clay slopes. After eleven years, the sprouts have become trees and the deposit seemed deeper and harder to work, so I finally quit searching for them. Especially, I didn't like to dig in hot weather and during the tick and chigger season. If I did, I always powdered my ankles, legs, and waist thoroughly with powdered sulphur. It is tasteless, odorless, non-offensive, and doesn't stain clothes. Chiggers and ticks don't like it, as any outdoorsman or naturalist knows. Of course, one always takes a bath when returning from the field and puts the clothes into the laundry.

And so, this summer (1988), when the owner and development company cleared and scraped the area to promote sales of the land, we were quite excited to find the geode area exposed again, and only twenty-five feet from a parking area. I hope to take pictures of the area. The land is a long hill that rises from a small rocky creek at the south end to a stony ledge at the top, probably a quarter mile in distance to the north, and is at least 100 feet higher in elevation.

The stony top is not evident to the casual observer, but as one walks back and forth much rock is seen and seems quite hard.

Eventually, this hill will be developed and landscaped so these geodes will be gone forever. I have scouted around most of the hill and found a few of the geodes with coarse, yet still milky, quartz crystals showing up. I've hunted the creeks and draws much farther north, looking but finding nothing. The eastern exposure may turn up some more, but it needs extensive exploration and digging that should be done in cool weather. The southeast area of the hill is filled ground and landscaped, so there is no future digging there.

So, in the immediate future, we intend to gather as many geodes as we can, saving them for gifts or trades to other collectors, especially overseas.

Of course, it will always be a mystery why white, milky, quartz crystals form in an environment that has no white sand or minerals or chemicals present. The limestone mentioned in this article is sandy and buff-colored, not white. ❧

Dewdrops and Diamonds

It was September, as I remember, and I said to my wife, "Bobbie, why don't we drive to Keokuk and collect geodes? We could leave around four in the afternoon after work, stay in a motel Friday night and come back Saturday afternoon if we have good luck. You've never been there and I know all the good places to explore."

Bobbie had always been my secretary in our sign business and was willing to go and see for herself what "geodeing" was like. If you don't know what a geode is, a simple statement is that it is a hollow rock. That's one way of saying it. I had been to the area three or four times with the St. Louis Mineral and Gem Society but she hadn't gone. This would be her first experience. The geode area around Keokuk, Iowa is quite extensive. Over 200 locations have been pinpointed on a map I have in my possession.

A large limestone quarry has been worked out of the side of a hill across the Mississippi River from Keokuk. At the lower end, towards the southwest, trucks enter and haul out the limestone daily, except Saturday and Sunday.

The upper part is covered with a two to four foot layer of gray-black shale and occasionally it has to be removed by power machinery and dynamite so that the limestone can be quarried out.

Rumors that this shale has been blasted gets around to rockhounds even as far away as St. Louis, about 200 miles south. They usually rush up and poke around, breaking up the shale into smaller pieces, looking for geodes. Even the smallest piece of shale could conceal a geode.

But the geodes of the Keokuk area have many interesting

minerals and crystals inside them. I have heard that at least nineteen different kinds have been found, such as quartz, calcite, dolomite, sphalerite, millerite, kaolin, marcasite and chalcopyrite, to name a few. Most of these geodes, however, have quartz crystals in size from very fine to 1/4" in height, lining the inside walls.

This area is a classic area for mineral and crystal collectors. There are many classic areas all over the world, like the hourglass selenite from Jet, Oklahoma, Lake Superior agates from the northern shores of Lake Superior, copper from N. Michigan, or bladed barite and drusy quartz from S.E. Missouri.

Saturday morning, Bobbie and I awoke to the light pattering of rain. Of course, I was disappointed but rockhounds are like Boy Scouts who have a campout planned and they go weather or not and usually everything works out OK. Perhaps a phrase might be made that "Mad dogs and geode hunters go out in the midday rain!"

So we ate breakfast, sort of slowly, hoping the rain would slacken, which it seemed to. So we drove over the Mississippi River from Keokuk to the quarry on the Illinois side. We took the upper road and parked outside the cable that barred any entrance by a car. Bobbie had newspapers to read and I put on a light jacket and got out into the rain with my rock bag, hammer, and umbrella. I couldn't wait to start popping the shale.

There was no sign saying "Keep Out," although the cable across meant keeping out, so I decided to trespass until they kicked me out. I knew there were no workers on Saturday and besides, it was raining. Who would care to bother me?

I walked about fifty steps or so and now I was in the middle of the recently blasted shale. The pieces were probably wheelbarrow size and not hard to shatter. You didn't need a chisel or heavy tools, only a regular rock hammer was good enough.

Of course, you kept your eyes peeled as you broke the shale, watching for the familiar oval or round shape of the geode, nestling in the shale. They were the same shade of gray and could be overlooked. If you were lucky, perhaps two or three or four would show up close together. They might be 1" to 4" in diameter. After working them out, being careful not to shatter them, for as a rule the outsides are only 1/4" thick or even thinner. Some, however, are solid quartz and diggers often derisively call them "cannon balls" and put them aside immediately.

On our first geode trip, the St. Louis Rock Club went to this location. Our guides had strung out a heavy rope attached to iron stakes, forming a safety barrier that no one, especially children, was allowed to go beyond, for the quarry edge was a scant thirty feet away and a big hazard. All children had to stay with their parents.

I will never forget seeing the long line of diggers, at least twenty-five of them, digging in the shale, happily talking as they dug, announcing loudly when they found a keeper or a nest of geodes. Of course, they groaned, too, when a "cannonball" showed up. Those were the days.

Here I am now, however, standing among the big chunks, hammering away, holding an umbrella in one hand and picking up geodes with the other, maybe one or two every five minutes.

I dug out a fairly large one, about 3" in diameter, and after hefting it a bit, I thought it pretty light so I decided to crack it open for a look. Usually you don't crack them open on the site, for if they're broken open, you want to put them carefully back together and either

40

wrap tape around them or put a large rubber band around them. They should be kept clean to stay in good shape. Rattling around loosely in your bag with other dirty geodes is not good for an opened geode.

I gave my newest find a gentle tap and it cracked open easily, a perfect division of two halves. I gasped at what I saw! It took a few seconds to realize that I had found a diamond dewdrop geode! I had seen only one before and it was a small one at a small rock shop at Niota, Illinois. I closed it quickly, not really believing that I had found it. I opened it slowly again and looked at it very carefully. Again I closed it and took out my handkerchief and wrapped it carefully and placed it in my pant's pocket. No rock bag for it!

Now I must describe a diamond-dewdrop geode to you. The geode is lined inside with a white, porcelain-like coating of chalcedony from which quartz crystals stick out all around the cavity. They are very clear and perfectly formed with the six sides that quartz crystals always have. But at the ends of each crystal the top edges were smoky in color, which is very unusual in a quartz geode from this area. Besides that, each crystal is embedded in a pool of clear quartz around it at the bottom. The white chalcedony was below that. What a sight!

I couldn't wait to get back to the car, but before I did, I decided to look some more in the shale at the exact spot where I had found the diamond dewdrop. Maybe the conditions there would be just right to form more of them. But, after a half hour, I found no more. I guess I was getting "piggy." Too bad.

By that time, my back was soaking wet and when I got back to the car, I peeled off my shirt and put on a dry one; also a spare jacket we had brought along. Bobbie enjoyed seeing my prize and said dryly that she hoped I wouldn't sell it.

I kept it around the shop several years, showing it off, but one day a lady from New York made me an offer of $25.00 for it, so I weakened and I sold it. I figured Mother Nature had given it to me and I had enjoyed it all those years. It had been in several rock shows, and after all it didn't cost me anything and this lady would probably take good care of it back in New York. Good specimens may move from collector to collector, sometimes winding up in famous museums. Who knows?

So you see, this is another thing that happened to me that I can't forget.

February, 1991

Bonanza!

Quite a few years back, Hugh Filley, Principal at the Brentwood School, was seated with me at our regular weekly Rotary Club meeting. We were eating dinner, as usual, before the evening program. I mentioned I was driving to Denver, Colorado and was going to explore old gold mine camps. He said if I would drive west, past Boulder, up into mountains toward Nederland and Ward, I should stop at a little general store in Ward where he knew the woman who owned it. It seems he had been a scout master too, and had taken his boys camping in the area near Ward and once in a while would come into town to the general store for supplies and treats for the boys. "If there's any old mining dumps worth looking into, she would know them," he said.

So, we drove up the curving, two-lane mountain road toward Ward. We could see, occasionally, the yellow, ocherous and rusty tailings from holes dug into the sides of the small cliffs along the road. They seemed well worked over, almost pulverized rocks and sand, quite rusty from the iron pyrite that was dug out. We never stopped to investigate, for it seemed to be a waste of time to excavate and literally shovel the stuff in order to get to any crystals, etc. I don't know if anyone ever finds anything in those kinds of prospects.

We finally got to Ward. It was certainly in the high country. There we found the general store and the woman that ran it. She remembered Filley, but couldn't give us any clues as to where to prospect. My daughter, Carolyn, and my wife decided we should have some ice cream so we sat in a booth and ordered. I suppose I was talking loud enough about the material we brought along to trade, for before we finished our ice cream, a young man from the next booth came over to talk to us. We talked a little about collecting and I could see he was very knowledgeable and when he offered to show us his collection we decided to go see it. He said his home was back in the hills and we should follow him along the gravel road, or trail, that had been the road bed of a railroad that went to mines in the area. We drove and drove and finally came to his house; a nice, big, peeled log-style home. We went in and found we were in a very large room, all varnished knotty pine wood; very elegant and neat. Around the edges were various pieces of testing and weighing devices, scales, etc., all under glass cases.

Hal Miller explained that he was a mine assayer and that that was his business. People from all over the west sent him material to be assayed and valued. He spent many hours analyzing and cataloging the ores that were sent to him. He wrote up lengthy reports and mailed those reports back to the people who sent the material. Evidently his opinions and evaluations were highly respected, for he had built up quite an operation there, way back in the woods.

We walked around looking at his equipment and often he would open a drawer and say, "Do you have any of this?" And then he'd hand me a piece or two. Most of it I had never seen or heard of. I might have seen the names in the index of my books, but that's all.

After an hour or so, looking and learning, he invited me outside where there were long, wooden sheds with doors that opened to the outside, and he began to open them and take out corrugated cardboard boxes about 12x12x8 that were full of material sent to him for assaying. He'd said it would cost too much to return this material and I was welcome to take the whole box home with me. Each box had a printed white label stapled to it with a complete breakdown of the minerals, chemicals, etc., in it.

By this time I had my car trunk open and Carolyn was carrying the boxes to the car and packing them in. Soon it was full, for we had suitcases in there too. So we started to load inside the car. I knew the springs would get overloaded if I didn't distribute the weight in some kind of scientific manner. Finally, since Carolyn took up a third of the back, we could balance the other side with boxes and then load up the middle all the way to the front of the car, even up to the dashboard. When we finally finished loading, boxes were between my wife and I on the front seat almost to the ceiling. We had a good large Oldsmobile that was capable of carrying the load so we didn't worry too much.

Our list of goodies consisted of Enargite, Alabandite, Huebnerite (a kind of tungsten), Ferberite (another tungsten), Pyrrhotite, Boulangerite, Calaverite, Coloradoite, Syvanite, and Tellurium. (These last four were types of gold ore). There was Enstatite, Covellite, Endlichite, Jarosite, and Rhodochrosite, and others I can't remember. It was quite a haul, a real bonanza, and when we got home the first thing I did was get a bathroom scale and weigh every piece and box. It came to 658 pounds. It took me quite a while to sort, label, and present all this material for sale in my tiny rock shop that I had in connection with my sign business on Brentwood Blvd. I learned more about minerals too, from seeing the material and reading more about it in mineral books and magazines. I also gained an insight into mineralogy that has stuck with me to this day. It was really a lucky day when we went up to Ward, Colorado. ✿

Scientific?

Years ago at Brentwood High School there was an inspirational science teacher by the name of Duggan, and it's too bad that I can't remember his first name. Every student who had him couldn't do enough for him. Even the dullest youngster learned from him. Even the athletic inclined boys did their best for him.

And so it was for my two children, Steve and Carolyn. Every day when they came home from school it was Mr. Duggan says this and Mr. Duggan says that. It didn't surprise me, for I was into the scouting program then and I met Mr. Duggan there where he was giving his all to that program.

Steve was the oldest and somehow always knew what he wanted and what he wanted to do with his future. And so when he wanted to do a science project, he knew exactly what it was.

Every year, all the students entered a science project competition. The best ones went to the finals, city and county-wide, to try to get ribbons, prizes, money, etc. Steve decided he wanted to demonstrate how a radio tube worked, etc. He made an elaborate drawing and explanation on heavy cardboard and won a blue ribbon. I don't remember how far he went at Washington University or if he got any money or not. We were very proud of him.

Two years later, science fair time approaches and Carolyn wants to enter but she doesn't know what to do. About once a week she says, "What am I going to do for science?" I would rack my brain for a little while and then forget it. Making a living in the sign business was keeping me fully occupied. I will say this much, Carolyn was starting early, for the school year was nearly out and vacation was coming and then September comes when the science competition started.

So, she pesters me again, more and more, and finally, in June, the day we are to go on our vacation, a trip to Philadelphia, I hit on the idea. "Carolyn," I said. "You have to do the work on this project, totally, and here's what I suggest. Let's take a lot of paper cups and a trowel and get samples of dirt from every state we drive through. You can put paper covers over each cup and mark the state on the cup. And, when we get back, you can put the dirt in separate flat boxes in your display space and put a string up to a map of the United States, where our route will be marked, state by state. Then we can plant beans or carrots or peas in the boxes and see which state's dirt grows the best." In the enthusiasm of the moment I didn't think about the fertility of the dirt in each cup, but was caught up in the fun of doing something a little bit different as we were riding over the highways.

We got out a United States map and marked the states that we were to go through. Of course, starting with Missouri through Illinois, Indiana, Ohio, West Virginia, Pennsylvania, and New York going and coming back through New Jersey, Delaware, Maryland, and back to Pennsylvania. All the way mostly over Highway 40; ten states in all. I told her it was her responsibility to remember to call out when she wanted the car to stop for her filling the cup. As I remember, she always remembered. We had a separate box in the car trunk where she kept all her scientific paraphernalia.

We visited her Uncle Curt in Philadelphia and got dirt outside his apartment. I remember getting gas at a station near him where the whole building was composed of mica-schist, a type of rock

47

prevalent in the Philadelphia area. I noticed a lot of small reddish stones, about the size of rice only more rounded, and I asked the owner what they were. I already had guessed they were garnets but I was in my early learning years in mineralogy and really wasn't sure myself. "Oh, those are rubies," the owner said proudly. "They're all over." When he wasn't looking, I pried 1/2 dozen from the wall at the back, figuring he would never miss them. After that I saw garnets everywhere in the schist walls around Philadelphia. In fact, I researched Pennsylvania after I got home and found garnets are fairly plentiful in Pennsylvania, New York, Maine, etc.

Next, we went to New York and got a room on Manhattan Island where the parking was so restricted that you had to move your car every twelve hours, no matter what! We got used to that, but what bothered Carolyn was, there was no dirt anywhere for her to put in her cup. Everywhere was nothing but sidewalks, paved parking lots, no gardens, nothing but concrete and asphalt. I reassured her we'd find some dirt somewhere, but on the last day, she said, "What are we going to do?"

I said, "When we go out to see the Statue of Liberty maybe we'll find some."

And, so it was. I was drinking soda from a cup when I saw around the edge of the raised brick and stonework on which the statue is placed, dirt that had geraniums, etc., planted in it. We went around to the back where pedestrians were scarce and I dumped my soda out and scooped up the dirt for her. It was no trouble to take it out from there; everyone who might notice would think we were drinking soda anyhow.

Once, on the trip going home, we went through Delaware so

fast that we forgot and had to go back to get dirt from a small cornfield.

Carolyn took good care of her cups of dirt until the next spring when she planted her seeds and dutifully watered them for the science project. She got good marks for it, but later we all realized it wasn't scientific at all, but a lot of fun. I know she and I and Steve will always remember that trip and their projects. ✿

Hard As Granite

I heard a car door shut and looked up from my bench on the front porch to see my sister-in-law approaching. It was especially good to see her after the two weeks she had been away to the northeast. She said, as she came closer, "I've got a couple of friends for you in the back seat - you can get 'em, they're too heavy for me."

At first glance out to the car, I couldn't see anybody, but after giving her a strong welcome home hug, I went to the car and glanced in. Nobody there, but upon opening the door I saw on the floor a paper bag. I picked it up. It was quite heavy and I carried it back to the porch where she was waiting. "Betty asked me to get some round rocks from the bay at Nova Scotia that she could paint," she said.

I was opening the bag, looking at the two stones, when one of them muttered, "I hope she doesn't paint me." I was startled a little, for here was another rock, talking to me like the one a few months ago in the Meramec River.

This one's voice was much deeper, but anyway, I answered right back, "Oh, you're too pretty like you are."

"Well thank you," he said.

"But you're such a nice piece of granite, I'd never let you get painted," I said.

"How did you know I was granite?" he came back at me.

"Well, I can see all the physical parts of you like feldspar and quartz and mica; everyone knows that's what's in granite," I told him slowly, because I wasn't sure he knew about such things.

"Well, I've always known I was granite ever since I fell in a great crash from a cliff way up in the bay, a few million years ago. A lot of us fell that time, all shapes and sizes. We were a rough lot, banging and scraping each other, for the longest time. We tumbled a long way before we got to the bottom, where we settled in a small river."

"Well," I said, "Marion picked you up a long way from a river. She said you were barely rolling around along the edge of the bay. Do you suppose you came down with the glaciers from a long time ago?"

"I guess that's right," he mused. "I know for a long, long time we were under a lot of snow that kept coming down for years and years so that all the lights went out and we didn't seem to move at all. Then one day I felt water trickling around me and some of my buddies; and before long we were moving along, grinding and shoving our way. We were a rough bunch, crushing and punching, day and night. After what seemed an awfully long time we started to see the light of day - mostly because we were covered with beautiful clear blue-green ice. I could see hundreds of feet sideways on either side and I saw strange things, moving along with me, although a lot slower. Things like grass and sticks and logs and animals, all suspended in the ice and all in a frozen state like the day they fell in the snow or water or whatever. Of course we were at the bottom of all this, tumbling along, and the scene was constantly changing. I thought I saw planks of wood and boots, too. It was very intriguing."

"Well, you have had a long, interesting trip and now you are far from home, and you're not doing a single thing productive," I said.

"What do you mean by 'productive'?" my friend asked.

"When you were back up in the bay at Nova Scotia you were making sand and creating rock dikes, building up the shoreline, helping to stabilize a place for plants and birds and animals to live.

5 1

Now you're down here, maybe you'll be part of a rock garden, looking pretty amongst exotic plants and flowers. Or you could get sliced up and studied by a geologist. Which would you like?" I asked.

"Well, I've had a long time to think," he said. "All I know is, I'm pretty tough, and if I'm left in a rock garden or sitting on a shelf or mantel piece, I'll be here a long time after the house is gone that has the mantel piece. I'll still be here when all the fine Cadillacs and Rolls Royce's are gone or even all the trees I see all around here. Even if I get thrown in a trash can and even in a land-fill, I'll still be here."

"That's right," I said, "you are nearly indestructible. Everything and everybody could go and you'll still be here."

"Unless, they slice me up," he retorted. "Maybe I'd be better off back in my bay up north, rolling around, grinding away, softly and gently, until I become, after another million years, a grain of sand in a sand bar."

"Yes, I think you'd be better off. We'll see what we can do about it." ❧

I Remember Cristobalite

Reading, seeing, and hearing so much about the moon landing twenty years ago brings to mind the mineral Cristobalite. But at least I'd like to start at the beginning of my acquaintance with it.

Remember snowflake obsidian? The first time I saw it was in slab form; a black glassy slab with white specks in it that were 1/4- to 3/8-inch in diameter. Much different than banded agate or wonderstone, etc. I learned, too, in those beginner days, that obsidian was called volcanic glass and lots were found in the Western U.S. and down into Mexico. In fact, Pough in his books says, "Obsidian is not too old, high in silica and is the uncrystallized equivalent of rhyolite and granite."

Quite a few years back I put a small ad in a traders' magazine and picked up at least 1/2 dozen persons who wanted to trade. One of these traders was a woman who lived near the borax mining area in California and I traded quite a bit of Missouri minerals with her for the various borax types. Her mailing address was "Onyx," California, a very small town whose postmark looked like it came from a rubber stamp made in the 1800's. She was a faithful correspondent and loved drusy quartz. Her letters were crude, with lots of misspelled words, but her knowledge of minerals was great, especially in the borax area. She went on lots of field trips, mostly on her own, and I could tell by her remarks that she was up in years.

One day I received a package that had three lumps of obsidian about 2"x3"x3" in size that had a few greyish-white balls interspersed through the rock. She wrote at length on these balls, saying, "Remember the spots in snowflake obsidian? Well, those spots were underdeveloped balls of cristobalite, and if you look inside of them, you will see a tiny, dark olive crystal peeping out. That is a form of olivine, called fayalite." This was quite a discovery for me and I was very grateful to her for these rare specimens. Later, I wrote to her asking if there was a chance of getting more, but I received a letter from a neighbor saying she had passed on. I'll always remember the knowledge she passed on to me.

A few years went by and I was invited to hear a talk by Professor Walker of Washington University on the moon rocks. When the audience was asked to submit questions, I asked if there was any quartz found on the moon, and surprisingly, the professor said the only form of quartz that was found was a lot of cristobalite, and I was quite pleased, for I knew what that was and it brought me to a closer realization of what the surface of the moon was. ✒

Quartz Fascination

At the risk of talking or writing about rocks and minerals and my interest in "rock-hounding," I take the chance of showing how much or little I know about the subject. As in any hobby or interest, focusing all your spare time in attending club meetings, field tripping, reading and attending lectures and movies and rock shows, all add to a lot of knowledge that you gain.

Before I joined my first rock and mineral society, I didn't know that amethyst crystals were purple, that diamonds, real ones, were found in Arkansas and didn't know one fossil from another. After 35 years, I know a lot more, but I've traveled many miles, and spent many hours getting that knowledge.

Quartz is a very abundant mineral, in many colors and forms, and I am writing primarily about it. When I joined the Civilian Conservation Corps in 1934, I discovered quartz crystals in the rocks about our camp at Reform, Arkansas. We were in an area of small mountains, quite wild and away from civilization, where there was practically no farming done and the inhabitants there were cutting timber mostly. The crystals were white or milky but six-sided hexagons, not large but interesting. In my spare time, I collected the better groups and asked local people where to find larger and clearer ones.

Several of my buddies in camp told me of some of the other fellows finding large 8 to 10 inch clear crystals that they had taken from the graves in the local cemeteries. Seems as if the poor natives would stick the crystals in the ground around the edges of the grave. I finally visited a cemetery and saw for myself, but was horrified to think that anyone would take or really steal from private property. The temptation was great but I resisted although I know several boys returned home with crystals, clear ones, almost as big as a football.

Anyway, I collected when I could thru August, September, October and had a nice, large candy box full of clear crystals, intending to take them home on Christmas when we had leave. Every night, in my upper bunk, I would sort and high-grade my findings and sometimes at night, I would take walks and throw the culls away for others to find, come daylight. What a sneaky trick! On one occasion, a near bunk-mate told me that he had seen a lot of crystals on the road, where his crew had been grading. So we got up early one morning on a Saturday at 3 a.m. and after getting some bag lunches from the cooks, set out for Crystal Mountain, several miles away. It was a bright moonlit night, and we were as happy as skunks, anticipating great discoveries. In those days, when we were young, we weren't fearful of the weather or wild animals or the mileage; we were as free as birds. Of course CC boys were free to do anything on the Saturday-Sunday weekends. They only had to be ready for work on Monday mornings. We also had to stay in camp if we were on fire call for occasionally there was a forest fire and the crew names were posted on the bulletin board by the mess hall. You were on fire call for a week and also had to do kitchen police or table-waiting for a week, when it was your turn.

We got out to the location, but couldn't see a thing - it was too dark, so we lay down by the side of the gravel road and by using our canteens as pillows, we tried to get some sleep. I couldn't sleep but tried to rest somehow. Bill finally got up and said we ought to go up the hill to do some exploring and digging. It was getting light, and we found some pits, small ones, only 2 or 3 feet wide. We had brought some window screen and sifted for crystals. They were small and clear, but not very large. At one time, a large centipede, which I had never seen before, ran across Bill's pit and he shuddered, saying they were very poisonous. It was at least 6 inches long with many black legs attached to a bright yellow body. Each leg contained a very strong poison.

Gradually, exploring every chance I got, I assembled larger and clearer specimens, sometimes finding a 3 x 4 inch plate full of crystals. Some single ones were 2 to 3 inches long.

When we moved to Greenville, Missouri in October, there were no more crystals to hunt for, so we looked for other rocks or minerals. It wasn't long until we discovered iron, northeast of camp. It lay loosely in clay, and stalactite in form, very heavy and rusty-looking on the outside, but sort of bluish on the inside. Some were 5 to 6 inches long in clusters, stuck together like organ pipes. I took a small box of these home when I got leave at Christmas.

Our camp moved after Christmas (1935) to Sebastopol, California, about 10 miles from the Pacific Ocean. I had been transferred to Co. 733 at Fremont, Mo. before we left. Together we went to California, where we did soil erosion work. The rock from the quarries was dark and hard, not like the limestone of Missouri or the sandstone of Arkansas. I didn't learn much about it although I did find some small flecks of Mica. Occasionally we found sandy fossil impressions of shells in some of the deep trenches we dug. My buddies and I were more interested in the new strange country of California, where we explored the redwoods and made weekend beach trips to the ocean. We became beach combers, collecting starfish, sea urchins, and sand dollars, also abalone and Japanese green glass fishing net floats that had floated all the way across the Pacific to Bodega Bay.

Later on I was discharged from the CCC, after being active in 1934-35 and 1936. I came out with an assistant leader's rating, and went home; and after 4 years of learning the sign business, I got married and had two children, a boy and a girl. As they grew, the family learned about nature which included rocks, trees, etc. When my son Steve was of scouting age, a friend of mine, who already had two sons in the Scouts, saw my quartz collection and asked me to a special meeting of the Scout Leaders (fathers).

They offered me the job of being Scout-master, to a troop that seemed to be failing. They figured if I had worked in the pine trees and redwoods CCC style and liked rocks and nature, I would make a good leader.

I took the job and went to camp Irondale with my first group of 16 Boy Scouts. During the two weeks I was there, I donated one of my large quartz crystals to the camp museum. Another leader saw it, and combed the whole camp looking for me, inviting me to my first meeting with the St. Louis Mineral and Gem Society. I went and then I was hooked. I started going on field trips everywhere. I talked to experienced rock hounds, teachers, asking them questions continuously so that soon I knew a lot of people who were enjoying the hobby as much as I was.

Naturally, accumulating pounds and pounds of material and through trading with others and even trading with out-of-town collectors, I discovered I could sell my specimens over the counter at my sign shop. I made many new friends and acquaintances, some of whom were from overseas and who came back whenever they were near.

Going back to 1940, the year Bobbie and I were married, I remember discussing with her picking a place for our honeymoon. It was September and I knew the foliage in Arkansas would be turning color and I wanted so badly to see the mountains again and even explore for crystals, so jointly we both decided to go there.

Three or four days later we were in central Arkansas, north of Hot Springs, and as we pulled up to our motel in the general area of crystal mining, we noticed a small crew of photographers and others going into the rooms next to ours. They were carrying plates of crystal inside and I went over to admire them. They gave me a large plate, about 6x8x10 triangular in shape covered with crystals 1 to 2 to 3 inches long. They explained they were from the Chicago Daily News and were doing a big story about quartz crystals on location. It seems as if the U.S. Government needed a lot of clear quartz for electronic use; this was before man-made quartz of silicon chips were made or even invented, and since Hitler had taken Czechoslovakia in 1938 the source of good quartz crystals had dried up. They asked us to go with them the next day to the mine where they were taking pictures.

We got up early the next day, with great anticipation. Imagine, falling into a situation like this one and even on our honeymoon. We seemed to go about 15 or 20 miles back into the mountains and finally came to a large, open area where we were led to an open 10 foot by 12 foot hole that was straddled by a 3 legged wooden tripod, from which hung a heavy chain hoist.

Two men were in the hole attaching a chain around a large

plate of quartz crystals. The plate was about 4x5x7 feet and covered on one side by 3 to 6 to 7 inch crystals. It was breathtaking just to look at it.

The reporter from the newspaper said it was being shipped special to the Smithsonian for display and to convince Congress to authorize spending money for subsidizing the exploration of quartz mining in Arkansas.

On top of this, they asked us to stand by the plate, to give viewers an idea of the size of the plate. What a happening! Our honeymoon was to be in a newspaper, complete with the biggest quartz specimen I had ever seen. Later we were mailed copies of the paper, some of which are in my archives, somewhere. My brother and sister-in-law in Chicago couldn't get over this Historical Honeymoon we were having.

During the years, I've probably mined mine dumps, quarries, beaches and road cuts in at least 21 states. Sometimes 4 to 10 places in one state. You not only get to see friends and relatives, but lots of scenery which you actually get into and bring a small part home with you. Being a serious collector, I inevitably study the areas where I collect, doing research from maps, charts and books that I get from libraries and friends.

I recently began research on the chalk and flints of East Anglia, England, particularly in the Cliffs of Dover area. I finally got a young fellow in Basildom, Essex to do field work, etc. for me and he sent by sea mail (which takes about 35 days) quite a few specimens, even including sand-boulder clay and fossils overlaying the chalk. In return, I've sent 18 pounds of specimens from our area, about 30 pieces. Our club also has sent 15 pounds of material in a cooperative effort to stimulate trading between the clubs...a sort of International Earth Science Study. I don't know if other clubs in the U.S. have done this before, but it's a first for any club I've been in.

It's a lot of satisfaction, knowing that all over the world there are people, young and old, bending their backs, searching, studying and collecting from the Earth's surface, who are willing to trade material, information, and opinions, even photos about geology.

I've noticed that our hobby has caused even mediocre students to want to read more, spell more accurately, and enjoy getting outside and learning to take care of the treasures (to them) they find, and I've known a few to go right ahead to become professionals in some fields of geology.

I've also noticed that many outdoor people finally get curious about the rocks they walk on, whether it's on the beach, cliffs or road cuts. I'm sure joining a rock and mineral club would give them a lot of satisfaction and a better understanding of the Earth's secrets and marvels.

These few pages have maybe given you, the reader, a little insight into my feelings for quartz and other minerals. I hope to write more about collecting and field tripping in the future. There is so much to tell and I want it to be not only interesting, but also personal from me.

I forgot to mention in among these notes that I worked as a carpenter, sign painter (beginner), bridge builder, tower builder, tower lookout, etc. during my three years in the CCC's.

During the depression my father was a struggling lawyer, who had been a barber, studied law at night and during the bad times went back to barbering on Saturdays and evenings to make ends meet. So my joining the CCC's helped our family out a lot. They didn't have to feed or clothe me for most of three years.

We enrollees put in an eight hour day, vigorously, too. It was President Franklin D. Roosevelt who created the Civilian Conservation Corps as a program of unemployment relief for millions of young men between the ages of seventeen and twenty-eight. The outcome was the most productive conservation program in the history of this nation.

We were under the jurisdiction of the Army, who clothed us, fed us and sheltered us. They also provided educational facilities and went to great lengths to provide good recreation in scores of ways. Like taking, all that would go, 50 miles one way to a skating rink, organizing athletic teams in competition with other camps, some which were fifteen or twenty miles away.

We planted over forty-three million trees in Missouri alone. We built two hundred and forty bridges, cut one thousand six hundred miles of banks sloping and terracing in various soil erosion projects. We were paid thirty dollars per month. Twenty-five was for going home and we spent five dollars for snacks, books, clothes or a Saturday night on the town. Assistant leaders made thirty-six dollars and leaders made forty-five dollars. A lot of our money went for stamps and some for tobacco. We did our own laundry, but later on, local people would come up to the camp, pick up our clothes and charge very little for the service.

The Forest Service, State Parks, and conservation agencies supplied trucks and tools, lumber, road graders, bulldozers and materials for bridge building, tower building, axes, saws, etc.

So you see, I was very busy in between my rock hunting trips. ☙

Earth Science Club of Missouri Goes International

Friday evening, June 2, Gene Dodel, owner and editor of the Brentwood *Pulse* newspaper, and his photographer were invited to the final meeting of the Earth Science Club of Missouri at the Brentwood City Hall, in order to publish a photo-news story.

The club, which was chartered in Brentwood, Missouri in 1966, over twenty-three years ago, is still meeting regularly, and has a regular attendance of forty-six to sixty adults and about ten juveniles. All are avid students of various phases of rock collecting, whether it's for minerals, fossils, gemstones, crystals, jewelry making, or geology, etc.

Once a year a pow-wow is held in a county park, where the public is invited to picnic and share in trading and buying specimens or participate in silent and live auctions. Many members usually have surpluses of materials gathered from taking field trips once a month, or gathering materials on their vacations. Also, once a year in November the club has a live auction at their regular meeting in the City Hall. Monies from these auctions go to financing the many activities of the club, such as equipment, supplies, and postage for editing a monthly bulletin. At present, a fund is being collected to buy a new film projector. The club also donates to a scholarship fund that is organized by a federation of all the Midwest rock clubs. This federation is only one of many scattered across the nation, all united in a National Federation. The funds go to two deserving students of geology each year.

July 7, 1989 will mark the 1st anniversary of our international club trade project, started by Howard York, Special Projects Director. Understanding this will take a little explaining.

About four years ago a contact was made with the English Mineral Society in Essex who said, "yes," they would trade boxes with a club over here. Several trades were made, and soon a contact was also made in LaBaule, France. Since then, club bulletins have been exchanged, together with boxes of interesting rocks, crystals, minerals, and fossils.

About a year ago our special projects director noticed a listing of rock clubs around the world in the Lapidary Journal, a magazine of high caliber that caters to all kinds of collectors. Reasoning that the foreign clubs were listing names, addresses, and phone numbers for a possible trade, our director mailed out letters to twenty clubs, proposing a trade with their members as a co-op venture. As members around the world always have surpluses, he thought he would send the first box if they would be willing to send the box back, filled with their material. The proposal written to them was a typed page and half long. The letter contained a photo of our club with a self-addressed envelope for their reply. By the end of September, eleven answers came back from across the oceans, all willing to participate. Our club hoped that most of the clubs that were written could read and write English. Surprisingly, the first country to answer was Argentina, a Spanish speaking country. The person who answered knew three languages but wrote back in English, and since he was the first to reply, his club was sent the first box.

The boxes sent weighed from eleven to fifteen pounds average and were made of 1/4-inch plywood. All went by sea mail, much cheaper than air mail, but still some took sixty days one way to their destination. All were labeled "rough rock, no commercial value." That way, inspections were waived at each country's port. Our boxes cost from $11 to $18 to ship. One country, New Zealand, had a club who apparently realized we had to wait such a long time to get our box back that they air-mailed theirs with a cost of $22; all in colorful stamps on the top of the box. Many of the stamps were large and together they almost covered the box.

To date, nine boxes have come back, all with pleasing results. The club in Scotland didn't think they had enough nice material to send, but we sent them a box anyway, and their return box was better than most that came back.

When the latest box came in from Western Australia a week ago, we decided to open it up at our regular meeting, a process we have invited all the foreign clubs to do, and most of them did, writing letters of acknowledgment and surprise. We have had a lot of correspondence from these clubs and met a lot of individuals, however, by mail, that we enjoy writing to. We intend to start another wave of boxes going back containing larger specimens, which most of the clubs want. Our original boxes, in the experimental stage, contained smaller pieces so that we could get more in. We have also asked the other clubs what they preferred the second time around.

A bonus couple of boxes also came in, one from Japan and one from West Germany. A Japanese friend from Tokyo, knowing my hobby, asked if he could hand-deliver a box to a teacher in Tokyo who took his class out every Sunday to research and collect. After almost two years a box came in, mostly of fossils and old, old shells, which he had classified very expertly.

The box from West Germany came about through someone's

hearing of this international trade through (German) relatives traveling in Alaska. He wrote, and we immediately dispatched a box. Thirty-five days later we had a box back from him. We are expecting boxes from Sweden, England, and Ontario this summer.

A box expected from Argentina must go through lots of red tape and has not arrived as yet. The president of the club there sends the Spanish-written club bulletin every month, faithfully, with apologies about the no-show of the box. A member of our club has translated some of the bulletins, and the Brentwood High School Spanish class some of the rest.

Our club is very grateful for the interest of the *Pulse* and hopes the exposure will attract more members. We meet on the first Friday every month of the year, except July and August, at 8 p.m. at the Brentwood City Hall. The public is always invited. Be sure to use the north door.

P.S.: To date, we have received boxes from Capetown and Johannesburg, Africa, Sweden, France, England, Nova Scotia, West Germany, Victoria, New South Wales and Western Australia, New Zealand, Japan, Turkey and Sri Lanka. ✺

Earth Science Club Exhibits in Great Britain

For the first time in its 25 years of existence, the Earth Science Club of Missouri, chartered in 1966 and has been meeting at the Brentwood City Hall ever since, has sent a rock, mineral, and fossil exhibit to Essex, England.

The Essex Rock and Mineral Society's annual show accepted the specimens which filled two of the club's display cases. The Essex Club was founded in 1967, one year after the club here in Brentwood. Incidentally, the exhibition hall was located in a shopping mall near the towns of Brentwood and Basildom, England.

Specimen trading has been going on for over five years between these two clubs. Ron Flack, an officer in the club, initiated the first trade, by sending an 8-pound box of chalk and flint he had collected from St. Margaret's Bay near the Cliffs of Dover, to Howard York, a charter member of the Earth Science Club of Missouri. This international trading project has expanded to more than 12 clubs participating around the world. Gerald Lucy, treasurer, and Ron Flack, liaison, both wrote back to say the ESCOMO exhibit was well received, and many spectators were surprised and asked many questions. The Essex Club hoped to exhibit the material in other shows this spring.

Specimens sent: Missouri 9, Illinois 5, Oklahoma 3, Michigan 2, Colorado 2, Arkansas 2, Indiana 2, Iowa 1, Pennsylvania 1, and Tennessee 1. ✺

July 1, 1989

To All Cooperating Clubs and Societies:

It has been almost a year since I sent the letters proposing a world-wide trade with the Earth Science Club of Missouri. I'm sure you all remember receiving the proposal of a trade that was mailed July 7, 1988.

Slowly the boxes of specimens were mailed out. Slowly, because I was ill for several weeks, but finally the last box was sent (Sea Mail) by the end of October.

The first boxes were sent somewhat as an experiment and were perhaps meager in contents, I realize now. Of the original twenty proposals sent, eleven clubs responded with a willingness to participate. I have enclosed their names and addresses and copies of a few of their letters. Some have sent wonderful pictures of members (often on field trips) and these help add a more personal touch to our long-distance correspondence. I also enclose pictures of a map showing the scope of our success to date.

Needless to say, it has been very gratifying to get all the kind letters from everyone. Waiting two to four months for a box to arrive is often difficult, but the euphoria when it finally does come is almost too much.

At our club meetings, the "Escomo International" report is the last thing on the agenda, but everyone listens intently for the progress of the trades. I usually read any correspondence I have received and these are published in our bulletin also.

I hope now, that somehow, a group picture of your members

could be sent to ours. Photos of clubs on field trips would be great—showing how people all over the world enjoy doing the same thing in the name of Earth Science.

A few of the clubs have expressed a desire for perhaps fewer, but larger specimens. In the future, we will try to send at least 3"x3" pieces whenever possible. Of course, very beautiful, small specimens are always appreciated, and often that is the only way they occur. Naturally, there will be fewer specimens per box and shipping will probably cost more, but I think most of our treasuries can support this.

The hundreds of clubs in the United States are organized into Federations, comprising several states and these have regional conventions yearly. This June, I was sent as a delegate to the Mid-West Federation convention and show in Kalamazoo, Michigan. I was happy to go and observe how business was conducted on a higher level and hear all the various reports. There was also a chance to go on a field trip to collect beautiful orange gypsum found in a commercial mine once operated under the city of Grand Rapids, Michigan. The mine is closed now, but collectors are allowed in to take all the gypsum, satinspar, and alabaster they want.

The Program Chairman of the convention heard of our international trading and unexpectedly asked me to speak to the Federation about our project. Because this is so dear to my heart, I was able to speak without notes, and the idea was met with surprised enthusiasm. Afterwards, four members of individual clubs came up to speak to me and get more specific information.

So the idea is spreading, due to your members and their willingness to trade. It has been very exciting for me in my senior years and I hope we can keep it up. As we all get older, overseas travel becomes more and more difficult, but receiving your letters, pictures, and specimens and then returning ours to you, has been one of my greatest joys of this past year. Thanks again for your participation.

Sincerely,

Howard F. York

ESCOMOS Meet Russians

Dear Gene:

It was my good fortune to see the article in the July *Pulse* about the Russian students who were in this country helping to dig 9000 year old artifacts from a "dig" at Kampsville, Ill.

I thought, "What a good chance to practice our kind of 'glasnost' to the 23 members of their group." I called Kampsville, and got in touch with Katie Egan, who agreed to meet our Earth Science Club of Missouri (ESCOMO) on Friday the 13th.

I got in touch with our members, and proposed that we meet and present the students, all hand-picked from high schools all over Russia, with specimens of rocks, minerals, crystals, and fossils we had collected from our Middle West part of the U.S.

Nine members responded (they were the only ones who were off work on this particular Friday). We met at 10:30 at Kampsville (about 80 miles) and at noon met the students at a park pavilion and presented them with over 35 lbs. of specimens.

The students agreed to divide up the material after the work day. Probably each got 3 or 4 a piece. Later, at home in Russia, they could show what the rock hounds of the U.S. did as a hobby.

They signed a register sheet and about 10 gave addresses. I have since written to 3 of them and one of the chaperones, who was an engineer from a large University in Gorki.

I hope to get a response and maybe start a trade for specimens found in their area. Even if it's only pebbles from a creek, or river, or ocean beach near them, it would be a start.

After the introduction and presentation, Katie Egan, director at Kampsville, took our group out to the "dig." Kevin Conroy, our field trip director, wrote up the enclosed article on what the ESCOMO's saw.

Howard York

Coal in Brentwood?

Charlie Clark blinked. Coal in Brentwood? Yes, there it was on the chart, a four-foot vein about eighteen feet down from ground level at Eager Road near Bobolink Avenue in the Brentwood Forest apartment area.

Charlie is the Chief Building Inspector for the City of Brentwood and has a multitude of inspections to make in his daily work, from sign inspections to skyscraper inspections. As he looked over the soil and rock profile drawings from the new Landmark Bank and garage site, he spotted at 475 feet above sea level, a seam, or vein of coal about eighteen feet down, which in some places looked to be at least four feet thick.

Later, at the coffee shop just north of St. Mary Magdalen Church, he shared his unusual information with Howard York, a rockhound. Howard, he knew, is a member of the Earth Science Club of Missouri, a club he helped charter over twenty years ago and that regularly meets in the Brentwood City Hall.

Howard had also maintained a small rock shop for many years near Pine and Brentwood Blvd., and asked to see the charts. Charlie obligingly showed them, including pictures of the actual cores taken from the drilling sites.

Strangely enough, Howard wasn't too surprised, for perhaps ten or twelve years ago some teenage boys had brought in samples of coal that they had found on the north side of Highway 40 near a large drainage pipe, or culvert, that ran under the highway at the south edge of the then Stix parking lot (now Dillards). The coal had bits of pyrite (fool's gold) in it and also was accompanied by small, diamond-shape crystals of selenite (gypsum). Interestingly too, was the fact that about the same time, Howard had picked up the same size gypsum crystals from around some telephone poles that were installed at the new Milton Building at Lawn and Brentwood Blvd. These poles usually are set in holes of six to seven feet or more and the crystals were scattered through the clay at the base. He picked up perhaps a dozen or more. To a rockhound, this was an interesting find.

Probably coal has been showing up in a lot of the borings made in the Brentwood area and the public has not known about it. Maybe in the distant future, when fossil fuels really get scarce, there will be a need for citizens to avail themselves of such a close deposit. Who knows? ❧

Coal Fever Hits Brentwood!

Early in 1988, Charlie Clark, Bldg. Commissioner, and Howard York, Director of Special Projects for the Earth Science Club of Missouri, examined some charts and graphs of the projected garage for Land Mark Bank to be built on Eager Rd., a few hundred feet West of Brentwood Blvd. They saw that about thirty-five feet down a layer of coal three to four feet thick had been penetrated. This newspaper covered this story.

Monday, again Charlie Clark and Howard York were invited to actually visit the excavation at the site of the garage and take samples of the coal.

They went down at noon when work shut down and took out about thirty or forty lbs. of good black coal from a seam about 24" thick. It was very exciting for Howard, for although he had been in various other mines in the U.S. for such minerals as gold, iron fluorite, feldspar, galena, he had never dug coal in his own home town.

A professional geologist could probably estimate the number of years it would take for this deposit of coal to form. From an amateur's view point, the chalk at the Cliffs of Dover, England was estimated to have formed at one inch per thousand years. Imagine thirty-six inches of coal forming in Brentwood could be estimated at 36,000 years. And what about the other thirty-five feet of dirt on top of the coal? Where did it come from; winds, ocean, rivers? Makes a person feel mighty small and insignificant.

Perhaps at one time Brentwood was in the middle of a large swamp full of trees, ferns, and plants extending over to Illinois.

We hope samples of the coal and the fools gold (pyrite) found above it are preserved in a suitable manner, possibly by the Brentwood Historical Society. ❧

Russia

I'm not qualified to write about Russia, but lately things have happened to me concerning Russia and Russians.

Last summer I wrote to a Russian high school student who had participated in a "dig" at Kampsville, Illinois. Our rock and mineral club made a contact with the twenty-two other Russian students who were spending two weeks at the "dig" looking for 9000 year old artifacts.

The *Pulse* gave our rock club quite a nice write-up about us donating about thirty-five pounds of Midwest U.S. specimens to the students to take back home.

Before they left, they signed a sheet listing their names and addresses. I took a chance, writing to two of them and one of their chaperones. I hoped that at least one of them would write back in English. Perhaps a liaison could be developed, if not in mineral collecting at least in correspondence.

On September 29 I got an answer. My letter took forty-five days to get through to Artem Vartanian. His answer took fifteen days to get back to me.

One thing he wrote in the letter was that his grandmother was born in 1912. The same year I was born. Another was that he (Artem) was born in Sevastopol, which coincidentally is the name of the city (Sebastopol in N. California) where I spent almost a year in the C.C.C. (Civilian Conservation Corps).

This brings back a lot of memories about Russian things.

In the C.C.C., evenings, Saturdays, and Sundays we were given permission to leave camp, provided we showed up for work at eight in the morning. Our work in the Sebastopol area consisted mainly in erosion control.

On one of our evenings spent in town, I met a girl about my age in the town ice cream shop. We had a lot of common interests and became friends. Eventually I met her parents, who were school teachers, and on several Sundays they would take me on a fairly long auto trip, exploring the country around Sebastopol, Petaluma, Santa Rosa, and the Napa Valley.

One trip we took was Northwest up to Fort Ross, where the Russians had established a colony years ago. I might mention here that the Russian Bear still adorns the California State flag, showing that theirs was quite an influence in the Northern California area. Odd, too, was the fact that in the south part of the state the Spaniards were creeping up, establishing missions, the farthest one north being Sonoma. So the Russians and Spaniards almost met in their colonizing efforts.

All the houses and fortifications at Fort Ross were made of logs. The National Park Service has made a National Landmark out of the area. Even the church we attended was made of logs and was quite primitive.

I remember standing for a real Russian Orthodox church service, during which a long-bearded priest walked around and through the congregation, swinging a smoking lamp and chanting the words of the service in Russian. This truly was a first for me.

During my stay in the CCC in Sebastopol, I discovered that there was a sign shop about twenty miles away in Santa Rosa, so I hitchhiked over there on a Saturday morning and walked in and told the man that I'd like to work for him for nothing just to learn the trade.

He agreed, mostly, I suppose, because he was working single-handedly at that time and with spring coming he would need help doing a lot of signs along the highways of the area.

I watched him do a few sho-cards and I could see he had a real touch. He invited me to do a card for him which said "restrooms" and I really made a mess of it - it took me so long - I was quite embarrassed about it, but he was kind and didn't seem to mind.

He asked me to come back next Saturday and we went up on a one story roof to paint a long panel sign that had to be repainted "Safeway Store" in large black and white letters. The two of us worked together quite well and he said there would be more to do, but somehow this connection fizzled out and I never did any more work for him. I suppose hitchhiking the twenty miles was too hard to manage.

Later, after I had returned home from the CCC camp, I settled down, reading newspapers, etc. I began to think for myself. I began to enjoy reading the editorial pages with more interest. I suppose reading some of my father's letters on the editorial page protesting this or that had something to do with it.

The papers were full of anti-Russian communism propaganda (1936). I reasoned for myself that the Russian people can't be too different from me. They couldn't be as bad as they were painted. I had worked with Nick Russ who had come over from Russia to California to start his sign shop. He didn't seem to be a monster; although he maybe did get out of Russia under some kind of pressure, he never talked about it. We never talked politics.

I've always felt that I could get along with the average Russian person. I've always enjoyed work - even hard work. I was partially skilled at carpentry, painting, and even dug ditches. I enjoyed reading and art and music and nature and people. I could get along with any of them I was sure.

For this attitude, quite a few acquaintances have accused me of being soft on communism, which I have only resented. After all, all I ever knew about communism was what I was told by the media. I never had any idea of pulling up stakes and moving there; I just wanted to have an open mind.

So now comes my contact with a real Russian family, especially the grandmother, a person my age who has lived under a Czar, survived two World Wars, lived through the Trotsky and Lenin days, and even has a medal for her participation in putting out roof fires in the siege of Leningrad.

I hope she will correspond with me, too. Of course, what she writes will have to be translated before it comes over to me.

Seventy-eight years is a long time to wait to get my first letter from Russia. In the last few years, because of my rock and mineral hobby, I've traded specimens and corresponded with people all over the world. I hope this letter that I have received develops into a lasting correspondence. There are so many questions I want to ask. ❧

Tiff (Barite)

Recently, at the local donut shop, I had an interesting talk with Rod Schumert. He is a regular patron and we had talked before about his early years living near Potosi, Missouri. Potosi had always been a favorite area of mine because way back when I was in high school I always remembered that the pine trees in southern Missouri always showed up there first along Highway 21. From there on south to the Arkansas state border you could see them.

I asked Rod about them and he said he had relatives around Potosi, who owned several hundreds of acres covered with pines. Besides having lots of pines, Potosi is center of the barite mining in S.E. Missouri. What is also interesting is that it is called "tiff" down there. Before I get too far along in this story, I shall have to explain that I use the terms tiff and barite interchangeably. Rod said that during the depression days of the 30's many natives dug it from the ground where it was very close to the surface, sometimes being only two or three feet below.

Barite, chemically is barium sulfate, and is very heavy, being the heaviest white mineral in the world. Usually its surface is cross bladed and stained with iron (reddish) stains. Driving south on Highway 21 you can always tell when you are in barite country, for the soil exposed in the road cuts and plowed fields is quite reddish. Sometimes, if you dig a little in the gullies along the road, you can find nice pieces of bladed or crested barite. Of course the highway department frowns on your doing that so don't get caught.

Looking back, when I was a sixth grader visiting an uncle who had a home in Florissant, Missouri, I noticed he kept a cantaloupe-

81

sized and very heavy doorstop. He told me it was tiff and he got it from a factory nearby. It was a bladed piece but most of the blades had been broken off and it wasn't very pretty, but it did a good job as a doorstop. My uncle said he didn't know what they made at the factory. I've since learned that it was used as an extender in paint, also in paper-making and in fluoroscopic examinations in hospitals. Later, when my uncle moved to Jefferson Barracks, he gave it to me and we used it also for a doorstop for many years when we lived in University City.

My father was a lawyer and sometimes had foreign clients and at one time took care of the affairs of an English firm who owned property in the barite mines near Potosi. When he made visits to the courts for titles, etc. down there he discovered how little money the miners were getting for digging the tiff. He advised the English to sell their holdings for they were a poor investment. I don't know if they ever did.

The miners were getting, if I remember it right, less than thirty cents a pound. "Poor as a tiff digger" was an expression used in the area for many years. My father, seeing how bad the situation was, organized a bunch of friends here in St. Louis, who regularly took clothes, food and other articles down there to help out.

Barite has really been in and out of my life a lot and talking to Rod brought back more and more memories. Rod told me how he and his brother would walk the gullies and creeks, digging up lumps of tiff and sometimes finding chunks of lead (galena) that they would pile up for recovery by the caretaker of their aunt's property. They would work like dogs and only get eight or nine dollars for all their efforts. He said they would find iron and zinc and copper, too, but not enough to keep.

Once, he and his brother awoke one evening hearing strange noises. They got up, grabbed their flashlights and guns and went out in the darkness to discover some poachers had driven right through their fences, proceeding to dig tiff right and left. On other occasions thieves had stolen timber, too, but were hard to prosecute. Rod seemed to think the law looked the other way and let people get away with anything.

Tiff (barite) is a valuable mineral. It is very heavy and the oil industry soon discovered that barite, when ground up, made an excellent drilling mud. It kept the diamond bits lubricated and cool at the bottom of the drilling. It way heavy and didn't flush out. Missouri, for many years, shipped out tons and tons of barite to all parts of the world. Why the miners didn't get paid more for such a valuable commodity, I can't understand.

In the 1930's & '40's and even now, large mechanical shovels strip the earth to get at the ore, sometimes going down 10 feet or more. They load dirt, rock, ore and even trees into large dump trucks that take it quite a few miles to mills, where the ore is separated. During World War II, much of the galena (lead) found with the barite had to be kept separate because it contained, in some cases, an amount of silver that the U.S. government wanted.

Lots of pretty, sparkling drusy quartz was found in the rock and rock hounds are always searching in the dumps for nice specimens. Many nice pieces of barite are found, too, some bladed and criss-crossed, other shaped like turtle backs. Of course, they are all brown-stained, (not the drusy quartz) which gives them a nice, distinctive look. Sometimes the blades are glassy and almost clear.

These are rare and collectors really prize them. Smart collectors always wrap their specimens on the spot, for the edges are fragile enough to break off, exposing the white ore underneath, besides ruining it to a collector.

My first field trip with the St. Louis Mineral and Gem Society was to barite pits at Old Mines, Missouri, on Highway 21. It is a very small town, easy to pass through as you whiz down the highway. I diligently worked along the edges of the old dug out strip mine. Most of the nice pieces of barite were right along side the highway, right under the black top. I found my first two turtle backs and showed them inquiringly to our field trip director. He gave me the greatest of praise, saying, "You have certainly found some 'keepers'."

From then on I was really hooked on barite. I no longer called it "tiff". We found good drusy quartz there, too, which our director said to keep, for drusy was prized by collectors out-of-state.

Whenever our family got the chance we went to the barite area. Once, my daughter Carolyn and I found an enormous abandoned strip area that looked like no rock hounds had discovered. We found quite a lot of nice pieces of both bladed and turtlebacks. We loaded up the back of the car and at the last minute we discovered an enormous piece, about half the size of a sidewalk section. We decided to turn it over and covered it with dirt and decided to come again some other day to get it. It must have had thirty-five or forty nice 4" turtlebacks on it, all fresh and unmarred. But we never went back. I don't know why.

I took all my good stuff to my first rock show in Decatur, Illinois and Ed Harmon said I was the hit of the show. All I sold was barite and so many of the Illinoisans and Iowans had never seen it.

Mr. Lafayette Funk of the hybrid corn fame bought three large pieces for his museum at Bloomington, Illinois.

Rod said his aunt sold the property at Potosi, some years ago. I'll bet there are some nice spots there even now for exploring for barite and lead. Maybe Rod and I can go back and look some time before the weather gets too hot and the ticks and chiggers are not out.

I remember the first year that our family went to New York City on vacation because after we got settled in our hotel on Manhattan Island, we visited the Museum of Natural History. While the family browsed, I immediately went upstairs to the geological room, really enjoying myself and losing all track of time. As I wandered around, I noticed that there was no specimen of our Missouri barite.

I finally cornered the curator and asked him about the omission. He could see that I was very serious, so he invited me to go to another private room where there were more cases of crystals and minerals. There he showed me milky-blue barites that were from Missouri.

At that early stage of my collecting career, I hadn't really heard that there were such types of barite, but I didn't let on. I told him I still thought he should have some of the criss-crossed bladed types. He was very indulgent and friendly and said hopefully, "Maybe you can send us some."

I went home, charged with the responsibility of doing just that. The very next week Ed and I drove down to the barite pits near Washington State Park, about 40 miles south on Highway 21. We drove and drove and explored every pit we could find but couldn't pick up a decent specimen to send to New York.

I finally went to two of the top collectors in the St. Louis Club, Elmer Headlee and Ted Boente and each gave me their finest piece of crested barite. They weighed together over twenty pounds.

Shipping was the next problem. The blades or edges of the crested barite are not very strong and are hard to pack for shipping. If just one of the blades are broken, the specimen was ruined and not fit for display.

I decided to send the pieces in a wooden box similar to the old fashioned rabbit trap of which I had built many during my high-school days. I used all 3/4" thick boards and started with a base board about 6" wide and 2 feet long. I placed the specimens, one behind the other on a foam rubber pad and then cut 1 1/2" strips of thick rug to use for straps to hold the pieces in place. I tacked them over and around and soon they were bound so securely that they couldn't move. I shook them and wiggled them, but they remained firmly anchored. Next I packed crushed newspaper and excelsior all around and above the specimens. Finally I fastened the top to the sides and ends of the box, with screws only so that the specimens could be taken out easily. We called the trucking company the next day and shipped it out.

I mentioned to the St. Louis Club that the New York Museum didn't have any of our typical barite and I was thinking of sending some but I had done most of this project on my own except for the donations from my two friends. So when I received a letter from Museum about two weeks later that our barite had arrived safely, I was quite elated. But to top it all off, they sent me, under separate cover, a real, parchment award scribed in Old English type that the St. Louis Mineral and Gem Society's donation of barite would be displayed in the Hall of recent notable acquisitions in the museum. That was something I won't forget. The club cheerfully paid for all the expense.

There's more to this story of barite, for once I had heard of the blue crystals, I began inquiring on where to find them. We found out that in Morgan County, north of the Lake of the Ozarks, there were mines where blue barite was found, particularly in the Buckshot mine at Versailles, Missouri.

It seems that a collector had found quite a few large crystals there and was selling them at his shop in Southeast Missouri. He had moved to Denver and opened a shop there.

Anyway Ed and I decided to find the Buckshot Mine. After writing several letters, we finally located a real estate dealer on the south side of town who wrote telling us told us to go south along a poor country road and follow a fence on the west side of the road, looking for openings. When we came to the third opening that would be the path to the Buckshot Mine. The reason it was called the Buckshot Mine was that when the original ore body was found a lot of small 1/4" cubes of lead (galena) were interspersed through the ore.

I forgot to mention that on our first trip, Ed didn't get to go but Fred Powers and Tim Dineen went instead. On the way up we had two flat tires and had to buy two new tires, about $75.00 worth. I was undaunted, however, so we kept on. All the blue barite we were to find, I hoped would pay double of what we spent on tires. I figured if we needed tires, we needed them wherever we were.

Well, we couldn't find the third opening in the fence. It went through meadows and woods and now it was getting past midafternoon when we discovered an old wooden gate made of rough wooden boards about four feet high, all covered with green moss and trumpet vines. We opened it and drove in about 300 yards through a pasture and through a small woods.

We parked. We could see that we were in the lower edge of a deep pit. Walking further in we saw another car and heard voices on the other side of the pit. The place was quite overgrown with trees.

We could see people now and called across to them. They said they were from Kansas City. We went over to see what they had found. They showed us plates of massive barite with lots of small clear crystals of barite covering the plate. They seemed happy with what they had but I was disappointed. They told me they were packing the red mud over the crystals to keep them from bruising. I remember noting in my mind, "here's that red mud again."

Anyway once on our side, Fred had gone to the car to lie down, complaining of a headache-he had been a paratrooper in World War II and he'd get headaches occasionally for no particular reason. Walking along the south side of the pit I had noticed some lumps of calcite sticking out of the ground. I started digging them out. They were not little crystals but most were grapefruit size or even football size. The good part was that they were a beautiful, almost clear amber color.

So I resolved to dig out as much as I could and sell it at home in my shop. I got a lot of it but I could see the shadows of late afternoon gathering. It was after five and even though it was a summer our side of the pit was getting darker and still no barite.

All at once I dug up something new- and it wasn't calcite- about a foot down I had run into a 4" blue barite crystal. I cleaned off the red mud, put it into my pocket and began digging like mad, at the same time trying not to hit a crystal.

Fred and Tim crowded around and we all made the dirt fly. We were finding more calcite too and by the time it was really dark, we had about seventy-five crystals in various lengths from one to five inches.

The Kansas City bunch came over to see what we had found and I could see that they wanted to snuggle up to our claim but the steepness and position of digging was not conducive to their getting in. So they left.

It was a great haul, but weeks later when I led the St. Louis Club to dig in the same spot we didn't find a thing.

We got home about ten that night from Versailles and I assured my wife, Bobbie, as I washed the mud from all the crystals, that even though we spent $75.00 on tires which we needed anyway, we would get it all back from the loot we had found. All the calcite I broke up into hundreds of attractive rhombohedrons, which I sold for several years at my shop. Some were clear as iceland spar only they were of a nice golden color.

One more last thing about the Buckshot Mine. I took a new friend, Ron Venezia, up there and we spent a whole day exploring all around the pit, not finding much, and as we left, Ron was lagging behind digging at an earthen bank about shoulder high. He kept digging at something sticking out of the dirt. We were fifty feet away from the pit and finally he shouted "I've got a big one." When he got it out it was a blue crystal slightly scratched and worn that later we found just fit in a shoe box. What a find!

And one last memory concerning the Brentwood Library. I do

a lot of business with the Brentwood Library including copies, displays, borrowing books, etc. and recently offhandedly, asked the head librarian, Miss Frisbee, where her hometown was. She said Versailles, Missouri and she knew the real estate man we had contacted and had even heard of the Buckshot Mine. Small world!

March 1, 1991

Along the Meramec

I walked out on the narrow gravel bar near the river and sat down on a rock about the size of a small footstool. It was a bright day in late fall and the warm sun felt good on my face and shoulders.

I looked down and picked up a tan-colored rock, about three inches by three inches. It was irregular in shape but not angular or sharp. As I picked it up I said, "Hullo - how long have you been here?"

To my surprise the rock answered back, "It's been about three or four months, I suppose."

"Hm-m, a talking rock," I said to myself. Maybe he could give me some answers I've been looking for. I felt he was male, for I can't imagine rocks being female, although at the time, I wasn't thinking of gender.

The rock spoke again, saying, "When the flood came last spring, I was at Pacific but here I am now almost to Valley Park."

"You're quite a traveler," I rejoined.

My new friend spoke up again, saying, "Remember the flood a few years ago that wiped out Times Beach and the water was over eight to ten feet deep in the streets of Valley Park? Well I came all the way from Sullivan on that trip. Boy-O-boy, did I see a lot of old friends on that trip, big buddies I haven't seen in four or five thousand years went rushing by me, just barely rubbing shoulders, and it seems to me they were a little smoother and rounder than way back then, and prettier too. Did you notice my nice color?" he finished. I said "yes" and he went on, "I wasn't always this color or this smooth."

He then told me, how, through the years various minerals and solutions in the river water had coated him, until now he had a considerable coating almost a sixteenth of an inch. "Break me open, I'll show you," he said. I gave him a sharp rap with my rock hammer. I always carry it when I'm exploring. "Wow," he said, "there's three of me."

"But, you're chert, a pretty buff chert inside - I thought you were jasper!"

"Everybody thinks that, but they are only partly right. Only the coating outside is jasper," he said.

"Well, I'm sorry I broke you," I said.

"That's okay, maybe now I'll be moving along faster and see more in the world. I guess a lot of people look at me and think, 'you stupid rock, what good are you?' Well, I have some ambition. Maybe I'll wind up in a high forty-story building in a sort of stable, fixed home. That wouldn't be bad after roaming everywhere for these past few million years. Or, even be part of a beautiful, arched bridge somewhere. There's lots worse things."

"You are pretty important, I realize, but of course I've felt that way a long time ago," I answered. "I wonder how old this river is and where all this chert came from and especially, where did you come from?" I mused.

My rock friend, now in three pieces, still continued to talk with one voice, quite amazingly. I didn't dare to question how he did it but he said, "I might have broken off of some larger piece way back up the river or maybe over in some valleys still farther away. You know how families gradually split up and go their various ways."

"But," I mused, "everything has to start somewhere. Do you think you used to be silica, real fine stuff like the powdery grit that settled over the west when Mt. St. Helens exploded?"

My friend said, "You're getting a little deep for me. All I know is that I've been on the river for thousands of years taking my lumps. Maybe I'll make it to the Mississippi River some day, but I'll probably be so worn down that I won't enjoy it. It's not very comforting to know that some day I'll be a little grain of sand, but then again, maybe down in Louisiana I'll be scooped up on a sand barge and used to make a beautiful fountain or a winding sidewalk near a southern mansion."

"But, it's hard to imagine you as a grain of sand," I rejoined.

"But I will," he retorted, "although I've had loftier hopes as I've told you before."

"But," I persisted, "I know you've never seen your far off cousins that are found in the Mississippi and Great Lakes area, but they are rounder than you even though they are of much harder material like basalt and granite and gneiss, and porphyry. Do you suppose traveling in glaciers and long distances in rivers caused them to be that way? Is the Meramec River (where all this talk has been going on) younger and the rocks haven't traveled so long and so far to get rounded?"

"It gets quite involved," he said. "Why don't you throw me back in the river and say bon voyage. I've had a good time talking with you." And, so I did. ❧

Meramec River

We stood on the bluff on Big Bend Road in St. Louis County looking down on the flooding Meramec River. The river was way out of its banks and yet it looked very peaceful. Of course, we were close to a mile away.

We drove west down Marshall Road which ordinarily winds along the north bank of the river but now the road was covered with water perhaps three or four feet deep. But in a few more days, it would cover Marshall Road over eight feet as it ran through Valley Park.

I turned to my friend and said, "I wish I had a plastic bubble that I could get in and go to the middle of the channel and watch what goes on down at the bottom of this flood!" Continuing, I said, "Of course, the bubble would have to be anchored securely to the bottom and be made of clear material so I could see in any direction and strong enough to take a hit from the boulders that probably were rolling along at a pretty good clip." My friend looked at me, incredulously, but said nothing.

I imagined a lot of things going on down there on the bottom of the flood. First it might not be clear and visibility would be poor and yet in good sunlight as it was now, maybe I could see the powerful action of boulders and rocks and gravel and sand shoving and pushing their way down stream. What a sight that should be!

I wondered how far all these rocks had come. The flood had been going on for about ten days. Perhaps some of this material had come from up the river at Pacific or even Sullivan. At fifteen or twenty miles an hour, day in and day out, a lot of material could have traveled that far. How could we find out? I came up with an idea that I'll tell you later.

Up on top of the flood, moving islands of logs and brush, and weeds and grass were moving down, with snakes and small animals hanging on, probably hoping their refuge would go near shore so they could all get off. And where do the fishes and other water creatures go in times like these?

It would be nice just to sit in my bubble at the bottom with a buddy and take all this in. Probably with two of us it might steam up and we wouldn't see anything. We'd have to engineer a method to keep that from happening. The whole idea of a bubble in this awful circumstance seems very improbable the more I look at it. Anyway, I can imagine all the tumbling action just the same. I wish it were possible to do it and view it.

I thought again about measuring how far material came during a flood. Maybe we could paint a lot of fist-sized boulders a color and dump them in the river near Sullivan and then check for them at Pacific or Eureka or Castlewood or Times Beach a few years later. But I know that's impossible, for paint would wear off or deteriorate in a short time in a sandy river like the Meramec.

Then I hit on it. A tough, reddish rock like our red Missouri granite from Graniteville would keep its color and toughness through the whole route.

Dump three or four truckloads in the river at Sullivan in appropriate places, not impeding the flow or making a dam. Check in five years at specified places for any granite "travelers."

Measure the river somehow to ascertain the distance traveled and how many days, etc. it took to get where it was picked up. Perhaps after twenty-five or fifty years it could be checked again. The pieces would probably be rounded by then, to some degree for the river acts like a giant tumbler to all the rocks it carries along.

Just some funny ideas a rock hound gets when he lets himself get carried away: and not by the river either. ✒

Gifts To St. Matthias

At the Brentwood Post Office there is a man named Matthew Knuckles. But, he is not what this story is about. However, he started it all and I have to give him credit.

Matt is fairly new at the Post Office, but already he has hundreds of friends. He is friendly, courteous, and knowledgeable, but most of all he is effervescent, gregarious, patient, and goes out of his way to help the customer satisfy his wants. We have built up great rapport ever since I started mailing heavy ten to fifteen pound boxes of minerals and rocks to various foreign countries. He'd ask me what was in the boxes, etc., so I started to bring him small samples of nice crystals, geodes, and minerals. I noticed he had small gifts from other people, too, which he had piled up high to his right in a sort of shrine. I noticed a year or so later it disappeared, probably because the Post Office authorities don't exactly approve of that kind of adoration. He has always called me Brother York, no matter if he waited on me or not. We have arm wrestled a half dozen times or so and he always wins, but I think I surprised him at my staying strength.

Anyway, one day he asked me to call a certain woman who had asked if he knew of anyone who knew about rocks. I suppose she had noticed the material in his little shrine, so he mentioned my name. I called her and she gave me a name of a teacher at St. Matthias School down in Lemay on Buckley Road. I called down there and the teacher asked if I could spend the day talking to the Grades 1 through 6 on sedimentary rocks which they were studying at the time, which was before Halloween.

We set up a date and I was to be at the school at 8 a.m. I didn't let on that this was a shock, for lately I've been sleeping until that time.

I found out a long time ago that giving a talk in front of a group of people, if you had objects in your hands which you had a knowledge of, you could manage to keep your equilibrium and not get mixed up talking. So, I gathered a lot of material like limestone, onyx, marble, clay babies (from glacier deposits), etc.

After I had filled up three or more shoe boxes, etc., I had easily 100 pounds. As I talked I would give out samples that would help illustrate what I was talking about.

When I arrived at the school it was pouring down rain, so I went in a door by the gym and found my way down a long hall to my teacher. I asked her for a couple of stronger boys, maybe a couple of Boy Scouts, and she gave me three and we unloaded and carried the material to what they called the music room. The teacher said she would bring in the sixth grade first. After they had filed in and sat down, I commenced. As I look back it seemed like there were only seventeen or eighteen students, but every forty-five minutes a new class would come in. After the sixth grade left, I noticed that each class got bigger than the former and I was giving away rocks like crazy. I tried to be orderly and had a boy or a girl walk amongst the rows, handing them out. I had about seventy pieces of each category.

I tried to explain sediments and how much sediment was going to the rivers and down to the gulf and building up the big delta there. I rambled quite a bit on various subjects, keeping things simple. I talked about the chalks and flints of Dover, England and about the glacier deposits and loess around St. Charles. In those deposits there are found little two and three-inch nodules, or concretions, that have odd shapes and have been nicknamed "clay babies." Right away I could see I didn't have enough "clay babies" so I limited the giving out to only the girls.

At noon we called a halt and I ate with the teachers and nuns. I was invited to specify what I wanted and they sent out to a restaurant and got it. My request was simple; only a ham sandwich and a Coke. They had chips and pie and cake, etc. for me besides. I was the only man there, so with all the teachers around me it was quite enjoyable. I guess there were seven or eight.

In the afternoon, on came the kids. About 2:30 I had talked to all the grades except the first and third. But, my material was running out so I asked for a reprieve and was invited to come back a week later. This time I would talk to the first and third grades only.

So I went back with another load and when I got to the school, it was cold and windy. I got four or five more boys to help unload, and we went to the music room again. Miss McTigue explained that the first grade wasn't coming so I had the third grade all to themselves. So they all listened and I gave out more material so it seemed like when they got up to go that their little hands were clutching almost more than they could carry. I had visions of rocks flying around in the classrooms later, but it never happened - at least I never heard of it.

At the end of the session, one little girl came up and said almost tearfully, "I didn't get a 'clay baby'!" So, impulsively, I gave her a nice specimen of some other material I had brought.

During the talk, at one point, a little boy in the first row looked up at me and said softly, "Can't you come back tomorrow?" I said that maybe I'd be back, probably, but not tomorrow.

After I got home, I informed Betty that we should make another trip out to St. Charles and get some more "clay babies" and we did the next day. I mailed a small box of the "clay babies" to Miss McTigue and mentioned that if the class ever wanted a talk on trees, I would do it. Trees have been a second hobby of mine for a long time so I felt I could have some fun sharing that subject with them. I also sent a couple of short stories I had written about chert and granite.

Well, in about a week I got a large brown envelope with twenty-six letters from the third grade class of Miss McTigue. As I read them I got a tremendous lump in my throat. These children were thanking me for the talk and the specimens I had given them, even saying they were starting their own rock collections now.

I had passed around pretty specimens for them to see from my collection, such as ruby from South Africa, sheet mica from North Carolina, garnets, mastodon tooth, and gastropod from Israel. They thanked me over and over again for spending my time and being so generous. They liked my stories about chert and granite. All of their letters were on colored paper and in colored lettering with drawings and wishing me a Happy Halloween with drawings of pumpkins and turkeys and pilgrims, etc.

I wrote and thanked them and later on, in about a week or so, Miss McTigue called and arranged a talk on trees. She gave me about a week to prepare.

Immediately I went out to the woods and gathered about twenty-five leaves and taped them to large 9x11 white sheets of paper with large titles under each one. I gathered green pine cones along with old dried ones, along with green gum balls and old ones and also some sycamore balls, green ones only, for the old ones were gone, since this was late October. I took a black walnut log section to show the rings and growth in dry and wet years, white and brown birch bark, catalpa cigars, green twigs of sassafras, etc., everything I could find that would help the students understand and appreciate trees.

When the day arrived, I drove to the school but didn't have to get there before 9:00. A small group of boys came to the car and helped me in. As I talked, I explained how white birch bark burned even when it was wet, because of the heavy tarry pitch that was in it. I explained that the green pine cones and gum balls and sycamore balls expanded when they dried out and literally exploded sending their seeds out over the ground. I passed out the sassafras twigs and had them break them. The kids could now smell the fragrance. They really enjoyed that, one boy exclaiming that it smelled like root beer, and I told him he was right, and that was what was put into root beer to make it taste so good. I had also picked up about forty pin oak acorns and the same of scarlet oak acorns, putting them in small individual plastic bags, two in each.

They planted two in a small six-inch black plastic pot with dirt I had brought along. Then I gave each a pot and a bag of acorns to take home and plant right away in their yard so that in the spring they might have their own oak tree sprouting. Of course I had various students passing out the bags and pots which they always enjoyed.

After I had talked about each of the leaves I had brought, we compared them to the leaves they had brought. They had been instructed to bring at least six different ones to school. I went from pupil to pupil comparing, and the rapport between us was wonderful and to watch a whole room of kids sniffing the sassafras and exclaiming about it was worth all the trouble.

As I was leaving, nine of the girls helped carry out all my material and outside they posed for a polaroid picture. I had copies made up along with a shot I had taken of Miss McTigue at her desk. I mailed the pictures to the school about a week after and in another week comes another group of "thank you" stories and drawings. These were mostly of Christmas, etc., and were very humorous, for they were all telling me about the pine cones exploding and the gumballs popping out and what a mess the sycamore balls were making.

They told of planting their acorns, one boy mentioning that his mother was happy that she'd have another oak tree in her yard. Another wrote that she wasn't allowed to climb her tree but she did it anyway when her parents weren't around.

Of course I read these letters two or three times and showed them to my friends who thought I should display them somehow, somewhere. The thoughts and art work are priceless as far as I'm concerned. One boy wrote in the last bunch of letters, "What are you going to do next?"

I hope all you readers who have read through all of this have enjoyed it as much as I have had doing it.

Through the last three months, Matt, back at the Post Office, keeps remarking, "Boy, you made a hit down at the school," etc., etc. And he keeps saying, "Can I be your agent?"

And I said, "Yes, you can have half of what I make!" ✺

Letters From St. Matthias

We had such a nice response from writer Howard York's story *"Gifts to St. Matthias"* featured in our February issue, we decided to run more thank you letters sent in from the kids to Howard on his talks about Rocks and Trees.

Howard did a great job on this, we're glad he shared his vast knowledge with the kids.

Pulse Publisher, Gene Dodel

Dear Mr. York,

I can't tell you how excited and grateful the third grade and myself are for your generosity. Not only do we appreciate your time, expertise and patience, but also your friendship. We all would love to see you again before the school year ends (May). I will be in touch.

Thank you again for everything!

Yours, Kathy McTigue

Teacher

Dear Mr. York,

Thanks for putting us in the newspaper. I was real excited. When I got home I told my mom and we were looking and looking but we could not find it. We were looking for it in all the newspapers we had. And then I remembered our teacher said she would give us a copy. And the next day we got it. My teacher was excited too. All of us were. Now I am going to show my mom after school. I'm sure she'll be excited too. My whole family will love it. You know your a nice friend. A very very nice friend. I've never been in the newspaper.

Your Friend, Jamie

Dear Mr. York,

I was really excited about the newspaper. And so was Miss McTigue. She was thrilled to see us in the newspaper. She couldn't even wait to show us. We got copies. I can't wait until I show my family that I'm in the newspaper. This will be my second time in the newspaper. The first time I was in the newspaper when I was seven now I'm nine. It probably be a long time until I'm in the newspaper again.

We had a Valentine's party on Feb. 14, 1990 it was a lot of fun. And it was my teacher's birthday on Feb. 15, 1990 she spoiled us I will never forget it. But I must say it was fun.

Your Pal, Kristen Suter

Dear Mr. York,

My grampa collects rocks too. Thank you for the samples I like the story you wrote. But how could a rock talk. The sand baby was interesting mine looks like a turtle. Did you ever want to be a scientist some day. But how do you make a bow and arrow?

Love, Justin

Dear Mr. York,

Thank you for coming to St. Matthias school and showing us your rocks. It was fun. I really like your mica. And how you told us that in one inch there was 1,000 sheets of mica. I'm glad you came.

From, Sarah Richard

P.S. Happy Halloween

Dear Mr. York,

Thank you for spending time with us! I enjoyed it. It was fun. I love your rocks! Some I have not seen before. You are very funny! Your collection is neet. Happy Halloween!

Love, Julie Reelman

Dear Mr. York,

I think you are the nicest guy ever! We read one of your stories it was neat. Please write me soon.

Love, Nick

Dear Mr. York,

Thank you for your time. You had some good samples. I like the rocks you gave me. Guess what, you started my rock collection. Your a real interesting guy and I bet people would like you.

Love, Katie Gale

Dear Mr. York,

I didn't know much of what you was talking about. But I really enjoyed what you was saying. Thank you for the acorns.

From, Justin

Dear Mr. York,

Yesterday was fun! I planted my nuts. I went outside to get some dirt. I hope they grow. My family is moving. It well be fun. I hope. I have a cat too. But he is going to another home. I am sad.

Love, Jenny

Dear Mr. York,

Hi do you remember me? We're the third grade class that you came to talk to.

Guess what? The seeds you gave me already grew. Now it is about one inch tall! My mom is glad we're having a new tree but when I put it out side my dad might not see it and cut it with the lawnmower. What should I do?

A few days ago we had a Valentine's day party it was fun. Well got to go now.

Love, Sarah

P.S. Happy late Valentine's Day.

Dear Mr. York,

I can't believe you put us in the newspaper! I hope you come again because your so good to talk to big groups. Today is my teachers birthday Miss McTigue. We had a Valentine's party yesterday. Today we made and just talk about inventions. I talked about a dog wash machine because if you want to do something and you wash the dog all you have to do is put the dog in and on a conveyor belt and the dog will get a bath and dried and the dog can't run out because it's on a conveyor belt.

Your Friend, Kevin

Dear Mr. York,

Thank you for putting me in the newspaper. My mom cleaned my room and she threw away my rock collection away but, I'm going to start a new one. Miss McTigue's birthday is today and we broght in some inventions! My Dad hasn't mowed our lawn for so long time.

I think one time he hit the tree.

Your friend, Katie Gale

Dear Mr. York,

Thank you very much but I was not in the picture, I was in the bathroom! I love you. I don't mind.

Love, Angela

Dear Mr. York,

I was excited when my teacher told me that you wrote a story in the newspaper about St. Matthias School called the Gifts to St. Matthias. I hope you will come again.

From Paul

Dear Mr. York,

When I heard where in the newspaper. I felt famous it was awesome dude every body screaming in our class. Thanks alot publishing are class in the newspaper. Hope to hear from you soon!!

Your pal, Marty Walsh

Dear Mr. York,

Thank you for putting us in the newspaper. I was excited. I could not believe it. Thank you for putting Miss McTigue in the newspaper.

I hope you had a Happy Valentine's Day. I got a lot of candy and Valentine cards. I got some money from my grandma. I got a game from my other grandma and grandpa.

Miss McTigue got some copies of the newspaper. We each got one.

From, Nick R.

Dear Mr. York,

I was so excited when I heard about the newspaper! You really didn't have to do that.

Did you have a nice Valentine's Day? I know I did. At school we had a Valentine party. My Mom helped me at the party.

The acorns you gave me are growing fine.

Your Pal, Kristin Payton

Dear Mr. York,

I was very very pleased because I've never been in the paper. I'm really excited to tell my mom and all my friends.

That was very nice of you to do that. On Valentine's Day we had a party in our class. The party was very nice.

P.S. I hope you had a good Valentine's Day.

Love, Cindy Jokerst

Dear Mr. York,

I was excited that I was in the paper. Miss McTigue got copies for everyone.

My tree is growing and my rock collection is getting bigger. I found a little piece of Mica.

Did you have a Happy Valentine's Day? I sure did! We had a party for Valentine's Day!

But I had to go to the dentist!

Your Friend, Abby Solovitz

Dear Mr. York,

I told my mom, dad and my brother that don't run into the tree with the lawnmower.

About the rocks my brother and I had a rock collection but you made it bigger and I like that.

What are you going to do next?

From, Bobby

Dr. Mr. York,

I am surprised that I'm in the newspaper. Thanks for putting me in the newspaper.

I had a Valentine's Day party and my tree is popping up.

I have a vary big rock collection now.

Your pal, Patrick

Dear Mr. York,

Last Saturday I went to the Science Center. They had this pencil with all kinds of little rocks! It was awsom. Thank you for putting us in the newspaper.

Your pal, Nick T.

P.S. Please come back soon.

Dear Mr. York,

Just a few months ago I took down a tree that was dead. It was small too and my dad didn't like it, I said "Dad can I plant a tree where the old one was?" He said "Yes". Then the next day it was sunny. I asked my dad if I could plant it now. Then he said it was too late so he said yes. I planted it and I almost watered it too much.

Then a few weeks later it was growing. I was so excited that I jumped up and down. And now it is about 4 ft. tall.

Oh yah I almost forgot thank you for putting the girls in the newspaper. I have never been in the newspaper. Your the greatest.

Your Friend, Julie

Dear Mr. York,

I was very excited when I heard that are school was published in the newspaper! When I got my copy of the paper I was really excited! I was excited for two reasons. 1 reason was because I saw my picture and the other reason was that we get the hole paper.

Well I have nothing else to say. by, by!

Love, Lorien

City Rocks

Every once in a while, maybe two or three times a year, I get asked to help a teacher or a scout leader on the subject of rocks. I've been collecting rocks and minerals and fossils for over forty years and after being in four or five clubs and collecting in over thirty-five states and reading constantly I have picked up a superficial amateur kind of knowledge. I try in my teaching not to get into deep water expounding on geology and theories about geology. Mostly I talk to students about the fun there is in rock collecting and I try to inspire them to start out for themselves, collecting, exploring and reading, etc.

Last fall, I went to the Brentwood Middle School to talk to two separate fifth grade classes that met on alternate days. I took samples for them and talked about the samples. I asked the teacher to have her students bring in material that they found in their neighborhood or pieces relatives had given them.

Some of them brought several boxes or even buckets of stuff, a lot of it being duplications but a different color.

But one day a little girl from the inner city, who probably was bussed in every day, came up to the front of the class with her plastic bag of material she had found in <u>her</u> neighborhood.

I had noticed her before, first because she was so dark and so little and also I noticed she wore the same dress the whole two weeks I was there. It wasn't a school dress but more of a party dress, made in tiers of purple sort of a velvet, one tier stacked up over the one below, getting smaller as it reached her top. It always looked clean. She looked bright but talked to me so softly that I had to ask her to speak a little louder, as I am a little deaf in my old age.

Anyway, here is what she had in her clear plastic bag. A piece of limestone which I guess came from a wall in her area. A piece of mortar, probably out of a brick wall, and another piece of pink mortar from another brick wall. There was also a piece of slate, asphalt, concrete and brick. If I remember, there were about nine in all.

I realized at once that this material was from her world of rocks: all man-made. Quick as a flash, I told the class that hers was the most unique collection I had seen. I think it made her feel good. There she was, so tiny and humble in this fairly well-to-do class of white kids, whereas her collection was unique.

The whole incident affected me so that I went home and made up a collection of about twenty-four rocks and minerals, all labeled, that I gave to the teacher to give her sometime when the other students weren't around.

I don't remember her name and I haven't seen her since, but I'll always remember her in her purple dress showing me her city rocks.

April, 1991

A Few Sign Stories

When I got out of the CCC (Civilian Conservation Corps) in August 1936, I thought I was a sign painter. I had built, lettered, and installed signs for three CCC camps, painted signs for the highways near our camps, lettered names on hundreds of metal footlockers in five or six CCC camps in Arkansas, Missouri, and California, but when I got home there were no jobs for sign painters, not even apprentices.

Finally I saw an ad in the newspaper put in by a moving company on Gravois near Jefferson Avenue. It paid the great sum of $7.50 a week. My father and I decided since it wasn't too far out of his way to drop me off and pick me up every day and that I should try it.

The owner of the moving company believed in advertising and immediately I began painting everything that had a flat surface with copy that read as follows: "Bonded Moving-$2.00 per Room." I painted stove backs, icebox tops and sides, etc.; anything that was exposed to the reading public. And since his property faced on two streets, Sidney and Gravois, he had plenty of exposure. He also had two moving vans that needed lettering. His office consisted of a house typical of many houses in south St. Louis in that it was a string of rooms all in one line from the living room in the front to the kitchen at the back. These houses were known as "shotgun" houses. You could see daylight from one end thru to the other.

Well, Mr. B. somehow had gotten hold of a roll of four feet wide window screen wire that he thought could be painted and lettered and put up high on some poles on the east side of his property. He planned to put it up quite high so that auto traffic could see it driving east on Gravois.

I told him it wouldn't show even if I put ten coats of paint on it, for the screen holes just wouldn't fill up to give the sign any legibility. He couldn't be persuaded, however, and so between the two of us we began tacking up the screen on the door frames leading from the living room straight thru to the back of the house.

We got it up pretty tight however, and at a convenient level for painting and lettering. Nevertheless, before I started I consulted with an uncle of mine who worked for a high class decorating firm in St. Louis. He was, I knew, a very practical man so I told him my problem. He suggested we somehow glue paper to the screen but all of us knew the glue wouldn't hold up in bad weather so I went ahead coating the screen with white paint in preparation for the red letters that would say, as usual, "Bonded Moving-$2.00 per Room."

My memory is dim about a lot of the details, but after I left his place I noticed, driving by weeks later, that he had put the sign up like he had planned and it was readable, if only barely.

Another odd thing about this job was trying to letter the moving vans. I would start out in the morning but the van would be needed for a moving job so I'd pack up my box of paints and brushes and ride along with the van to the house to be moved. Then I would hop out, get on a ladder, and commence painting again. However this didn't work out, for when a bunch of rough-neck movers are bouncing around in a van, loading, etc. there was no chance to do a good letter so I gave up and went inside the house, helping to load up with the men, thereby earning my pay.

I learned a lot of interesting things along the way about the habits of moving men. They would always rush into the house, trying to be first in the rooms where all the large overstuffed furniture was and run their hands under the pillows and cushions, looking for coins and bills. Mostly they found scissors and combs, for they had a big box of them back at the office. It was so amusing to see these grown men rushing into houses and feverishly going thru the furniture for the treasure. But they were good to me always, saying, "Carry the light stuff," like end tables, kitchen chairs, pictures, etc.

One evening, it was in late November, I had to catch a Manchester Road Streetcar going West to get home, for my father had called that he couldn't get me and I found myself waiting under a large V-sign that hung over a hamburger shop.

I looked up at it and admired it greatly, for the letters were so cleanly executed and the layout was perfect. At the bottom it was signed Gaskin Sign Co. All the letters were so skillfully airbrushed and subconsciously I wished I could do work like that.

I broke with the moving company and decided to solicit work in my neighborhood in Rock Hill. I soon started to get jobs from everyone and since we were living in a two-car garage that I helped build, there was no room for me to build and letter signs, especially since winter was coming on.

A man who operated a large fruit and vegetable store asked

me to build him a large 3' x 16' metal sign, double-faced to be mounted between his store and a large elm tree in front. Cars would pass under it to park and it had good exposure to Manchester Road, both ways. It was called "Better Stop Market." I remember that his name was Mr. Daniels and he became a great booster of mine. He asked the blacksmith next door if he would rent me space to operate a shop in the back of his place of business.

When I looked at the space available it looked at first that you couldn't turn a 4' x 8' piece of plywood around in it, but I saw possibilities in it. So I rented it for $20.00 a month and got in, moving tons of iron and all kinds of rusty implements, etc., etc. I worked a whole day moving until my back ached, but finally I had a room ten feet by sixteen feet.

I built a slanted work table to do drawings on and put in a small supply of lumber. The table I covered with beaverboard and I felt great about what I had done.

Meanwhile, I had to build the big metal sign for Mr. Daniels. My father had a friend in Maplewood who fabricated sheet metal that agreed to sell me two pieces of galvanized iron, two feet by eight feet. I had ridden the bus into Maplewood but I had no car to transport my metal back so I rolled it up into a roll about sixteen inches in diameter and putting it under my arm, walked out onto Manchester Road, hitchhiking back to Rock Hill. The load wasn't heavy, but lucky for me I had only walked about a block when a man in a little truck from Glencoe picked me up and took me all the way to my new shop. What luck!

Anyway, the big sign was finished and put up. Mr. Daniels wanted to keep me busy so I lettered a lot of windows in white paint and even sprayed Christmas trees for him in white and pink and blue, for that was all the rage then in 1936.

One morning after it had rained all night, I discovered the roof over my shop leaked and had warped the beaverboard of my drawing table. It was a disaster, for there was no way to fix it.

Anyway, I finished up a 4' x 6' metal sign (double face) for a grocery near Charleville and Manchester and was wondering how I was going to hang it when I read in the paper that a sign company needed a helper to build displays and do odd jobs in their shop. It paid $14.00 a week, so I wrote a long letter with all my qualifications but I didn't hear anything for two or three weeks. Then I got a call a few days before Christmas that a Mr. Gaskin was calling, asking if I still wanted the job. This was the Gaskin that had made the beautiful hamburger sign I had admired on Manchester back in November. I was overjoyed!

He came out to my little place behind the blacksmith shop with a young fellow about seventeen years old, a helper I found out later, who was doing the kind of work I would be doing. Gaskin said he had hired another man who had turned out to be a rascal, running off with some pistols and other things that Gaskin owned.

Gaskin thought of my long letter of application and remembered that he hadn't thrown it away so he decided to give me a chance. I went to work there and stayed eight or nine years. There were a lot of adventures there in those years that I hope someday to tell; learning all the aspects of sign work, cabinet work, spray painting, sign installation, wall sign work, gold leaf, etc. When he was drafted into the army, as most of his help was, too, in World War II, the shop closed down and I got a job in a glider factory spraying planes, lettering insignias and signs in and out of the plant. "A" & "B" Buildings were on both sides of what is now the Arena Building on Oakland, where the Blues hockey team plays now.

November, 1990

Dangling On A Rope II

Sometimes you remember a happening in your life that's worth writing about and could possibly be interesting to others. This happened when I was in my forties; strong, and no job fazed me. Looking back I can hardly believe I did it. Anyway, the man I worked for got a telephone call just after lunch and I heard him tell the caller, "I'll see what I can do." He came back to where I was lettering some real estate signs. I was a journeyman sign printer and had experience in all kinds of sign work, from building signs and erecting them, gold leaf lettering, wall signs, silk screening, etc.

Cliff said, "There's an emergency out at McDonnell Aircraft and that call was from the painting company that has just completed painting the outside of the building at the airport." He went on, saying, "The problem is that management won't accept the job, in fact they are furious because the top of the 'A' in Aircraft is rounded off instead of being pointed like it is in the company logotype, and they want us to go out and fix it—now!" Then he gave me the sixty-four dollar question, "Have you ever been up in a chair?" A chair, I knew, was a seat that was pulled up by ropes and pulleys that enabled one man to paint, or letter, smokestacks, steeples, pipes, etc. "How high can you go?" was his next question. I had done sign work on a stage as high as three stories with no fear, but I didn't know what my reaction would be if I went higher. He continued, "There shouldn't be much to it—they'll pull you up, you paint the point on the top of the 'A,' and they let you down."

"OK," I said. "I'll go out and look at it."

To prepare for the job, I drilled a hole in the end of a yardstick and fastened a piece of wire to it. That I would hook into my belt when I went up. I also made a small bucket out of a tomato can with a wire handle fastened to it like a regular paint bucket. I knew the building was a smooth, stucco-like finish so I took a small and a large fitch brush, which I stuck in my back pocket later when I went up.

When I arrived at the building I drove around where I could see the lettering over the large open doors. The space from the ground must have been forty feet. Aircraft have high tails, and need plenty of clearance. The lettering was in a space of at least another thirty feet. The "A" looked to be at least twelve to fifteen feet high.

The ropes were already in place, the top pulley was hooked into a large iron hook that was fastened to the edge of the roof. I knew how the whole thing worked, for I had placed plenty of hooks on roofs myself. They had also played out a safety rope which you held as you went up. I sat in the chair, which was only a board with a rope fastened at each end. I adjusted my yardstick behind me, checked my brushes, and kept my eye on the half filled can of black paint hooked on my belt and said, "Let's go."

The man on the ground who was to pull me up called out, "Be sure to keep your feet out straight so when you get to the wall you can sort of walk up. That will keep you from bouncing off the wall, hurting yourself, and spilling the paint."

Up I went, fairly quickly, dangling over the open space and when I came to the wall surface the upper man called out, "Keep walking on the wall, you're almost there." Well, I walked and it wasn't bad going and soon I as opposite the top of the "A."

It was a modern script letter and I personally thought it looked better rounded, but anyway, I went to work sketching in charcoal the area to be filled in. The part I added was probably thirty square inches and it was finished before I knew it. The man above kept talking small talk, probably to keep me from feeling nervous. I told him I was finished so he signaled the partner on the ground to let me down. I again walked down the wall and was back on the ground in a few seconds. Then the ground man said, "Now we do the other side." So I had to do it all over again. I glanced up at my work and I still didn't like the point, but the fellows said it was fine.

So I went up again and painted the second "A." They lowered me to the ground once more and believe me, I was relieved. The man up above shouted down, "Hold the rope tight, I'm coming down!" I watched as he swung around off the building, grasping the pulley rope in his hands and slid down bare-handed right to my side in a few seconds.

I was astounded and remarked, "How could you ever get nerve to do that?"

He answered nonchalantly, "When you work on ships and around dockyards as long as I have, you get used to going up and sliding down. I looked at his features and could tell immediately he was an Indian, and then it flashed through my mind that I had heard of the Mohawks and other Indian tribes from upper New York state were great skyscraper workers, having perfect balance and no fear of heights.

When I got back to the shop and reported in, we took the whole occurrence as just another job. I didn't tell my wife about it for a long time, and when I did she said I should have refused to do it—didn't I think of her and the two youngsters at home and the consequences of doing such a dangerous job? At the time, I felt the job was the main thing. I was strong and I had to prove something to myself—so I did. 🐦

Christmas Trees

I worked for a sign company full time but in my spare time I picked up extra jobs which were done for my friends, and I figured it didn't hurt my boss's income.

I did some airplane lettering in the evenings and I was introduced to a man with the county bus company that mentioned that 3M wanted him to experiment putting a new material called Scotchlite on his buses. It reflected a car's lights at night and the bus company wanted me to put it on the rear of their buses.

I can't remember what the outcome of this was, but I know I was one of the first in the St. Louis area to fool around with it. A big candy company put it on their signs along the highways and it looked great.

I accumulated quite a few scraps of red and green and when the shop I worked for started using it, we had more scraps of blue and yellow, etc. that I appreciated.

Around the first of December I hit on an idea. Why not cut out small 1/4" plywood Christmas trees about 18" to 20" high, paint them dark green and outline their edges in quarter-inch strips of green? I added discs of yellow, blue, red, etc. for ornaments and cut out a few stars to complete the decorations. Lastly, I added a small stake at the bottom so the whole thing could be stuck in the front lawn.

So, thinking I could make some money, I cut out about twenty on my band saw. I sharpened the end of a piece of pipe I had and cut out discs. I made two sizes of the Christmas trees.

The problem was how should I market them? You couldn't

sell them in the daytime for they didn't reflect. Finally I prevailed upon a friend of mine, the owner of a Countryside Florist on Manchester Road in Rock Hill, to let me put eight or so in front of his place at night.

They really made a show. Whoever saw Christmas trees that glowed at night? I put up price tags and sat back in my car in the dark waiting for customers. I don't remember my prices but I think they ranged from $6.50 to $10.00.

It wasn't long before cars would come to a squealing stop and come back and buy a tree or sometimes two. I think I sold out the first night. I went home and glued some more tape and ornaments on the extra trees and went out again the next night. I felt strange sitting there waiting for customers but every night up until Christmas I sat out there and peddled my trees. I sometimes wonder if anyone still has one. That's been forty-five years ago.

November, 1990

$10.00 From The Past

The telephone rang. Betty called from the kitchen, "It's for you. It sounds like Jerry." Jerry, of course, works at York Sign Company, my old business that I sold seven years ago. He said, "We opened a letter sent to the shop, but it's to you and inside it's got a $10 bill inside."

I finished shaving, ate my breakfast, and drove to the shop. Then, I read the amazing letter. There was no date, salutation, or signature, only the following message and a $10 bill.

"When I was much younger I took a couple of things from the rock shop without paying for them. I am now in a program of recovery which tells me that I must make amends for the past. Please accept the enclosed for those $10 items. I am sorry. I feel much better having corrected this to the best of my ability."

The story behind all this is that about forty or more years ago, when I first went into business on Brentwood Boulevard, I decided to have a small rock shop in the front, combined with the sign shop office. Rock collecting was a beginning hobby with me and I went on many field trips with the St. Louis Mineral and Gem Society. Soon I had a surplus of specimens that I displayed and sold to various interested people that came in. I put signs in the windows and soon I was taking a few extra dollars home in the evening. I started making up labeled boxes, hoping to catch the educational trade, too.

Anyway, the little rock business kept growing and I began reading about mineralogy, going to rock shows, attending lectures, movies, etc., and in the years since, I feel like I've been going to a long, long college course in geology, mineralogy, paleontology, etc.; maybe thirty-five years worth. I've met scores of nice people and had foreign visitors from Sweden , England, Germany, Mexico, Japan, etc.

At the shop, all my specimens were out in the open, for people to select, etc. Sometimes we left the visitors unattended, since we were busy in the rear with our prime business, sign work. I realize now the temptation was great, and a weak person might take something.

The rock business was not great. I think our peak year was $3,000 in sales; that's about $10 per day. It wasn't worth it, so after all the years at it, I decided to sell out everything to a Chicago man, who took everything I had. A year later, I retired, also, from the sign business.

Whoever this person was, or is, it was a fine decision to make and although I don't want to moralize about it, I wonder how many times all of us have wished we could make up for some of the shady things we've done in the past. Thought this whole episode was newsworthy. ❧

Brentwood, My Story

This story may be of no historical value, except to satisfy my ego; however, it is an interesting zigzag narration of my involvement in affairs in my life concerning Brentwood.

Chronologically, it started in the summer of 1929 when I was a junior in University City High School. Economic times were booming before the crash and subdivisions were going up through-out the county. Consequently, there were labor-type jobs available.

I was hired as a water-boy and sewer pipe carrier and started to work at the area north of Litzsinger Road called Parkridge Subdivision, an area being developed by Joe White, father of Tom White, whose developments are well known in St. Louis County.

I used to eat my lunch sitting in the grass, on the east side of Van Horn's outdoor restaurant, leaning against a wild cherry tree, gazing north across the subdivision area, an area scraped clean of bush, grass, etc. and showing only mud and clay. I'd look north to the trees of what would be called in the future, Audubon Park. I'd daydream about the beautiful girl I'd marry and how we'd build up there, near the beautiful woods, and so on, never deciding on a plan or anything in earnest, just enjoying living and working day by day. I was putting all my earnings in the bank to pay for graduation, etc. in 1930.

We put sewer pipe down the middle of St. Clair and Parkridge and I had to carry water from a 1" water pipe that stuck up out of the ground near the west end of Stafford Ave., north of McGrath School. We had a crew of about eight or ten, about half white and half black workers, and I picked up three or four songs from some of the fellows.

The ditches were six feet deep and in many places we ran into fire clay, refractory clay and yellow clay, which were tricky and dangerous to work in. Once, about four feet down and twenty feet long, a section of earth slipped suddenly in the ditch, burying a black digger (who, on Sundays was a minister in his community) up above his knees. He got out, a little shaken, but continued to work further along the ditch while I helped shore up the sides that had slipped with 2 x 12's and braces put in between.

I worked for Kelly off and on in Crestwood, Webster Groves, Maplewood, and Kirkwood. I could write a book on those experiences but I really want to show how Brentwood has infiltrated my whole life.

In the winter of 1933, economic times were so bad that the government caused the WPA to be created. My father, a struggling lawyer who had to barber on weekends to make ends meet, called from downtown St. Louis and told me to apply in Clayton for a job.

I went to an office on the south side of Forsyth, about two blocks east of Central, and signed up. They gave me a card and told me to show up - where else? In Brentwood! Our first job was to clean the snow off the sidewalk on the south side of Manchester; the area along Schnucks eastward to the Kirkwood-Ferguson car tracks. Our foreman was Mr. Kick, who later became an electrical contractor and also building commissioner of Brentwood, I think.

Gosh, when I look back, my strength was boundless. I could

shovel all day and never feel it. Later we dug ditches all alongside Cliff Wright's sign shop, which was then the County Dog Pound, where a couple of times I had to get my dog out. We lived in U City then and it irritated my father to pay the fine to get him out.

There are so many incidents that come to mind when I look back on that time. We put a ditch across eastwardly toward Breckinridge Material Co., and in one area we had to widen and deepen a creek. My shovel struck something very hard but still moveable and I thought it was a rock, and when I finally dislodged it, it turned out to be a 16" snapping turtle.

It was so ugly and slimy, I wouldn't touch it. However, the crew thought I had possession and had to keep it. A bit of good fortune because, when one of our crew, an Indian by birth, offered me a quarter for it. I asked him what he was going to do with it. He said, "Take it home and eat it - it was the finest delicacy you can have." I found out later, he was right. Incidentally, "Frenchy" the Indian caught a rabbit bare-handed and cooked it at lunch; ate it without salt or any seasoning. I even tried it, but unsalted it was pretty flat.

Later on our crew was moved up to the High School, where we dug out the area in back for the football field. It was cold and the ground was frozen about 4" thick and we had to use a team of horses, attached to a special piece of equipment which had a heavy hook on one end that lifted up huge slabs of frozen clay that we broke up with sledge hammers and threw on the dump trucks. I remember "English" was the name on the side of some of the trucks.

We would shovel all day long, throwing the clay over our heads into the truck. When the truck was full we would shout with glee, "Take it away."

Years later, after I was married, I would remember as I sat watching fireworks from the seats on the east side of the football field, how I had shoveled in the bitter cold in years gone by.

There is a certain camaraderie between workers, and gradually I found myself in a four or five man group that liked to sing. At first, I found out that I could get a ride with fellows that would pick me up at my home for twenty-five cents a ride both ways and we got to singing in the car and I could sing a feeble harmony and so we had a good old time every morning. I made a small sign that we put in the back window of the car, something like "The WPA Singers." One of the fellow's name was Freeman, who later helped create the building stabilizer company called the "Freeman System".

The football field needed rock to build a wall on the north side and a crew hauled rock in from an area in Brentwood. I was assigned to a crew of two, to stack it neatly until the stone masons had the excavation ready to receive it. We stacked it about seven or eight feet high in an area twenty-five feet south of the original High School.

It was after a 1/2 day's work on Saturday going home that turning east on Moritz off of High School Drive, I turned over in a Ford touring car. I was riding in the passenger seat and as we turned over rather slowly none of us got hurt, except I had a very badly bruised shoulder and couldn't work for a week. My brother, Gordon, worked in my place no questions asked, piling the rocks on the stack.

Later on, in the spring, we were working back down in the Manchester Ave. area, along the street car tracks when Mr. Kick came to me and said he had been instructed to cut back on the size of the crew and that he should keep only the men who had dependents that really needed the money. We were getting about $14.00 a week then. He said, "Howard, you are such a good worker, where as some of these other lazy men just lean on their shovels. I'm going to keep you on the job." Makes you feel good even if you are only a laborer. Years later, as a sign painter I lettered his trucks and office windows.

In 1934, I joined the CCC's in August and spent the greater part of three years in Arkansas, Missouri, and California. After I got back in 1936, I worked as an apprentice sign builder and painter until 1940 when I got married.

We lived in St. Louis during the war and one day after I was working at a Glider plant, my wife showed me an ad in the County Observer - lot for sale, fast sale wanted, owner to leave for Florida immediately. They wanted $800 for a 40'x150' lot on - guess where? 9125 Lawn Ave., Brentwood - right where I had gazed, daydreaming at the woods near Audubon Park! Fate was creeping up on me.

We took all of our savings and bought the lot. We had no hope of building. Every month or so we'd go out and cut the grass and rake it and have a picnic. We had Steve, our son, by then and they were nice days. Finally, after the War II, I got a job with Cliff Wright. His shop had moved from Maplewood to where? Brentwood! After about four years we built our two-story home on Lawn Ave. and moved in one day before Christmas 1948.

Both children started at Frazier School, my wife Bobbie became active in school affairs, made many friends. She always said her hobby was people and she really proved it by becoming School Board President for a number of years. She's gone now, but she left her mark.

During the school years, I got roped into being a Scout Master, simply because I had had CCC experience, knew trees, collected minerals, had three years National Guard experience, etc. I knew nothing about the scouts organization only having tried out scouts food and bridges and lean-to's when I grew up in U. City. I certainly never dreamed of being a leader of scouts in Brentwood.

About the same time, I was asked to join the Parkridge Improvement Association. I immediately volunteered to make a survey of the subdivision trees planted along the parkway, the space between the curb and sidewalk. When I finished the survey I asked for money to plant trees, but there wasn't any. After I got into the scout program, I saw a chance to plant along the north side of the High School, getting money and help from the boys in the troop, doing a community good turn. We got approval from all parties and planted six trees. The boys were to take turns watering them and I went on a short vacation and they all died. I've always blamed myself for that fiasco.

I separated from Cliff Wright after about eight years and went into business myself, temporarily working out of my garage which was illegal, I know, but I was desperate. I kept everything clean and neat and only when I tied a sign on top of my car did the neighbors know what I was doing.

This lasted about a year, when we rented a small store next to the shoe maker from Jerry Howe for $60.00 a month. We got established there in about a year, when Mayor Parker called me in to help decorate the town with signs and overhead street banners. The Brentwood Merchants had an organization that wanted to cooperate with the city on their 25th Anniversary. All decorations to

133

be blue and silver. I made a budget and stood up before the Alderman and read it off. I was scared, but they didn't know it. I'd had professional experience at Cliff Wright's, but I was no public speaker.

Here I was, suddenly a scout master, a sign shop owner and town decorator in Brentwood in three short months. Those were expectant, fulfilling days for our troop; won 1st prize with our float in the parade ($100.00) and made over $100.00 selling ice cream and soda from a portable booth that the Pepsi company brought in. It really seemed that Brentwood was the place to be.

In a few years the business people organized a Chamber of Commerce. We had a lot of lofty ideas and we made most of them work. One of the most controversial projects was improving side-walks, which we did and I'm sure now everyone is glad that we, the Chamber of Commerce, sponsored it.

I saw my chance to get trees planted and proposed it to the Chamber. Together with Ernest Purkey and the Women's Garden Clubs, we made a complete survey of the city, block by block, tree by tree, with sizes, etc. This, by the way, was done in conjunction with the sidewalk survey. I compiled all the findings onto a 4' x 6' map and took it to City Hall and asked for an audience with the council. It was granted and here I am again in Brentwood, speaking about a special project that I was convinced we needed.

I guess my enthusiasm was sincere enough that I got a letter from Mayor Parker to see him and come up with a budget, etc. for a tree program. It took a year for the Alderman to pass an ordinance to make the park area between the curb and sidewalk public property, meaning the city would have to maintain it, even to the extent of cutting the grass. I despaired of even getting the tree program started and even called the City Attorney, at that time Jack Nangle (now a federal judge), about why the program was so hard to get started and he said to me in words that I have never forgotten and have used infrequently since, that "A Democracy moves slowly!" Anyway, Mayor Parker calls me in and says I can be City Forester at a dollar a year. Well, I took it, although I have never seen a dollar but that didn't matter, I'd gotten a start. I hired two men and bought a truck and tools and was given $500 a year to spend on trees. Tex was the leader of a crew of two and he certainly knew his way in foresting. He had worked for Davey Tree Service and knew grafting, pruning, etc. He'd methodically stop doing other jobs to water trees, especially when they were getting settled in. My only regret about the whole program was that he assured me that pine oaks and sweet gums had roots that went downward and not spreading. As it turned out, the oak did follow that growth pattern but sweet gums did not. And of course, the roots have caused serious sidewalk problems, and as I take walks now, twenty years later, I see bad sidewalk situations and I want to apologize to Brentwood for that. And even with the trouble we have with leaf raking, gum balls, and sidewalks, could anyone imagine our city without the trees, their shade, coolness and park-like setting?

Sometimes, when I purchase flowers from the Brentwood Florist's shop on Litzsinger, I look out north past McGrath School and remember that there wasn't a house or tree or even grass all the way across to Audubon Park woods, and that Litzsinger was called Lay Rd., and Bremerton was called Lay Rd., even McKnight was Lay Rd. and ran north all the way to Clayton Rd. It was a zigzag way to go north, then to the city of Clayton, except if you drove over North and South Road, now called Brentwood, all the way to Page Ave.

After a few years in the little shop next to Sam's Shoe Repair we inherited a small sum of money and bought our second piece of property in Brentwood at 2111 Brentwood across from Mobil gas. We built a building, tailormade for a sign shop, and sold out the building and sign business separately after eighteen years.

But we are still not thru with the rendezvous with Brentwood. Planning our first visit to Europe to see our son Steve at Wurzburg, Germany, where he was getting his discharge, we went to City Hall to tell them where we were going and to alert the Police Dept. on watching the house, we ran into Ann Schall, the City Clerk who performed her job so admirably through many years, who suddenly got all excited and said would we take some letters and newspapers and photos, etc., etc. to Brentwood, England? It seems the day before we were to leave, the city had received a letter from that city, who was celebrating their 200 or 300 Anniversary and they were contacting three other cities in the world named Brentwood to exchange material. Of course we were delighted to have such a responsible task, especially since we were to land in London to meet Steve and Brentwood, England was only forty-three miles northeast of London and we could catch a train for such a trip.

We flew to London, then to see Brentwood and it seemed so strange to see Brentwood School and Brentwood on signs everywhere. We finally found the newspaper office who sponsored the celebration of the anniversary and when we walked in carrying all our photos, newspapers, etc. from Brentwood, Mo. they were astounded. Imagine, they had only mailed their letter to Brentwood, Mo. a few days ago and here we're personally there to see them.

Well, we were greeted and then doubly so when they found out I was a Rotarian and they were too, so we went over to a restaurant and visited shops, etc. What a coincidence. This happened in 1976.

About 1966, a group of rock-hounds, ten in number, founded with a charter an Earth Science Club called The Earth Science Club of Missouri. We worked a full year on our by-laws and constitution. The group asked themselves, where would we meet. I thought awhile and decided to ask Brentwood City Hall, who else? We have now finished our twentieth year. We are grateful that we still have our meeting place, although we now pay rent whereas for many years got space free.

Recently, Mayor Oppenheim asked me to be one of the Traffic Safety Committee, and I gladly accepted. I've also joined the Brentwood Historical Society. Now when I see Brentwood School No. 1 go down in dust and see the block where I had my first sign shop plowed under and planted in grass seed, I think it is time to put all this down on paper. The St. Louis County Community Chorus began rehearsals at the Recreational Center ten years ago this year and of which I am a member those ten years. I am married again to Betty, formerly a Meisenbach who for many years had an art studio in Brentwood. Carolyn, my daughter, is an administrator in the Kansas State Institute for the Visually Handicapped, owner of a bed and breakfast inn with her husband, Ed Litchfield. She is also a writer of an unpublished book of recipes for the blind, in print and braille.

Steve is a producer of documentary films in Washington D.C. At least a half dozen or more have been televised on the Public TV Networks.

At seventy-five, there are so many forks in the road in my life that need writing about, but I doubt if I ever take time. Needless to say, Brentwood has been uppermost in all of it. ◆

A Visit to the Brentwood Post Office

I parked the car on Essen's parking lot and walked to the Brentwood Post Office. I had a small letter to mail and two brown envelopes to get weighed and stamped before I could mail them out. It was about thirty-five degrees and windy as I approached the entrance doors. I noticed to my left that a young woman was approaching the entrance, too, and quite fast. It was chilly and she had on only a short skirt and a thin blouse. I stepped aside, opened the door ahead of me, and said, "It's too cold for you to be out without a coat on."

She said, "I'm from across the street and didn't know it was so chilly."

She went in and sort of fell into a line along the window not bothering to pull a number for service. So, I gallantly pulled two numbers, crossed over to where she was standing and gave her number forty-two and I kept number forty-three.

"Oh," she said, "It's my first time in this post office!"

I answered back, saying, "Do you go to one up north of here?"

She said, "No, actually I'm from L.A. We've only been here for three months."

I said, "Isn't that funny? I'm mailing a newspaper to my brother in Laguna Hills. That's not far from L.A. is it?"

She said, "No, I've been there, it's a pretty area."

We're standing in line waiting for our number to be called so I started to venture another question. (All along I had noticed she was very pretty and slim and dressed nicely.)

She started first however, saying her husband had been

transferred here so she transferred, too, to a branch of her company in St. Louis.

So it's my turn to talk and I ventured, "Do you have a hobby?" In the back of my mind, I thought since California had so many rock and mineral clubs, maybe she had been in one.

She said, "No, no hobby." So I gave her my Earth Science Club card and invited her to one of our monthly meetings. I do this sort of thing all the time and occasionally get a few new members. I told her about our field trips looking for minerals, etc. and that we have refreshments at our meetings and movies, and lectures. She was politely impressed but that was all. Her number was called and away she went. Mine was called, too, and so I left.

That's the end of a pleasant visit to the Brentwood Post Office.

December, 1990

Chapter Six - Green Bottles, A Fantasy

A Green Plastic Bottle

"This is too pretty to throw out," I thought to myself. In the middle of throwing out the trash, I came across this pretty, green, plastic 7-Up bottle and I mused, "What can I use this for?" I had seen this same type bottle carved and sculpted into various decorative things, but since I am not such an innovator or designer, I was stumped for a while. Suddenly, I thought this would be a good carrier of a message to someone down the river, maybe to the gulf and to a foreign country. I've always dallied with the idea of sending information in a glass bottle, having heard of some of them going all the way to England or to other places, some making it in a year or three.

Have you ever been on an excursion boat watching flotsam and jetsam going by? I remember the first time I saw those two words and looking them up. Anyway, watching some of the logs and jugs, etc. go by is mesmerizing. Imagine, some of those logs are eighteen to twenty-four inches in diameter, probably from a 150 year old tree that finally fell and lay in the woods another fifty years, and later when floods came, slowly began the journey down river. Even then it might get caught in a drift of backwater and get stuck another long period of time before it again moved at flood time. I hoped my bottle didn't get stuck.

Deciding to use the bottle, I reasoned it might go unnoticed so I painted broad white stripes on it and lettered "reward" on the outside on both sides. I really didn't want anyone to pick it up at Memphis or New Orleans. I wanted it to go all the way through the gulf, around Florida, and get caught in the northward flow of the Labrador current.

More ideas crowded into my head. Why not put a copy of our Earth Science Club bulletin in with a roster of our members. Also, why not put in a rolled up dollar bill and some coins and some small mineral and fossil samples. And, why not load the bottle up at one of our monthly meetings?

At our December meeting, the membership watched as I loaded the bottle; gypsum from Michigan, galena from Missouri, a Blastoid from Illinois, small geode from Missouri, St. Peters sandstone, etc., about eight or ten pieces went in. Then the membership present (41), signed a lined sheet, which was rolled up and put in, too. We put on the screw top tightly and sealed it. We planned to launch our "river satellite" on Saturday morning from the Jefferson Barracks bridge. There we could try to hit the center of the river, giving our bottle a good boost. I've since learned that the flow at this time of the year is about six miles an hour.

In the back of my mind always rose the specter of "Am I creating litter? Could I be arrested?" I reasoned no, and that it was a scientific endeavor, however long range and amateur.

The green color of the plastic, I reasoned, would filter out sunlight which might destroy or fade the papers enclosed, and the slight movements wouldn't cause the contents to grind a hole in the bottom. I had a lot of hopes in that bottle.

142

Anyway, Saturday after the Friday meeting the winds were too gusty. I had visions of throwing the bottle out, and it coming right back in the car. So we waited for Sunday. We would leave at three p.m., toss the bottle in and go on to Belleville for an evening dinner. Betty would drive and I would toss the bottle. We hoped for a little area of shoulder where we could stop a few seconds and I could hop out, and watch as the bottle hit the water. But there was no shoulder as we were on the old bridge, with the new one too close to make a good throw. So we drove on to Illinois and turned around and came back west. Betty slowed down slightly, letting traffic go by, and just about where the Missouri State line sign showed up, I lowered the window and let the bottle fly out. Marion, Betty's sister, was crouching in the back seat, avoiding the blast of air that came in. I don't know why I thought of it, but I thought of the line from the classic poem "The Ancient Mariner" where the sailor exclaimed, "And so I shot the albatross!" and he had bad luck ever after. I hope not for me!

A car passed us, honking loudly and shaking a fist as if to say, "You dirty litterer," to me, who has never littered a highway or road in my life, except to throw out an apple core or orange peel. So I immediately thumbed my nose at him. Then we turned around and resumed our ride to Belleville for dinner. A friend recommended a restaurant named "Fishers," which turned out to be very nice; good food, good service, nicely decorated, and nice prices. All during the meal, I kept thinking about the bottle. Was it really going down the river at six miles an hour? By midnight it could be as far as Crystal City. "How far is it to Memphis by water?" I wondered. What if it got beached at the gulf and a bather picked it up? It wouldn't be too bad

143

if it got that far and I got an answer.

But there is the bitter part. I didn't actually see the bottle hit the water, I realized. Maybe it landed on some of the working barges anchored under the new bridge being built nearby. Maybe it never even got a good start. So now, in my mind, I should launch another bottle and go down way south of the city where after a long walk out on the sand I could get close enough to throw it out and watch it go.

I'll probably do it. And now, doing it a second time, I could almost be considered a litterer. I wonder what the chances are of it ever getting across the Atlantic; pretty small, but one never knows unless they try. Wish me luck. ❧

Green Bottle Found

In April, 1988 I tossed a green plastic 7-Up soda bottle into the Missouri River, from the Weldon Springs Bridge on Hwy. 40 (now 64). It was an experimental scientific endeavor for it contained the bulletin of the Earth Science Club of Missouri, my card, a message to the finder please return the bottle and message to me. Also enclosed was a dollar bill to pay postage for the answer.

This was the first time I had ever done this. I had hopes of the bottle going all the way down the Missouri River to the Mississippi river to the gulf around Florida, to be caught in the current up the east coast and out across the Atlantic Ocean towards England and Europe. I had read about glass bottles making it across in a short time like 3 or 4 years.

And so I forgot it. However, last fall, I did it again as you read in this newspaper. This time I threw the bottle into the Mississippi instead of the Missouri.

A few weeks ago, while Betty and I were in California, my sister-in-law Marion got a phone call, while she was feeding our cats at our house. It was from Ed Spanberger in Granite City, Ill. He lives on Chouteau Island and said he had found the first bottle in a brush pile on the north end of Chouteau Island.

When I got home, I called him and he said he worked odd hours for the St. Louis *Post-Dispatch* and we arranged to meet at his house on Waterworks Rd. on the island. And so we met and he said he was checking some fishing lines he had set out for overnight catfishing. He noticed the bottle with the fluorescent orange stripes painted around its middle. He remarked to his girlfriend, "There's something queer about that bottle!" He said he had to split it open to get the material out of the bottle. He gave me the bottle and all the papers, etc.

I hadn't mentioned giving any reward, but I did although he took it reluctantly.

In conclusion, it seems quite amazing that I have the bottle back again. It had been in the water over half of 1988, all of 1989, and up to April of 1990. It had gone down the Missouri, past St. Charles and into the Mississippi. It got stuck in the brush at the junction of the canal at Granite City, where Ed Spanberger found it. ✦

Follow-up on the Green Plastic Bottle Story
(June, 1990)

To the Editor: Please notice this translation from the Swedish paper was made by a friend of my brother, Gordon, who now lives in Leisure World, Laguna Hills, California. Elsa is a retired Swedish opera singer, who graciously translated this from a Swedish newspaper that was sent to me by a Swedish rock collector to whom I had sent the story about the green plastic bottle that you had published last June, 1990. He immediately sent me the enclosed photos of all parties concerned and a picture of the bottle. It is a very involved but interesting story, I think.

Dear Mr. Howard F. York:

It's a pleasure for me to be able to translate this article for you—or as to present the "meat" of this fantastic story.

An 11 year old boy name Bjorn was on vacation in North Jylland Danmark. While there he wrote notes and put into 10 bottles with a hope to find a pen-pal. He had made sure to cast the bottles into the Sea when the wind blew outwards. He was mighty excited and found this to be a real adventure (which also I think it was)!

One bottle was found close by about a week later. It was only after 30 years that one of the bottles (old fashioned with porcelain cork) was found by Bengt Olsen. As a matter of fact—it was on the very day 30 years ago, July 6th 1960 that the bottle was found on a stoney beach of Gason outside Hamburgsund, Sweden. Bengt was walking on the beach alone because he wanted to find some nice stones for his garden.

147

He saw the bottle and became interested—picked it up and put it in his pocket. When he returned to his boat - the whole family were present and watching as Bengt opened the old fashioned bottle. The note inside was carefully rolled together and fastened with a safety pin. Only a drop of water had seeped into the bottle and it was therefore very easy to read the large printed worlds with the wish to find a pen-pal. Bengt then contacted the local newspaper and asked to help locate Bjorn in Danmark. Bengt could not help being curious about this 11 year old boy—and so contact was made through the so called, Person-registret, which was not an easy task, since Bjorn Olsen had changed his name from Olsen to Sondergaard. (Please mark that any name ending with sen is either Danish or Norwegian whereas in Sweden the names always end in son.)

"Oj-how exciting this is!" exclaimed Bjorn when he heard about his bottle being found after all these years. Bengt and Bjorn talked together for a long time over the phone, and in spite of language difficulties they came to know that they would very much like to meet each other. So this summer the Family Olsen will travel to Danmark to meet the Family Sondergaard. Bjorn, who now is a big boy of 41 years, with two daughters and a wife. Fini.

Fondly, Elsa Brozhate

October, 1990

"Huckster"

During the depression of the 30's I caddied for a golf course in University City and although I worked there less than a year, I learned a lot about golf and even got to play every Monday, which was "Caddies Day." Management conceded that since so few people played on a Monday, the caddies ought to be given a chance to play, and some caddies got to be quite good and later became professionals.

We could play all day except when our number was called to go out with a customer. We were allowed to have "steadies," meaning your number could be called out ahead of turn by a golfer who liked your work and conversation. I had several of these, some of which were women. Women liked coaching and special attention. You made better tips that way, too. Of course, the main thing was not to lose the ball.

The fourth hole ran along McKnight Road, the western edge of the course. On the other side of the road was a farm where we all got acquainted with the farmer because frequently a ball would go out of bounds, all the way across the road into a ditch near where he had a small stand that he sold tomatoes and cantaloupes.

One day he propositioned some of us caddies, suggesting

that on our off hours we sell his produce to our folks and friends. He would sell them to us at a very low cost so that we could mark them up and make some money.

Jimmy, a caddie a few years younger than I, and his brother jointly owned a touring car so we loaded up and started out, going door to door at first. After a week or so I could see he was losing interest so I decided to make a list of all my friends and my parents' friends. The list came to at least twenty.

Jimmy's brother, Mel, wanted the car so many times that it interrupted our venture so we decided to use my father's car, but after a day or so Jimmy decided he would rather caddy than sell vegetables. Several times we would get stuck with a load and he would say, "Well, we've got to get out and huckster!", meaning knock on doors, which we both disliked.

We separated as good friends and I kept going, although my customers frequently asked, "Can't you get some corn, or lima beans, or string beans and other things besides tomatoes and canta-loupes?"

Finally, while driving around in the country, I discovered a farm near Creve Coeur Lake where I saw a sign posted by the side of the road that said, "Fresh Corn," so I went up the long dirt road and met Mr. Seegar, who had lima beans, string beans, watermelons, and three kinds of corn, names I had never heard of before. There was golden bantam, a yellow corn, country gentleman, a white corn that had round, bean-shaped kernels, a sort of a pretty corn, and last, the evergreen type, with strong, large, white kernels. They were all good eating corn, not like "horse corn" which gets tough after a day or two off the stalks.

The prices were right and my customers were overjoyed to get all these fresh vegetables, with practically morning dew still on them.

My customers didn't want to see me every day so I developed two routes, seeing one group on alternate days from the other. Some days I didn't have any customers so I had to "huckster," going door to door, but I never had any trouble getting rid of everything, because it was so fresh. And bringing it right to the door was a plus, too, for me. Neighbors told neighbors so I didn't have to "huckster" so much, and the business kept growing.

My father had to ride the street car downtown to his law office, giving his car up so I could make my rounds. We took out the back seat and the seat back which gave me a lot of room. I needed it for all the ears of corn and boxes of lima beans, and with tomatoes, cantaloupes, watermelons, the back got pretty full.

One day a friend said, "I'll bet your good farmer out there in Creve Coeur has some chickens he'd like to sell." Well, this kind of threw me, but I tried it, still driving the route, with four or five chickens with their feet tied up in the back seat was a little hard to get used to.

Every evening when I quit, usually about 4:30 or 5:00, I would come in to the house and my mother would greet me, saying, "How did you do today?" And with great pleasure I would empty my pockets, which were so full of coins that they half covered the dining room table. There were a lot of dollar bills, too. It was a great feeling, that after being a caddy and coming home with three or four dollars for a days work. Besides, we had lots of good vegetables for the table.

Of course there was a lot of driving, for I covered Pagedale, Vinita Park, University City, and even into St. Louis to friends that lived around Hodiamont and Bartmer and Wells Avenue. I never had an accident, although I did kill a chicken on McKelvey Rd. near St. Charles Rock Rd. I regretted that and thought about retrieving it, but I was afraid that an irate owner might nab me. Even now, whenever I hear the phrase, "Why does a chicken cross the road?" I remember my chicken episode.

In those days, when tires wore thin, car owners would put boots in the tire at the worst spots, hoping to get by till they could afford to buy a new tire. And also the inner tube always had to be patched whenever there was a puncture. Sometimes we would have ten to fifteen patches on a tube. Once, early in the morning, I got a flat and needed a boot and didn't have one. I used two thicknesses of corrugated cardboard to cover the hole inside the tire and drove it the whole day before it wore out. Just made it in to the house at supper time.

Well, August ran into September and into October and the vegetables started to run out. My routes were drying up and finally did stop. My huckstering days were over, but my father suggested that I try selling and delivering canned goods and bread, etc. to all my customers on the routes I had developed. Somehow I didn't see the practicality of the idea, and he was quite put out about it. I found other things to do but that's another story and we still had a lot of hard times ahead. ✒

Recycling

Across the street from our house were quite a few empty lots. We lived in the west part of University City near Hanley Road and gradually houses were being built in our subdivision. In those days around 1931, basements weren't dug out by a tractor, etc., but usually a man and a mule, pulling a slip, dug them out with main strength and awkwardness. A slip was a large metal scoop, maybe thirty by thirty inches with two wood handles on one side for the man to grasp as the mule pulled the sharp edge front of the slip into the dirt. When the slip was full it was pulled out of the excavation and dumped in the proper place for future landscaping. This took several days and much of the excavation still had to be hand dug.

At noon, man and mule rested. The man usually found a shady place to eat his lunch and gave his mule corn to eat. I don't remember if the mule ate from a box or a bag. Anyway, this went on for several days until the basement was excavated.

The digging was done in the spring and after several weeks I noticed green sprouts all along the edges of the excavation coming up out of the new dirt. They were corn, I knew, and were about ten to twelve inches high.

I suddenly had an idea - why couldn't I transplant these corn sprouts over to an empty lot on the north side of our house? I wasn't working and it was the height of the depression; maybe I could raise some corn for eating.

So, not telling anybody, I dug up an area about four by twelve feet and after loosening up the dirt that was mostly clay, I managed to have three rows ready for the transplanting of the corn. I spent a whole day doing it. Later when my father came home he saw what I had done and he was pleased, but said, "We need to have some string beans growing with the corn, too." And, although it meant more work for me, I dug up a couple more rows for string beans and planted them.

All summer I watered and weeded and cultivated faithfully. Finally the day came when we had corn on the cob at our dinner table. And string beans, too. One thing I learned about the string beans was that they shouldn't be picked when the leaves are wet for that caused a rust-like fungus to set in and spoil the plants.

Anyway, as we sat eating, my father remarked, "You know, some of that corn that the mules ate could have gone all the way through that mule's stomach, etc. and never been chewed up and digested! It certainly didn't hurt the corn that sprouted!" It didn't bother any of us, for we enjoyed the corn nevertheless. But now when I hear so much about recycling I think back to the days when I recycled the corn from the house across the street. *

World War I

My mother often said to me when I was very young, "Howard, you sure have big eyes and so round, too." Now when I look at old photos, I see what she meant. I guess it also meant that I didn't miss seeing anything, either, for my memory goes back to before the end of World War I in so many ways.

Like remembering songs like "Long, Long Way to Tipperary," "Smiles," "Beautiful Katy," "Long, Long Trail A Winding," "Pack Up All Your Troubles In Your Old Kit Bag," "Over There," "Good Morning Mr. Zip-Zip-Zip," etc.

I remember cartoons depicting the horrible Kaiser Wilhelm of Germany. How we hated him. He was always pictured wearing the helmet with the pointed top. It almost looked like a weapon itself. The word Kaiser was similar to the Russian Czar and probably both names had their origin in Latin from Roman times. I think that the Czar and Kaiser were related also, maybe even brothers.

One afternoon in the fall of 1918, probably a Sunday, for my father was home, I was playing on the floor with some stone building blocks in our front room on Maple Avenue in West St. Louis when I heard quite a ruckus out in front. We lived on the second floor over a barber shop and had a good view of the street. Looking eastwardly I could see the cause of all the noise, for coming into view was the wildest collection of people beating drums, buckets, washtubs, and copper tubs, blowing all kinds of horns, harmonicas, ringing cow bells, and waving big and little flags, too.

There were all ages of people in all sort of dress and as I looked towards the end, there were more and more people joining up. They

155

were singing and shouting, "The War's Over! The War's Over!" as they paraded west to Hodiamont and North on that street.

My father said it must be that the Armistice had been signed and the World War was really over. Everywhere people came out of their houses. It was hardly believable. I had been born in 1912 and here it was 1918, so I was six years old. I had heard so many times about the terrible trench warfare from a Mrs. Nelson who visited us quite often. She had been the midwife to my mother when I was born and they had stayed good friends after. She had two brothers who were in France fighting. She always talked so sad and low and discouraged.

But the parade was for naught, for the next day the newspapers came out with an "Extra Edition" saying it was a False Armistice. The real one didn't come out for some time later, finally on November 11. I don't remember it, but I sure remember the false one.

March, 1991

Waterboy's Declaration of Independence

Part One

My grandfather was tough; I mean literally tough. He came from a line of adventurous pioneers who came down the valleys of the Ohio River, through Kentucky, Indiana, and Illinois to southeast Missouri. As a young man, married and with one child (my mother, who was in pigtails), he participated in the famous Cimmaron Rush through Oklahoma in the late 1800's. He staked out a homestead claim near the area where the small town of Medford is today. But, not being satisfied there, my grandfather pulled up stakes and moved north to Kansas.

My mother remembered the wild ride through Oklahoma and later into Kansas behind a pair of horses in a rough wood wagon. She said they didn't have a big canvas top cover like the ones shown in the movies, only a small canvas tied to some sticks that barely kept the sun and rain off them.

She remembered, too, the sod house she lived in. Sod houses were the only houses there, there being no trees to cut for log cabins. The sod was cut from six to twelve inches thick and piled up to form walls that were good shelter; cool in summer and warm in winter. I don't think she told me if they built theirs, but there were times she could see snakes that lived in the walls. They would weave in and out of their holes, disappearing as soon as they were exposed to the inside of the house.

Her mother, my grandmother, whom I never met and even to this day I'm not sure if her name was Louisa or Mary Louisa. My grandfather never spoke of her. I've heard that her maiden name was Thrasher, whose family roots were in and around Enid and Ponca City, Oklahoma.

Anyway, my mother said her mother was quite artistic and could improvise and make anything beautiful, like dyeing and designing and fabricating rugs for the sod house floors out of rough gunny-sacks, and dyeing and tying milkweed floss into beautiful, ornamental decorations that she put in vases around the sod house.

There were wolves out in that prairie country that seemed to know when anyone was sick and would scratch at the door of the house, causing apprehension to the family inside. My mother told me, too, that there was a man who lived about a mile down the road in a small shack. He was Mexican and was barely eking out an existence on his land. Whenever the Cagles, (that was my mother's unmarried name) went to town for staples, etc., the Mexican would break in a window and steal food, coffee, etc. It was a nuisance that they had to put up with, for they had no proof, so they couldn't make any accusations. But there were always bad feelings between the two families.

As luck would have it, after the Cagles left Medford, oil was found on the property they had vacated and that property became the center of the town. This story certainly would have been totally different had they stayed. What luck!

The Cagles eventually wound up in Kansas City, where my grandfather became a building contractor, building many houses in the early 1900's. My two uncles were born during this period and learned all the different aspects of building, like carpentry, plastering, painting, etc. Ithle was the oldest, and Marshall, his younger brother, was quite close to his father and stayed that way all his life. Ithle learned the decorating trade and it was soon apparent that he couldn't be domineered by his father so he left and came to St. Louis, where he got a good job with one of the top decorating firms in the city. He and his wife stayed with us when we lived on Maple Avenue near the streetcar barns on Hodiamont.

When my mother got married to a young soldier, my father, in 1899, my grandfather was so incensed because she didn't marry a fellow that worked for him that he disowned her and swore not to see her again.

My mother and father moved to St. Louis, where my father bought a small barber shop with some money that came out of his father's estate in Sikeston. The shop was in the Lafayette and Jefferson area. My father had learned to be a barber while in the Army. More about this later.

After eleven years my grandfather relented and came to see his grandchildren. I had been born in 1912, my brother Gordon was born two years later in 1914 and finally my brother Curtis came in 1916.

My mother had written letter after letter to Kansas City to her brothers there, but my grandfather was adamant and it was only after his wife died that he seemed to thaw out and decided to come down. He and my uncle Marshall drove down in a Saxon. It was a car that seemed to me, as a youngster, better than a Ford or Chevrolet. It was a great day when they arrived.

We lived in an upper story flat near Hodiamont and Maple and I can remember evenings when Papa (the family called grandfather that) and Marshall and Ithle (who had softened up a bit towards his father) would get out their violins and play like crazy. Papa had taught them to play and he had even made his own violin. No doubt he was a talented man. I remember seeing him scraping the back of his violin with a piece of glass because he said he didn't like the tone.

During the years in Kansas City, my mother had learned to play the piano, and my uncle Ithle learned to play it, too, but by ear only. He was a whiz! He could play four keys over a full octave, twelve notes, spreading his fingers that far and playing notes in between. He played everything by ear just like my brother Curtis did throughout his long musical career later.

So many experiences keep flooding through my mind as I write this. I feel impelled to put them down. No one in my family has ever attempted it so I guess I'll keep going, even if only to let my children and grandchildren know how it was in the years past.

Before he married, my father was a barber. He had learned barbering in the army, experimenting on willing fellow soldiers. He joined up with his two brothers, John and Jim, and went to the Philippines to help keep peace amongst the natives. My father, though short, was strong in the shoulders and could hold and fire a rifle steady as a rock when he fired on the range. A fellow sergeant noticed his accuracy and induced him to shoot at 1,000 yard range. My father made such a good score that he became the champion shot in the whole U.S. Army, abroad and at home, too. He held that championship for a little over a year until someone in the states beat him. I didn't hear this story from him until many years later, after I was married. He had such a short temper that I shied away from him and because of that I was never very close to him. I was more like my mother and everything I did seemed to please her.

160

While he worked as a barber, my father decided to be a lawyer, but since he had no high school education he had to go to high school and law college at the same time, at night! And so, with three children at home, working during the day, and going to night school several nights a week, he finally graduated from the old Benton Law School. I don't know how many years he did this but in 1927 he went to Jefferson City and passed the bar exam. That was quite a day in our house.

So since my grandfather was living with us and not doing any building, my father felt that with a law degree there were great prospects and expectations. The family decided to get out of the flat and build a house way out in University City. I was only nine years old and it was a big turning point in my life. And, of course, it was for my father and mother, too, for they had to borrow money for the big move.

The subdivision where they bought the lot was called City View Place. It was bordered on the east by Midland Blvd., which at that time was only an oiled dirt road. On the west it bordered on a pleasant, clear, winding creek that some people called River Des Peres, but it was really only a branch, for the real River Des Peres ran through Wellston, north and east of University City. It continued on southward, running through Forest Park and on down through south St. Louis. It wasn't a very nice river, for everyone dumped their offal into it. Sometimes, really most of the time, it was black and oily, and other times bloody from slaughter houses, dumping, etc. It was called "River de Stink" by many people who deplored the situation and the smell. Once I fell into it and had to throw all my clothes away. I really didn't fall but was pushed into it by some mean kids I was associating with and whom my mother greatly disapproved. My uncle Ithle was awfully mad when he had to clean me up. (He was supposed to keep me out of trouble while my mother was out.)

Out in University City, however, the creek was quite clear. We often caught crawfish from it and ate them with no ill effects. When my folks bought the lot, they had very little money and naturally bought the cheapest lot, which was on the western edge of the subdivision. It had quite a slope towards the rear and at the very end it dropped off in a fifteen foot clay cliff. It was very steep down to the creek; we never managed to climb it.

The big signs along Midland Blvd., about twelve by sixteen feet, advertised that everything was in place for the prospective lot owner. Sewers, sidewalks, electric, streets, etc. The only thing that was in place, however, was the "pink" sidewalks. Why they were pink, I will never know. The streets were graded and a thin two-inch coating of black cinders was the topping, but they washed away on the hilly parts and deep ruts eroded in the clay underneath. They were at least eighteen inches deep, so deep that a car had to straddle the ruts to be able to get through. It was only after I had finished high school that they were finally concreted in. They put in the sewer connections while the house was being built and we used coal-oil lamps quite a while before we got electricity. We used spring water until the water was brought in, too. Of course, the house was built without electricity; there were no power saws then, everything was done with muscle and sweat. And, even our kitchen stove was heated on one side with wood and coal. The other side was gas after the gas company piped it in. We didn't had an electric toaster or refrigerator. Looking back now, those were primitive times. Of course, it was over sixty years ago.

I was nine and going into the fifth grade after we moved into the house in September. I heard everything and saw everything that was going on in discussions about the house. Papa thought he could build a seven room house for $5,000, so a loan was made to do it. However, the costs went over, as they always do, and my folks couldn't meet the payments so we lost it during the depression of the 30's. ⚘

Part Two

Getting back to the building of the house, my folks couldn't see how we could start pouring a concrete foundation, there being no water. There was no such thing then as concrete ready-mix or made blocks. But my grandfather, pioneer that he was, said we'd buy a hand pump like the ones used on a farm, get some two-inch pipe and a big water barrel, hook it all up and pump our water out of the creek! But guess who had to pump it from the creek? Really, I only pumped it after the foundation was in, for I hadn't started to work on the project yet. But I did later, and a nine year old boy doesn't have the muscle to do that kind of work, although I managed to do it when they needed water for plastering, etc. Sometimes we didn't use the water from the barrel for a week or so and the mosquitos would lay eggs and they would hatch into little polliwogs, or larva, that I liked to watch wriggling around in the barrel.

Now when you have to hand pump water to use in your concrete mix, you know it will take a lot of hand pumping, so my

163

grandfather hired a couple of men that lived on the southeast corner of Hodiamont and Maple to help pump and carry the concrete. He offered them so much and transportation to and from the job. There were always a dozen men hanging around the barber shop and small stores on Hodiamont to recruit from.

So, after the concrete forms were set and the gravel, sand and cement delivered to the site, the men hand-mixed the concrete on a big board and then wheeled it to the forms. As a young boy of nine, I went out once or twice a week to see how the house was progressing. We would go out in the Saxon, for we didn't even own a car then. My father didn't know how to drive. He often said later that he learned to drive by following street cars, staying on their tracks and following closely, even when they turned. That way he got used to the mechanics of steering, braking, accelerating, etc.

The house was beginning to take shape after the subfloor was laid over the twelve-inch joists. Even at nine I was curious as to why the boards were nailed diagonally across the joists. It was explained to me that crosswise the boards acted as bracing so the floor wouldn't get out of the square. It's a principle that's used every day in bridge building, skyscrapers, boat building, etc., even today. Bracing and cross-bracing makes structures mighty strong.

The walls were starting to go up in the house. They were made of 2x4's and it took a lot of lumber handling, so one morning my folks came to me and said, "Today you are going out to help on the house." That was exciting, although I didn't know how I could help. They explained that for one thing I could be the water boy, for there was no drinking water for the men working in the hot summer sun.

My grandfather had discovered a spring about five or six lots away that drained into the creek. It was about four or five feet higher than the creek and was perfectly clear, cold water. If you carefully dipped your bucket in and didn't muddy things up, you had good drinking water. So several times a day I made the trip for the water. I don't know who ever tried it first. I did discover there was about a four-inch crawfish living in it that would back into his hole when I dipped in the bucket. Anyway, that was a pleasant chore for a city kid like me. The spring was in deep woods and I was beginning to notice birds and other wildlife as I made my trips back and forth to the house.

If I took too long getting the water I would catch dirty looks and sarcastic remarks from my grandfather, as sometimes he wanted me to be handy to pass up lumber to the men working up on the second floor, etc. Once I was walking across the joists above the first floor, carrying the water bucket, when I lost my balance and fell between the joists to the first floor. I landed feet first and somehow didn't spill a drop of water. My grandfather, working on a bench nearby, looked at me and said, "Boy, you sure are clumsy. Lucky you didn't spill any water."

I guess I was clumsy. I was only nine, and really quite green and timid. Other things he had said to me caused me to resent his attitude. I was willing but had to be shown and he probably thought he didn't have time to show me. I guess I was inclined to be lazy and many times I am sure I didn't anticipate the needs of the workmen. Often from sheer boredom I'd retreat to the workshed where we stored cement and nails and shovels, etc., and sit and catch flies and feed them to the spiders that had built webs in the corner of the shed or over cardboard boxes lying around. We had the fattest spiders in the neighborhood.

My grandfather caught me doing that one day and raised Cain, saying, "I want you to pick up all the scraps of wood and pile them somewhere, for this winter we'll need them to make kindling to start fires."

Well, that was a good job I could handle, so I really cleaned up the construction site. Except Papa griped that I was picking up all the good pieces, too. They looked like scraps to me! But he said things so sarcastically and mean.

One day he came to me and said, "I want you to pick up every nail you can find, even rusty ones and bent ones. I think we are going to run short of nails when we start nailing metal lath on the outside of the house tomorrow, and straighten out the bent ones, too." Well, reaching down around the concrete walls in all kinds of inconvenient places, I managed to pick up a lot of nails. Straightening them out was a different matter, for my young fingers weren't quite up to it, but I did it, as I remember. Papa was always complaining. He was never agreeable. I don't know what it was that made him that way.

One day he decided he only needed one helper so he let one go; didn't take him to the job in the morning. After working half a day the other one quit, saying he wasn't going to do a two-man job. I remember him saying it and I watched him walk over the hill to Olive Street Road and start on the two mile walk back to town.

One day, on the north side of the house, Papa came up on me sort of suddenly and yelled, "Why don't you get a board straightener for that pile of wood."

I glanced over to a sloppily piled bunch of odd-length pieces and asked, "How do I do that?"

He didn't reply but stalked off and I resumed doing nothing in particular when he showed up again and said, "Here's a board straightener. Lay a couple of 2x4's on the ground and lay all your boards as straight and neat as you can on the 2x4's. They won't warp and the crooked ones will tend to straighten out."

Well, I did what I thought was a decent job, but he came back and raised Cain again for my efforts. I'd been helping for six weeks and had endured his eternal griping and had reached a breaking point. I slammed down a board and said, "I quit," and hiked over the hill to Olive Street Road and walked the two miles home.

I knew the way and when I got home I told my mother, "I'll never go out there again!" I don't know how they got their water, maybe the water pipes were finally in, but I had really declared my independence, and even today I can remember breaking points in my life, or forks in the road, where I declared my independence and started on a new track. ❧

Conclusion

There's more to this story. I can remember looking at my grandfather's hands. Some of his fingers were curled and almost horny-looking, like talons. When I think of all the years he had handled the leather reins of horses, of the many handles of tools, saws, shovels, etc., I can see why they looked like they did. He worked constantly on that house of ours on Jackson Avenue in University City. Even after a Sunday dinner he'd go out and saw wood for the fireplace, and every night after supper he'd go to the basement and work on cabinets for the upstairs. The whole first floor was made of oak with cabinets and shelves, too. Oak is not easy to work, either, and a lot of it came from the saw mills my grandfather had owned and operated in Sikeston, Missouri. He had a lot of the oak he had sawn and milled down there sent up to University City for our house. I noticed lots of times the oak, when it was being worked, had a strong sour smell that was disagreeable to me. But Papa persevered and when all the woodwork was done and varnished, it was quite beautiful.

Once in a while Papa would inadvertently use a piece that had worms in it and on a still night, or even in the day sometimes, you could go into the dining room and hear the worms chewing their way through the outside of the board. It distressed my mother quite a bit, but we would just putty it up and hope for the best.

Papa had two saw mills burn down in Sikeston. Sawmills are a peculiar kind of business. It seems that the tiniest spark from whatever source could settle in the sawdust deep down and, unknown or unseen by anybody, smolder for years before bursting into flame. No one is ever allowed to smoke near a sawmill. Even flash powder used in taking pictures around sawmills has been known to cause a fire.

My grandfather only smoked cigarettes and once he put one in his mouth he never took it out. He would work and work and smoke and smoke the cigarette, leaving the ash hang on until it bent down in a curve. Only when the cigarette burned his lips would he spit it out. He always had a blister or two on his mouth.

In my grandfather's time there was a lot of speculation on perpetual motion. A machine that once started would never quit and would give power forever. This machine would revolutionize the world and my grandfather thought he had the solution. So in our basement, back in the corner away from any windows, he built his creation. We kids were never allowed to peek at it. It had blankets hung around it and we were warned and pledged not to speak of it to anyone or attempt to look at it. I had a glimpse of it once. It looked like a lot of 1" x 1" sticks bolted together in a zigzag fashion that fit into a 6' x 6' frame. It wasn't very clear what it was intended to do. I never heard any noise out of it. After a year or two it was abandoned, but years later, after I was married, he tried to explain it to me. It had something to do with weights, but he said the trouble with perpetual motion was that you couldn't get rid of friction and that you never could.

When my brother Curtis was ten or so, he learned to play the harmonica from my grandfather. He was so pleased, and they would play together by the hours; tunes like "Nellie Gray," "Old Folks at Home," etc.

After he finished the house in University City, he and my uncle Marshall, who had become quite a good architect, moved from Sikeston to Carrizo Springs, Texas where they built a lot of commercial buildings like theaters, offices, etc. Finally, they took all their money and put it into tomato and grapefruit farming. They did quite well, but eventually were wiped out by holding on to their produce too long for a better price. They were cleaned out completely and came back to Sikeston and started to build houses there again.

Incidentally, I feel that a lot of the houses that they built in Kansas City are still standing. My grandfather liked to build stone porches and since much of Kansas City, in certain areas, literally had to have limestone excavated before a house could be built on the site, they used the stone in the porches. The Hyde Park area abounds in these stone-porch houses and I feel sure my grandfather built some of them. I suppose the city records would show which ones. I would have to look up his full name which was George Washington Cagle. He was quite a guy even though he was a grouch. He looked so nice when he was dressed up and so wretched in his work clothes.

After I got out of the CCC's in 1936 and was working for a sign company, he came up to St. Louis from Sikeston for a short time, helping my folks, who were doing some remodeling on a small house in Rock Hill. He wanted me to quit and learn cabinet making from him and maybe get a truck and travel the country, painting signs and living like gypsies, which I didn't want at all.

And even now I can remember my father remarking on how much jelly or jam "George" would put on his bread or biscuit; about a quarter or an inch thick. And when I do it myself, today, I can't help thinking of him.

He finally died in Phoenix, Arizona at the age of 85, still building one and two room houses. My mother went out and buried him, but she never told me any details about that. ✺

Cigar Bands

When I was in the sixth and seventh grades, a fad broke out in our neighborhood. I don't think it was as prevalent in other neighborhoods. It might have been.

All of us boys started to collect cigar bands. As our collections accumulated, we started gluing them in Blue-Jay notebooks, usually there were eight to ten on each page and we used both sides of the page. We numbered them below each band. Our aim was to get a thousand different bands. That sounds impossible, doesn't it? But, it seemed there were more cigar smokers then, and at drugstores we could see the many different cigar boxes displayed on the glass cases of the tobacco section. Some cigars were made in six or eight varieties; long, short, mild, blunt, tapered, etc., and each had a different size band. The coloring was usually gold and red and the designs were quite beautiful. The art work on the lids of the boxes had exotic scenes and beautiful bare-shouldered ladies smiling at the beholder. We were always begging for the boxes, especially if we saw that there was only one or two cigars left in the box. Some of the proprietors were nice, some gruff, and some condescending, often saying, "Come back tomorrow" and we did, but sometimes a single cigar would go unsold for a week.

The boxes were made, then, of Honduras mahogany, and I learned right away it was nice to work with. We made many things from the boxes like guitars, small wagons, bird houses, etc. They were great to keep our treasures in like tops, marbles, baseball cards, pencils, rocks, shells, bird nests, etc. You always wanted more cigar boxes and sometimes you would hit it lucky and walk out of the drugstore with four or five, or more than you could carry. I was so disappointed, years later, when the boxes began to appear in the stores made of cardboard.

I remember once that three or four of us filled up a Chancellor cigar box (it was a bigger box, almost twice the height of a regular box) with our treasures, and secretly wrapped them with wrappings we thought were waterproof, and early in the evening of winter, dug a hole under the sidewalk of our subdivision and slid the box in and covered it up and smoothed the dirt all around so that no one could tell the ground had been disturbed; like squirrels do when they hide food. We each had contributed coins, tops, stamps, cigar bands, cards, etc. equally and solemnly pledged not to tell anyone about it and we never even glanced at the site if we went by it. We even drew a map for each of us, sort of like a Treasure Island map; so many steps from a tree or corner, etc.

We were a few of a larger group in the neighborhood and we didn't all agree on various things, so we thought it was unique and great that we had our own secret buried treasure.

Occasionally we'd sit on that special piece of sidewalk and talk generally to all of the group of how wouldn't it be neat to find a buried treasure and maybe we should all hunt for one, or even make one, never letting on that we were sitting on top of one. After a couple of weeks, after torturing ourselves about the whole thing, we dug up the box and divided the booty and forgot it. But we would do it several times through the years. We didn't have TV and very little radio and supervised sports like we have now.

Really this story started off about cigar bands. One of our gang read in a magazine that you could buy a thousand different cigar bands for $3.00 from a cigar company in Tampa Bay, Florida. It's name was Marcelino-Perez. I'll never forget that name. Anyway, one of us sent off for them. When they finally came it was exciting. There was one enormous one, about twelve to fourteen inches long spread out, and several smaller ones, seven to eight inches long. There were many bands named after athletic clubs, but I really was disappointed, for even though there probably were a thousand bands, many were duplicates; 650 different at the most. Even in those days scams were pulled off on youngsters. But, nevertheless the big ones were super and a marvel to look at. I suppose they went around bunches of cigars as a decoration. I never saw one in a cigar store.

Nevertheless, we all went around picking up cigar bands, once in a while fighting for possession if we saw one at the same time. In busy places like street car stops, in front of saloons, at ball parks (there used to be lots of hard ball parks in those days). We used to stalk cigar smokers for blocks, if he had a rare, or hard to find band. Sometimes we would get up nerve to ask him for it, if it looked like he was going to burn it before he threw it away. Many a butt was burned through before we found it.

Our favorites were the hard-to-get bands like a "white" Emanelo or an "Antonio-Cleopatra" or a "Red Dot" or Garcia Grand, Dutch Masters, Hauptman's hand-made, San Felice, Charles Denby, El-Roi-Tan, and Chancellor were quite common and didn't trade for much. "Red Dot" was a single 1/4-inch red dot and not a band at all, although another "Red Dot" was a big beautiful band. "Antonio-Cleopatra" was a rare find because it was a 75-cent cigar. I've picked up quite a few of them even though they were soggy and wet. You could always trade one for three or four others.

When we were out with our parents we were always cautioned not to be picking up any cigar bands in their presence and if we did we'd get punished later. We devised all kinds of sneaky ways to pick them up; like walking backwards or kicking them along to be in a better picking-up spot or even going around the block for another chance at getting this or that particular band. Around fancy hotels you could make a haul, sometimes finding several "white" Emanelos. Ordinary Emanelos were all gold and red but a "white" Emanelo had the lettering in the center of the band in white. Of course they cost more, too.

We kept filling up our Blue-Jay note books, hoping to reach the one-thousand mark. I never did; I think I got to 800 or 900. Anyway, going through my mother's trunks some time ago I found my cigar band collection. That was quite a shock! I kept them all through my first marriage, and later Betty and I took them to a paper show, sort of like an antique show, and showed them around. We got an offer of $13.00 or so. I know I didn't spend that much on them so we accepted the offer and I felt good that now someone else is going to enjoy them. I wonder how far they will go in some other collector's hands. ✒

Streetcars

There are a lot of people living, I suppose, who can remember the older streetcars that I'm writing about. However, I didn't live in the era of horse cars that moved so slowly and even had straw strewn on the floor around the seats to keep your feet warm. I don't think I would have liked that.

Anyway, my streetcars in St. Louis were electric, with trolleys that took power from overhead electric wires. The seats were of hard, finely-split cane, and had a built-in handle on the corner that faced the aisle. Believe me, those handles were very handy as were the overhead leather straps that many passengers hung onto tightly as the car lurched and weaved to and fro as it made its way down the tracks.

When you entered the car, the first thing you looked for was an empty seat. Many times there weren't any, so you hung onto the overhead strap or the corner of a seat until you could grab a seat when a passenger got off. Sometimes, there was a scramble for the seat, but if it was between you and a lady you always gave her the seat. Or if you had a seat and a lady came by, you would offer her your seat, although as a youth I always felt a little nervous doing it. I don't know why.

Smokers had to sit in the rear of the car, and usually a blind man selling brooms would stay in the rear with his load. He always had a youngster to help him on and off the car.

The windows were always heck to open or shut. Usually you would need help and sometimes the person sitting next to you didn't want any air or maybe the person in back of you would complain

175

about the draft, or the rain would come in. So, I generally left them alone. On the outside there were heavy iron bars to either keep you in or keep others out. And there were buttons to push to signal the motorman you wanted off, but sometimes they didn't work and you'd punch them two or three times, or go to the next seat and punch that button. Some cars had heavy cords that you pulled down to give the motorman a signal.

Good motormen would call out street names that were coming up next. That meant you'd better get out of your seat and start moseying up to the front. Some motormen had patience and some didn't. The motormen had to make their particular loop on schedule, for there were company car people checking them.

Streetcars were an important way of life back in the twenties, thirties, forties, and even fifties. Most of the main lines had terminals that were quite a few miles away. These terminals were called loops like Delmar Loop, Broadway Loop, Belefontaine Loop, Chain of Rocks Loop, Kirkwood-Ferguson Loop, Hodiamont Loop, etc.

A lot of these loops had amusement parks at the end. Of course, you paid another fare to go back to the other end of the line.

These parks had all kinds of attractions to entice you to spend your money. There were shooting galleries when you shot with a 22 rifle at moving wooden ducks, or tossing baseballs at various objects stacked on tables, where if you hit them all you would win a prize, usually a Kewpie doll; a flesh colored doll made of chalk, adorned with very few clothes and a pink feather glued to its body. We liked to find broken pieces of the dolls that we used to mark or write on sidewalks or fences or walls.

There were also big wheels that were numbered with small

numbers that corresponded to large numbers on a board or counter next to the player. When the operator gave a flip or turn to the wheel and it stopped on a number that you had put money on, you'd win a Kewpie doll or a cane or sometimes a ham even.

Many of the parks at the loop had picnic tables that were either out in the open or among trees or under shelters. Generally you went to loop parks in groups from churches or schools or other organizations.

On picnic days in the park, the city schools had the children assemble as usual in their classrooms, usually a Saturday, when they were given flags, balloons, noisemakers, and tickets that were good for rides, candy, ice cream, etc.

Usually the mothers would ride along with the kids. In those days most fathers worked on Saturdays and would come out later to join the family.

Next, we would walk to the nearest streetcar line where the cars would be lined up with flags in the holders on the front of the car above the windows. Incidentally, flags were flown there also on national holidays, too. The four schools in the district were Hempstead, Emerson, Hamilton, and ours which was Dozier. We all combined for this annual affair and there seemed to be an endless procession of streetcars with flags waving and singing and chatter. It was always a memorable occasion. One of the best parts, at least to me, was that our route was over a lot of strange streets.

In the early years I remember that we would go to the Chain of Rocks Waterworks Loop where we all went inside buildings and watched the pumps and machinery working away in the big pit below. We were quite impressed by that. St. Louisans were very proud of their new water purification system because for many years visitors wouldn't drink our cloudy, muddy water.

When our family moved to University City, Missouri, we were given tickets in addition to flags and noisemakers, that gave us rides on the ferris wheel, mountain-ride, airplane swing, etc. at a loop that ended at Westlake Amusement Park out on St. Charles Rock Road. It was a long ride from the Delmar Loop, where all schools boarded the cars to the Westlake Loop. We sang songs like "It Ain't Goin' to Rain No More," "Brown Eyes," and "Ain't She Sweet."

There were underground boat rides that ran under the decking of the park where, if you had the nerve, you could ask a girl to ride with you. Then maybe you'd take a chance and slip your arm around her.

It was always a long, weary ride back to the Delmar Loop, where we had boarded in the morning.

When we rode the streetcar, we always wanted to sit by the window so we wouldn't miss anything, and with two more brothers there was usually a scramble to get the window seat. It was even better still to sit up by the motor man, who fascinated us with his manipulation of the cranks and levers. He didn't have to steer, for he was on tracks, but he did have to use his brakes. All motormen wore a heavy canvas glove, although I never did learn if he did so because the handle was hot, or to keep his hand from getting calluses. He had a large box to his left that contained sand to dump on the rails when they were slippery or icy. If you got to ride on the sandbox you were very lucky. Most motormen wouldn't allow it for safety reasons, I guess, but some would let you and you'd get to talk to him and watch more closely what he was doing. The *Post Dispatch* once had a regular column in the newspaper called "The Man on the Sandbox" whose opinions, etc., were always considered to be wise and witty about sports and politics and things like that. Also, there was a large, round, metal button on the floor beneath the motorman's feet that was connected to a large bell that he would bang with his foot whenever something was coming into view that he might run into, such as a horse and buggy or pedestrians or a street cleaner's cart with the man behind it cleaning up manure from the horses that were quite common, then. Some motormen had a very heavy foot and seemed to bang the bell a lot unnecessarily.

All cars had a conductor in the rear where doors opened for the passengers to enter. This is where there was a lot of pushing and elbowing of people trying to get on first and get a seat. It was every man for himself. Gender or politeness was forgotten in the press to get on. When you did get on, you had to have your fare ready to drop in the box. Conductors hated to make change from dollar bills, for it slowed up all the loading. When you did have your change in the right amount you dropped it in a metal and glass fare box that had a crank attached which the conductor seemed to be constantly turning. It separated the coins in the box, at the same time counting up the amount taken in. And woe be to you if you accidently dropped too much money in the fare box, for you couldn't get it back. The conductor said it was counted and he'd have to take it out of his pocket to reimburse you. When you were a kid and had grown-ups pushing you from behind and yelling besides you'd get confused and maybe drop too much change in the box. Then you would be in trouble, for you might have dropped half of your money in.

In later years the car company did away with conductors and

passengers had to enter by the front door and the motormen had to make change and keep his car under control, too. There was a lot of hullabaloo about that for quite a while, but there was a depression on and the car company said they had to find ways to cut costs.

During World War I, the streetcars pulled trailer-cars. They were the same size as the front cars but they had lady conductors because men were going off to war. They collected the fares in the trailer-cars and looked so strange in their grey uniforms and squarish bill-caps and wore long pants long before Marlene Dietrich wore hers.

Streetcars had a trolley (a word seldom heard now). It was a metal pole and box attached with a swivel to the center of the roof of the car. At the top of the trolley was a bronze wheel that made contact with the bare electric wire that ran along above the car. The electric wire was strung above the car from poles and cross-wires to complete the route from loop to loop. This bronze wheel, I'd guess, was six or eight or ten inches in diameter. There was a rope connected with the wheel and bracket near the top of the pole and it went down the back of the car to the round metal box where it rolled up on a spring-like contrivance. The electric wire that ran along above would sag in places and be uneven, so the trolley would give and take to keep contact through the spring in the box on the back.

Nervy guys would sometimes pull the trolley wheel off the wire and run. Of course, the car couldn't operate without a contact. Anyone caught doing a stunt like that was arrested and treated pretty severely.

Speaking again of the bronze wheel, sometimes in bad or icy weather, when the electric wires got coated with ice and icicles, the bronze wheels would get clogged with ice and jump the overhead wire, creating a lot of sparks and noise. The poor car men would get out in the sleet and snow and try to get the wheel back on the wire. Sometimes they would have to give up and all the passengers had to get off and walk to their destination. Those were the tough days.

Of course, everyone used the streetcars. If you owned a car then, many times the roads were so bad even paved streets were not kept up; you could be late if you had flat tires, etc. The streetcars always got you to your destination.

When you paid your fare, you could ask for a transfer. This was a piece of paper that allowed you to go in another direction. It didn't cost anything, but there were time limits and you weren't allowed on certain cars that went back to your original starting point. Sometimes there were big arguments over this.

My brother told me of a time when a lady got on the Hamilton car that ran south from Hi-Pointe to the Maplewood Loop. She gave the motorman a transfer whose time had elapsed and when he objected and pointed it out to her, she got very upset and wouldn't get off the car so the motorman said he'd go get a policeman and he got off, leaving the car unattended. Whereupon the woman sat down on the motorman's seat and put the car in motion by moving around the cranks and levers. She seemed to be doing pretty well, but my brother thought there were times it seemed she was speeding.

She stopped the car, I guess at her stop, and got off, ran up the street and disappeared. Curt, my brother, said the motorman finally showed up with the policeman and took control of his car again and drove it to the Maplewood Loop, where everyone got off in relief. It was twenty years later that Curt told me he had made this whole story up. He only imagined it when he saw a motorman really having an argument about a transfer with an old lady!

When our family moved to University City, I was in fifth grade and we depended on the Creve Coeur line for transportation to school at Delmar and Kingsland, a distance of about one and three-quarter miles. I was given a dime for car fare, since I was the oldest of us three boys. The fare was three cents each, so I always had a penny left over, but lots of time I was only given nine cents exactly. I really don't remember what I did with the penny, but in later years my brothers told me that they always thought it unfair that I got the penny.

Lots of times, usually on Sundays, the three of us would be given money to ride the Kirkwood-Ferguson car out to the Meramec Highlands, way, way out to the Big Bend area near Couch Ave. It was a long ride, costing three cents there and three cents back and what a thrill the ride was through fields and woods and over three long trestles where we could see creeks and all sorts of strange views.

Our parents thought nothing of going to visit friends all over the city, south to Jefferson Barracks, by the Delmar-Broadway cars or north to Ramona Park beyond Wellston. Many times, after visiting friends in winter, it was dark and we'd huddle around each other as we waited by a nearby pole or building corner, stamping our feet and almost crying. We would pray that the streetcar would hurry up. We'd go out to the tracks and look back, hoping to see the headlight. And, too, we'd hope we hadn't missed the last car of the night. The last car of the night was called the "Owl Car." If you missed that one you'd have to walk home. It usually came along at midnight. We always managed to catch it and never had to walk.

Every spring, around Memorial Day, the Creve Coeur Line

put on "open air" cars. They had no windows. On one side there were bars and passengers couldn't get on or off on that side. The other side, where passengers boarded, there was a long sort of running board that ran the complete length of the car that the conductor walked on when he collected fares.

The seats were long and went from side to side. Maybe they were eight feet long. The step up from the ground to that long running board was difficult for ladies and children, too. The lades had long dresses and the children had short legs and had to be helped in a lot of cases.

Collecting the fares always seemed to be a hazardous job, I thought. Making change and holding on to a seat corner or pole was not an ideal job. Getting off the car wasn't easy, either. First you pushed a button, hoping the motorman heard you, for if you missed your stop it was a long, sometimes dark, walk down the tracks to your street. In our particular case it meant walking over a forty foot trestle, trying to step on the ties in the right place, in the dark. You could walk an extra four blocks and avoid the trestle, but you hated to walk all that distance so you held hands and crept slowly across, hoping another streetcar wouldn't come and scare the daylights out of you.

There were always hundreds of people going to Creve Coeur Lake on Saturdays, Sundays, and holidays for picnics, fishing, or boating. The ride out was always fun. It was breezy and there was so much countryside to see.

At the park, for a quarter, you could take a ride on a small-size scenic car that ran on a narrow gauge track up and down the hills in the area and at the end let you off by the lake. This ride saved you taking the many, many steps back up the hill to the concession area. One feature at the concession area was an observation tower at least one hundred feet high with an elevator that took you up to an enclosed platform. There you could see for miles with a great view of the lake and the Missouri River. I can remember looking up at the faces looking out over the restraining fence at the top. They looked like doll faces way up there and I decided I would never go up there, but I did four years later and got over my fears. It was a sad day years later when it was taken down.

No doubt about it, the streetcar loops and parks were the place to go. Automobiles were in their infancy with no starters, no glass windows to keep the bad weather out, and almost every long trip was marred by a flat tire or two. Roads were mostly dirt and graded, then oiled. Sometimes they got so many holes in them that the going was terribly slow.

Windshield wipers hadn't been thought of, and when they were they were hand operated, making travel on snowy days, even in the city, a gamble. Cars then were hand-cranked with a wire-choke that stuck out of the radiator. It must be pulled on at the same time while cranking. You had to remember to keep your thumb above the crank handle because sometimes the crank would kick back, and many wrists were sprained if your thumb was wrapped around the crank handle.

After I graduated from high school, I helped out as an assistant Scout Master at our church. We had four or five patrols in our troop #197 at Vinita Park Methodist Church. I promised the patrol that got the most points in a contest that I would take them to Cliff Cave for an all day outing. I had been there once with a friend

184

so I knew the way by streetcar and then hiking from the end of the line.

Well, the Beaver patrol won so we planned everything, packed our lunches and gear and rode the Creve Coeur streetcar to the Delmar Loop, where we caught the Delmar car at about eight in the morning.

It was a bright sunny day in winter, and the seven or eight of us were in high spirits.

We rode downtown and caught the Broadway car that went south to the Sauter Park Loop. From there we hiked down to the railroad tracks and headed down to Cliff Cave. I suppose it was at least two miles. We always kept an eye out for trains, for in those days there were many more on the move than now. We discovered they could sneak up on you very swiftly.

We had many big ideas of what we were going to do in the cave. First we were going to measure how far we went into the cave by tying a big ball of string to a tree outside and play it out as we went in.

Another thing that we thought was unique was that we were going to light our way with candles. Most of these candles were short discards from home. We lit them and placed them in nooks and cracks about every twenty feet along the walls. There didn't seem to be any drafts so the candles did very well.

We went in as far as we could and the passage got tighter and tighter until it was so tight I couldn't move my body and it sort of frightened me so I gave the order to stop and said we'd better go back out and head for home. I've always heard that if you persevered you could get through the cave and it came out somewhere on the other side of the hills. Later, in the Civilian Conservation Corps, I met fellows that said they made it through when they were boys.

We wound up our string and discovered that most of our candles had burned out. They weren't doing much good now and as we were walking out toward the light we had no trouble getting out, but lo! when we did get out, we discovered a three inch snow on the ground. It didn't scare us, but what a surprise!

We turned up our collars, (I don't think any of us had gloves), and headed back north along the railroad tracks to the Broadway Loop. About halfway back one of the boys lost the sole of his shoe. He retrieved it and managed to tie it back on somehow well enough to continue walking with it.

When we got to the loop it was dark, past eight o'clock, and when we finally got home it was past midnight. It was a hike none of the boys or I would ever forget and I never heard a bad word from the parents, who I know must have been concerned. Two of the boys are still my good friends today and we still reminisce about the good old (tough) days.

There are so many other things I remember about streetcars: the ads they had on the front of the cars and the "ads" inside above the cane seats, and the metal tokens you could buy ahead of time, thereby saving some money, and the little coke stoves that were supposed to keep the car warm but didn't unless you were lucky enough to almost sit on it.

The cars themselves weren't very pretty. They were square and boxy, except for the front and back ends which were shaped like a bay window with three sides. Very seldom did they have a new coat of paint and it was always a drab, dirty yellow. Many years later the cars were modernized with rounded streamlined bodies and red paint, with better springs; they seemed to glide down the tracks.

One of the last things I remember, and vividly too, was the time as I was walking home from school and saw about five or six of the old cars burning on a big open lot along the right-of-way. The wheels had been removed and the cars, which were mostly wood, had been set on fire, their window frames and doors black but their fiery outlines stood out against the evening skies. Though I didn't have much sentiment at that age, the sight saddened me.

October, 1990

A Few Golf Stories

Everyone should, at one time in their life, try to play a little golf. Of the many thousands that are playing, there are many, many more that aren't. The good golfers, ones that shoot par or under, are good because they practice a lot and discipline themselves in doing all the right things, while they are hitting the ball. That's all you do besides walking, is hitting the ball. There's no jumping, or running, or pushing or shoving, tackling or catching. You just walk a lot, uphill and downhill, trying to stay out of the rough, which is on both sides of the fairway. It's hard to hit a ball out of the heavy grass or weeds. Sometimes you even lose a ball.

My wife Bobbie and I always shook hands after the first tee shot, because she always hit her ball to the left (called a hook shot) and I always hit mine to the right (called a slice), so we rarely saw each other, except we naturally always met on the green and putted out. We played a few times and then the family came along and that finished that.

Back in the depression days, I was desperate for work and an older friend asked me, "Why don't you caddy out at the golf course where I work?" He checked tickets at the half-way mark and had lost his regular job, taking his present job for lack of any other job. The course was only a couple of miles west of where we lived.

I had always felt that caddying was a sort of lowly job, besides, here I was a high school graduate; I should get better work than that, carrying a bag around for some rich so and so. But, I swallowed my pride, went out to the golf course, went into the office at the first tee and told them I needed a job. I listened to the caddy master tell me what to do and what not to do. After that he gave me a big two-inch white badge with Number 89 on it. I should wear it at all times, near my watch pocket.

There are a lot of rules, terms, and courtesies in golf, and names like mashie and niblick, etc. If a player wanted a niblick tossed to him you better find it quick, etc., etc. Like the term "Fore!" meant a lot of things like, "Look out!" or "You're playing my ball" or "Give way, we're going through," etc. If you heard "Fore!" you had to expect anything.

I was bigger and older than the majority of my fellow caddies. Most were eighth and ninth graders. Some caddied as a lark and getting the privilege of playing for free on Mondays when activity was slow; others worked because their families need the money.

Most of the boys hated to caddy for a woman - they took too many strokes, gabbed too much with the other ladies, especially if four of them played together. Most of them wanted you to keep their scores and a few of them wore stale perfume. They didn't tip much either.

We were always called up to the starting tee by number, in rotation, depending on when you signed in. Somehow the boys always knew when certain ladies were on the tee and they would groan if their number came up.

We were paid by the golfer himself, sixty-five cents for carrying a bag for nine holes. If your player had a good round he'd probably pay, or tip you, another sixty-five cents or even a dollar.

And besides, he might play another round so you really pulled in the coin.

I soon learned that every golfer had his or her own peculiar antics and I kept my mouth shut, really keeping my eye on the ball and marking where it landed. Balls were expensive, even in those days, ranging from fifty cents to a dollar. Losing a ball for your golfer was a disgrace. You always went ahead, if it was possible, even running sometimes to keep it in sight over a hill or even worse, into a bad patch of rough.

When you found the ball you assumed a relaxed pose near it, with the bag standing upright by you, and ready to hand a club to your golfer. Many of my patrons and I would have long discussions on various subjects as we walked along, stride for stride. I usually enjoyed time like this.

There are always lots of things happening on a public golf course and the caddies would come in telling all sort of stories; like the one about two fellows that played every Sunday. They always took caddies and paid well, but they were real duffers, playing down the fairways, zigzagging back and forth, losing balls, swearing at each other, etc. On this particular Sunday, they had played all the way around to the eighth hole. This one player was losing, or had lost, every hole to his buddy and in so doing had lost quite a bit of money, betting on every shot, etc. He was so mad that he called his caddy over and started taking every club from the bag and began hitting the club around an apple tree near the edge of the fairway. Every club he wrapped around the tree. Next he took all the balls from the pocket of the bag and threw them in all directions and after that he took out a knife and cut long slashes and rips in the side of the bag, making it useless and irreparable. He threw away his cap and then sat down and pried out all the spikes in his shoes. When this was done, he stalked off to the club house. And, guess what, next Sunday he was out on Number 1 tee, ready to play, with a complete set of clubs, balls, cap and shoes. Unbelievable!

One day, some caddies came in and told quite a story. Out on Number 4 fairway, which was quite a long one, over 500 yards, the caddies had gone ahead to watch the tee shots come toward them. Lots of times the balls disappear from view because of the hilly slopes. This particular day M.S. and his wife were playing and they had hit their shots pretty well and the balls went rolling down the hill toward the caddies. They stopped about eighteen inches apart. The caddies, always up to no good, pushed the balls together. I might mention that M.S. was a very popular pipe organist at one of the downtown theaters for many years. When he and his wife saw their balls together, they were so overcome that they dropped their clubs, hugged each other, and told the caddies that they were through for the day and off they went, arm in arm to the club house.

One day, a golfer teed up his ball, a nice new one, and proceeded to hit it out and into a lake in front of him. He patiently took out another new ball, teed it up carefully and then hit it, "kerplunk" into the water again. Back to his bag again he took out another ball and did the same thing, right into the water. A spectator sitting on a bench near the tee couldn't help remarking, "Why don't you shoot an old ball?" The man on the tee looked up almost with tears in his eyes and said, "I've never had one!" ✒

Shadows

A long time ago, a teacher said to our class that there was something we would have all our life and no one could take it away, it would be with us wherever we went. It didn't weigh anything or need to be washed or tended to like other things we have, but it did grow larger or smaller depending on the season.

It was our shadow. From the time she mentioned it, I've always kept track of mine. Early in the morning I notice that it is very long and points west. In the evenings it points east. That is, if the sun is shining. But most important of all, it points north at 12 o'clock noon. And, in the summer, when the sun is almost overhead at 12 noon, it's very short, hardly any shadow at all. In the winter at noon it's very long. Even now in November my shadow at noon is eight feet long. Probably in January it will be ten feet long. I'm going to keep track this year, month by month on the same day, how much my shadow grows or shrinks.

However, this business of a shadow, pointing north at noon, gets complicated. I feel reasonably sure that every person living north of the equator knows, or should know, that his or her shadow always points north at noon even if they are Chinese, Italian, Turk, Spanish or what. It's a matter of keeping track of where you are, in many cases, and what your directions are.

What has bothered me for so many years is when a person goes south, very far south, south of the equator, does his shadow point south at 12 noon? It seems to me that it should. But, I've asked so many lecturers, travelers, planetarium managers, etc., and none could give me an answer.

193

As a youth, my mother was always complaining that plants wouldn't grow on the north side of the house; that it was too shady and in the winter the north side of the house was always colder. We never had any blooming things on the north side, only bushes. I've learned since that certain plants will bloom and thrive on the north side however.

Recently I attended an Audubon meeting and met the lecturer's wife who said, Oh yes, the south side of her home in Wellington, New Zealand was always the cold side, which means to me that the shadows do point south at noon, Wellington being below the equator.

The whole point of this article is, if a person traveled by air (of course, what else) to Buenos Aires, Argentina, getting there in two or three days, he might find himself walking on an east-west street at noon with his shadow pointing south! And, all the buildings on east-west streets would have their south sides in shadow and be colder, especially in June or July. I know I could get used to it, but the strangeness would persist for a while.

Of course we have many days when there is no sun and our ever-present shadow doesn't show up, but because we know our territory, it doesn't matter, however, going to another part of the U.S. it's nice to know what's north, and when you drive in a large unfamiliar city a map at your side is a must. And, even with thousands of directional signs you get lost. Knowing that in the Northern Hemisphere (above the equator) your shadow points north at noon and in the Southern Hemisphere (below the equator) your shadow points south at noon, seems very important to me.

November, 1989

Lovely Minka

My brother Curtis was a talented musician. Even as a five or six year-old he could sing so well that quite frequently people in our neighborhood would beg him to sing on a street corner near us and quite a few coins would be tossed at his feet from the by-standers and passers by.

A few years later, when our family managed to buy a piano at $25.00 a month, he would climb up on the bench and play by ear anything he had heard. So it was only a short time later that he was taking piano lessons.

All my young life from then on I constantly heard him practicing. I didn't mind and often we'd sing around the piano, while my mother played. I was generally doing things around the house, or working in the basement making bird houses or rabbit traps, etc. Always I heard him playing pieces like "Golliwog Cakewalk," "Clair de Lune," "Meditation," "Consolation," etc.

Sometime during our high school years (he was a freshman when I was a senior) I noticed him playing a little tune, over and over. It was his first original effort and was quite singable but the two of us just hummed it.

At the time, I was reading a lot of historical romances written by a Louisa Muhlbach, a German writer, whose books, about thirty of them, had been translated into English. They were about Napoleon, Frederick the Great, Henry the Eighth, Empress Josephine, Bismarck, etc. I eventually read them all.

In one book there were stories of the troubles between Poland and Russia. In one chapter, I remember that a young Polish laborer was doing forced labor with the Cossacks, their oppressors. He loaded gun powder in his wheelbarrow that he brought from home each day. He would load up and take the powder to a powder magazine for processing.

The Cossacks didn't know it but he belonged to a group of saboteurs who finally decided at one of their meetings to blow up the powder mill. He, the laborer, actually was to sacrifice his life to do it.

On the morning of the day set, as he walked along pushing his wheelbarrow, he hummed a song about his home and his family, which he would never see again. The words went like this.

"Lovely Minka, must I leave thee?
Leave thy happy, heather plains.
Ah! This parting does not grieve thee.
Though still true my heart remains
Far from thee, I roam.
Sadly see the sunbeams shining
Lovely all the night I'm pining,
Far from thee alone."

His habit was smoking a pipe as he walked, but when he entered the powder mill, he always emptied it because of the danger involved. This morning, unnoticed by the Cossacks, he kept the pipe glowing. And as he bent over a bag of gunpowder he dropped his pipe and blew the whole mill apart, including himself.

Well, the poem affected me quite a bit, and suddenly it dawned on me that Curtis's little tune had quite a plaintive sad air to it and that maybe it could be adapted to the powder mill worker's song "Lovely Minka."

So I went upstairs with my idea. Curt and I had done so many musical things together in church and school and other things that we had always agreed upon things musical.

Curt and I sang a lot together. He would play the piano and sing harmony while I sang the melody. And he would always put in extra touches as he played and finish with such flourishes that we always got applause.

Like the time we were invited to sing at the home on Arsenal Street for the insane. It was a big hall with the raised stage and a grand piano. We sang songs like "How Can I Pretend I'm Not Caring," and "Out Of The Dusk To You" and others. The place was full and they were generous with their applause.

We sang at weddings and even once at a funeral home, after which we vowed we would never do it again. We sang "Beautiful Isle of Somewhere." It seemed to us that everyone was affected by the song and was crying. It was too much for us.

Back in the old days when minstrel shows were popular, Curt and I would participate, piano and all at the Union M.E. church on Grandel and Grand. We were very young then, probably ten and fourteen years old. We sang the old songs like "Old black Joe," "Rufus Rastus Johnson Brown," "Dixie,"etc.

At University City High, the Music Department put on an annual light opera performance every spring. There were tryouts for the main voice parts and I always managed to get in special men's choruses, (about twelve to eighteen of us) but when Curt came in as a freshman he went for the tenor lead. His voice was developing fast and strong , although he always worried about hitting a high "A" in some of the songs. He got the part, and every year after that got the

197

tenor lead. Of course, we heard him practicing all the time at home.

Well, he looked over "Lovely Minka" and we began to adapt the music to it. We left out words and added some and finally it fit together.

Then, now that we had it, we thought, "This is great! We ought to dedicate it to someone!"

It didn't take us long, but instead of one, we decided on two sisters who lived in the northern part of University City, who were in school with us; Katherine Queal, who was my age, and Lucy, who was Curt's age. We had been to their house on quite a few occasions, singing (around a piano that had seen better days) with other people our age from the neighborhood. Seems like this group always thought of singing. We'd even hike all the way to the Municipal Opera Theatre in Forest Park to get to hear singers like Leonard Ceeley, Allan Jones, Guy Robertson, etc. We were a musical bunch.

We kept our tune secret until I had gotten hold of some nice paper and I hand lettered the title on the first page. Then on the inside page we dedicated it to Katherine and Lucy Queal. On the opposite page, Curt drew the lines and notes, like a real musical score and I put the words (lyrics) underneath his scoring.

Then one day, we marched up to the Queal House and announced our purpose, walking up to the piano and proceeded to sing our song. I carried the tune or melody and Curtis sang the harmony.

Well, the family was spellbound. And the girls were delighted. Imagine a song dedicated to them and they so young! We sang it over and over for them and they all joined in, grandmother and all.

For many years, whenever there was a gathering or reunion,

Curt and I were requested to sing it. Even after we were grown people with families we would do it. It was never published, really because Curt thought it quite amateur.

Curtis went on to Central College at Fayette, Missouri, where he did some more composing, but he finally graduated from Westminister Choir College in New Jersey. There he did some more composing, learned organ playing and took voice lessons.

His first composition, "Sing We All Noel" sold thousands of copies and was even sung in Japan six months after it was in print. The sad part was that he sold it for a few dollars and even then had to co-author it with another composer who already had some music printed. He did compose quite a few children's choir music, which he got royalties on. For quite a few years "Sing We All Noel" was sung in schools and churches in St. Louis.

After Curtis got settled in Philadelphia, where he played the organ in the Germantown Baptist Church and directed many choirs and even a Gilbert and Sullivan opera in town, we grew apart, only seeing each other at Christmas and vacation time. He taught music at the Episcopal Boys School, too, for many years in Philadelphia.

There's too much more to tell about Curt in this story. He's gone now, but he left a brilliant, exciting record.

The final words to "Lovely Minka" went like this:

"Lovely Minka, must I leave thee?
Leave thy happy plains.
Ah! This parting does grieve me,
Still true my heart remains.
Far from thee I roam.

See the sunbeams shining.
All the night I am pining,
Far from thee alone."

Note: You see Minka was a place, not a girl.

The tune keeps going on in my head. It will take a few days for it to go away.

December, 1990

Caught

When I was about thirteen or fourteen years old, we lived in University City. Our subdivision was still new and there were lots of open lots and also wooded areas west of our house and also to the north. Before you got to the woods there was a tract of open field, at least fifteen acres or more that was regularly farmed, mostly in corn. There was no house on this field but someone always planted it. We used to hide in the big shocks of corn, disturbing the mice and rats that lived in the shocks before the corn was harvested. We even took the ears to our little fires and roasted the ears until they were slightly burned or parched. This softened the hard kernels and we imagined they were quite edible although I'd hate to live on a diet of it. We had heard that the Indians ate it that way, in winter. And speaking of Indians, I personally found a number of bird points and arrowheads in that same field.

On the southeast corner of Midland, where Creve Coeur car tracks ran and Olive Street Road, some developers decided to build an open-air theater similar to the Municipal Opera Theatre in Forest Park. This theater was only about a tenth of the size of the Muny, however. The theater in Forest Park was built into the side of a hill, like the ancient Greek and Roman Amphitheaters. This new theater, to be called the Garden Theatre, was built upon concrete posts, with ramps, and elevated levels for seats, etc.

We watched the theater being built. I guess you would call it an artificial amphitheater. There was lots of open space underneath it and in case of rain the spectators could quickly leave their seats and run down the ramps for shelter. Besides, there was space for dressing rooms, rehearsal areas, restaurant, storage of scenery, counters for selling soda and popcorn, etc.

A buddy of mine who lived about three blocks away from the theater and I, who lived about five blocks away, were over there a lot watching what went on. A small creek ran thru the woods, along the back edge of the stage. Stage and scenery workman would throw scraps of wood and plywood and chicken wire into the woods where Phil and I would retrieve it. One day I picked up my first piece of quarter-inch plywood. Believe it or not, plywood was a sort of new material then and hardly anyone used it in outside construction, mostly because the glue in it wasn't waterproof and the material would come apart. The piece I found was about 2 x 3 feet in size. I later painted a big dragon on it with big green metallic scales, etc. We used it for a fireplace screen for many years.

The chicken wire Phil and I were always using for rabbit traps, etc. Once we built a 6x6x6 cage for three almost grown crows that Phil had captured in a tall elm tree in the woods behind my house. We only had the crows about three or four days. We tried to feed them one-inch balls of hamburger and bread but they wouldn't eat. We finally had to let them go because every morning about five or six o'clock all the family of crows would come over the cage making such a clatter that it woke up the whole neighborhood. My parents said, "Get rid of 'em!" Phil had the great idea that we could tame them and even teach them to speak. I always went along with Phil and his ideas although he was younger than I. He had read lots of outdoor hunting and fishing magazines and even had a license to shoot a 22 rifle and 410 shotgun.

After the theater was in operation, we used to watch rehearsals and I'd wonder how the actors would ever get anything accomplished well enough to present on stage. Some of the girls were so homely and unattractive, but at night, however, with makeup and costumes, they were so beautiful. It was hard to believe.

One afternoon after supper Phil said he thought he knew how we could watch the performance free by hiding behind a seven foot barricade high up in the seats at the top. The barricade was there, I suppose, to keep out noises from Olive Street Road.

We nonchalantly walked up the concrete ramp. There was no one around and it still wasn't dark. We went to the back side of the barricade and sat down. We figured that after the show started and everything was dark we'd slip out and find some vacant seats.

But we had barely settled down when a man appeared and asked what we were up to. I was quite embarrassed at being caught in the act but Phil didn't seem to be. He blithely said he thought it would be alright if we took seats later that were vacant.

However, the manager took a sterner view and said he could have us arrested for trespassing. But after a bit he seemed to relent, saying, "How would you guys like to sell soda for me during the intermission?"

Well, that was a relief to me, although I couldn't imagine myself doing such a job. I had watched soda boys at the Muny in Forest Park and sort of thought it beneath me to do a job like that. But we went below into the workroom and we each were given a large water bucket, I guess it held about sixteen bottles of cold soda, which we took out of a large open cooling tank. We threw in a few lumps of ice to keep the soda cold, picked up a bottle opener, put on a white coat, and were given a dollar in change before we started out. I guess there were eight or ten of us boys to cover the whole theater.

I didn't know what to say. I listened to the other boys calling out, "Soda here!" "Ice cold soda!" So I started yelling the same sort of calls. But somehow I discovered if I made my spiel a little longer and more colorful I would sell more soda. So I did and it worked! In a few more nights I was selling more than the others.

It wasn't easy, handling slippery, wet bottles and using a bottle opener that always threatened to slip out of hand, making change, reaching far out to get your correct change back and it was here that you made tips, for many times the buyer didn't want change back. We were grateful for that!

You always hoped that you would sell your bucket out but you dreaded to run all the way back to the soda area to get a new load, for the intermission time might run out. Some of the boys would carry a full box of twenty-four bottles to start out, but I felt they were too heavy for me. I would only use buckets.

Speaking of soda, there was only Coca-Cola, root beer, grape and orange sold by us soda-boys; in the days before Pepsi-Cola, Royal Crown, or Seven-Up.

We sold popcorn, too. At least two boys peddled it. These boys were sorts of pets of the manager we imagined and they made more money from their sales. And their load was lighter. About sixty bags were crammed into a corrugated box about 2 x 3 feet and six inches deep. A stout cord was fastened halfway into the short side of the box on both sides. This cord went around the neck of the boy, helping him to carry his load without spilling it.

One of the popcorn boys was a real smart aleck; not one of the crew liked him and one evening way down in the "rich" seats, he tripped and spilled his whole load on about three spectators. I'm sure all of us soda carriers snickered up our sleeves and had absolutely no sympathy for him. The whole load probably cost him six to eight dollars and he had to clean up the spectators, seats, aisles, etc.

Back in our room below where we kept the soda and supplies we had a popcorn popper, not like the modern ones, though. This was a medium-large pot with lid and was gas heated. We had to turn a crank that had to be turned constantly while the popcorn popped. It seemed like we always were turning the crank. It was tiring so we had to take turns cranking to keep the supply adequate. We had to know how much oil to put in and salt, too.

By the end of the summer the manager had put me in charge of the whole operation. I was older than most of the boys and he seemed to think that I had gotten everything organized the way he wanted and that I was dependable, etc.

Of course in September the theater closed because of cooler weather. It was called the Garden Theater because around in front, between the theater and parking lots, there were large pools and fountains and lots of planting and trellises and arbors that made the whole thing attractive.

I don't remember if the theater had musicals or not. I rather think they did occasionally. I know I watched several Shakespearean plays like "The Tempest," "Midsummer Nights Dream," "Taming of the Shrew," and even "Mourning Becomes Electra." I don't know how many years the theater lasted. Probably in the University City archives pictures and dates are on file. It would be nice to see them.

December, 1990

Winter Safari

Back in 1928, several of us neighborhood boys who were sophomores in High School got a chance to go to a log cabin at the Coldwater Fish and Game Preserve near Farmington, Missouri on our Christmas holidays. We would leave home after Christmas and come back New Year's Day so we could be back for school the next day. The four of us planned our meals and how much they would cost, duties we would each have each day, etc. We all had to come up with $3.00 each for meals.

I was apprehensive about my getting the three dollars and I quietly mentioned it to a close friend of my parents who was visiting before Christmas. To my great surprise he dug six fifty-cent coins from his pocket and handed them to me, saying, "I want you to have a good time so go ahead with your trip."

Roy and Ruth Wilson were my parents' close friends and they had always encouraged us three boys in our school and church endeavors and always attended the various performances, always went on picnics and barbecues, and encouraged my father to get his law degree. They had no children of their own with no prospect of having any so we were almost adopted by them in many ways.

Bob and Wooster and Ralph and I prepared for our trip. None of our parents were afraid for us doing the venture. Bob and Wooster were Eagle Scouts and Ralph was an experienced outdoorsman, having a hunting and fishing license. I was the rookie of the bunch and self-appointed photographer as I borrowed my parents' 116 Folding Kodak and shot about six pictures that I still have today, sixty-three years later.

206

We were to drive down in a two-door Chevrolet that Bob and Wooster's parents owned as a second car. It wasn't new but not old, either. Just well broken in.

The place that we were going to was in a very dense cedar (Juniper) forest south of the little town of Coffman, which was east of Farmington. A group of professional men had organized the preserve and built log cabins that were well-built and consisted usually of three rooms. They all cooperated in the building of the cabins and many times I heard Bob say, "No, we can't do this or that this weekend - we have to go down to Coldwater to help with the log-rolling."

It was then that I learned what log-rolling was really all about. You had to have quite a few helping hands to roll logs up a ramp to put in place on top of the logs already in place. Twenty-four foot logs are quite heavy and had to be rolled to position instead of being lifted. Notching out the ends of the corners was an exacting job, too.

Anyway, us four boys were to enjoy the benefits of all this summer-long effort. There was a stove inside in the main room, where wood was burned for heat. It had two removable lids on top and a front door that you opened to put in short sections of split logs.

I remember that there was a kerosene stove in the kitchen for cooking. I remember cooking some rabbit and squirrel stew on it.

There were no car radios then, but I got the brilliant idea of taking our old Victrola phonograph and some records like the "St. Louis Blues," etc. and playing it in the back seat as we drove along. The trouble with that was when we would go up or down on the highway, the needle would slip off. So we had to keep the phonograph level at all times. That was too much trouble so we gave up on music in the car and settled for it later in the cabin.

The weather cooperated with us the whole week, staying around forty to fifty degrees. Ralph, Bob, and Wooster decided after we had settled in, to go hunting for squirrel and rabbits and even doves. I didn't carry a gun, not owning one or even possessing a license, so I went along as a spectator, always being careful and carrying all the game we shot. Once in a while I got to shoot a 22 rifle at a can or tree.

A nondescript dog decided to tag along on our hunting trips and he turned out to be a real good squirrel dog, always running up to trees where he had spotted a squirrel, whereas we had no idea that there was a squirrel anywhere around. We got several right away. We came to a corn field and got a couple of doves, too. Near an old abandoned barn we shot a pigeon. Ralph said they were good eating, too.

Lots of times we crossed creeks and I began picking up interesting rocks; pieces with quartz crystals and banding in nice colors, which I realize now were agate, and I probably picked up enough to fill a shoe box.

The country we hiked over was rugged and covered with cedars so thick that they seemed like shelters over us as we walked thru them.

A large lodge was built in the center of the preserve. It had a long all-around porch on the outside and a large fireplace indoors. In one side room there were large dining tables and at one end was a player piano, which all of us wanted to play. I can remember so well one roll we played was "Roses of Picardy" and another was "Rain." I've remembered all the words to this day.

208

After a couple of days, one of the members came down from St. Louis with his wife and daughter. Of course, we were introduced and Dorothy, the girl, being our age, joined in all our activities. After a day or two, we all imagined that we were in love with her and she with us. We would go out of our way to do things for her and with her, like sitting at the piano, giving her our favorite rocks, all sorts of things. She was certainly a nice addition to the group. We found out that she lived in South St. Louis and went to Roosevelt High School. We all promised to write her later after we got home, but we never did.

There were various other members of the lodge who came in for the weekend. I remember one very serious man who owned an electric company in St. Louis who bawled us out for shooting fireworks on one of the side porches of the lodge New Year's Eve. He forbade it, saying it might cause a fire.

There was another member who also showed up with his family. He was a bossy, loud, arrogant type of person that we all immediately disliked. He was always going around telling everyone what to do, etc.

New Year's Eve, as we walked back to our cabin from the lodge, we all noticed the weather changing. By the time we went to bed, it was really getting cold so we put on all the blankets that were available. We even put our sweaters and jackets and clothes on the bed, too. Ralph even put his unloaded shotgun on, too.

We had bought a small pot roast in Coffman one day when we were close to the store there. We had cooked it and eaten about half of it and left it in the pot on the stove. Well, it got so cold that night that the next morning when we decided we'd eat it for breakfast, we couldn't. It was full of frost. We gave up on it, as we were in a big hurry to pack and leave. We had about 150 miles to go back home, most of it on gravel roads.

We had to put everything back in shape and good order before we left. All the outside wood panels had to be fastened again over the windows. We had to empty the portable chemical toilet we had used and give the place a good sweeping. The cabin probably wouldn't be opened again until spring, months away.

We rolled out about 9:30 am and we began seeing snow along the road after we had driven about a quarter of a mile to where we knew we would soon have to cross the creek. We figured it would be frozen but we had no misgivings about crossing it carefully. It was six to eight inches deep and we had crossed it a dozen times during the week.

Up ahead we could see our bossy, loud-mouth member already across the creek with the hood up of his big Hudson car. He had driven across the frozen creek with such wild abandon that he had splashed water all over his motor and shorted out all his spark plugs. We stopped to talk, but he assured us he'd be all right after he got all the spark plugs dried out, so we left him. I know what we were all thinking.

It was cold and the snow seemed heavier on the ground the further north we went. We had driven about ten miles when Wooster said, "Fellows, we've got a flat." Sure enough, it was the right rear tire. We didn't have a spare, I don't know why, but we all got out and got the car jacked up by the side of the road. We got tools out to take the nuts off the bolts around the edge of the wheel. There were four nuts to get off, spaced about sixteen inches apart around the wheel or rim.

But we couldn't get the wrench to fit the nuts. The creek water that we had come thru had coated the nuts with globs of ice. Wooster finally said the only way we can get these things off is to urinate on them and he proceeded to do so. He didn't get very far so we all had to help him. We made it, altho I've never had an occasion to do the same thing in my whole life since. It wasn't easy to forget.

It was getting so cold, even by the minute, and we knew we had to put a rubber patch on the hole in the tube and that required a warm place to do it. We glanced up a small road near us that led to a farmhouse. We would have to beg the farmer to give us a place to fix our tube.

When we knocked at his door, he was greatly surprised seeing us half-frozen kids with a tire in our hands. He caught on tho, and led us to his front room and welcomed us to do our job. I remember so well a large picture under glass, probably one of his parents, hanging on the wall above the place where we worked. We finished and thanked the farmer as much as we could. We put the wheel back on and took off once again.

The snow seemed much heavier by the time we got to the main concrete highway, but we drove mostly in the tracks made by cars ahead of us. Our Chevrolet had a small heater up front on the floor that consisted of about a 6x10 inch metal vent that was connected with a pipe to the manifold near the motor of the car. That was supposed to bring back heat but it was a poor excuse. Remember, this was 1928.

I sat in back with Ralph and we kept beating the floor of the car with our feet to keep warm. The windows were frosting up all

211

around and we scraped the back window constantly to give our driver some rear vision. Wooster had to keep scraping the windshield on the inside to help him see the road.

We kept looking thru the dark, trying to see the lights at Crystal City. We could warm up there. Bob, in the front seat, was crying and all of us were almost crying, too. It was still thirty miles to St. Louis.

Crystal City showed up and we got gas and went in to warm up. Finally we piled back into the Chevy and I think we got home about 10:30 pm. It's a trip I'll never forget and even now, when we get zero weather and our car frosts up a little on the inside, I thank God and all the inventors for all the improvements that have been made since that winter of 1928.

P.S. We found out later that the game warden was looking for us - said we were hunting squirrels which were out of season.

Another P.S. Also, when we cooked the pigeon it was so old and tough we couldn't put a fork into it.

January, 1991

Bamboo

Bamboo has always baffled me. As a young boy I was always making things out of wood or cardboard or paper or sheet metal or logs, etc. I made bird houses, scooters, rabbit traps, swings, small club houses (with the help of other boys in our subdivision, and pilfered boards and bent nails), sling shots, tree houses, log bridges over creeks, dug caves, etc., etc. All these things required dexterity, patience, planning, and perseverance but I got nowhere with bamboo.

I couldn't even break it over my knee. And, probably because I had tools that weren't very sharp, I couldn't saw it or drill it or nail it. Its surface was slick, round, and flinty. It would roll when I tried to do anything with it. You couldn't stomp on it to break it. Even at its thinnest end it would bend and bend and bend but never break. If it did, it would splinter into a useless piece of nothing. Even now when I see various things such as furniture, placemats, cages, and fences, I marvel at the craftsman who made them.

Occasionally I would come across a pole that had been thrown away or had come wound up in a rug that a neighbor had bought. It always seemed like such a waste to throw it away. And I saved them because I thought I could saw them into table legs or something useful. But it was not to be. It was hopeless.

A lot of things come to mind when I think of bamboo. One story my father told about when he was in the Army in the Philippines. He and his two older brothers enlisted after the Spanish-American War and lived in Army barracks near Cavite. They had joined because living had become too hard on the farm down in the Sikeston, Mo. area. Both parents had died and things were bad. My father told me that once someone had accidentally spilled Kerosene (coal oil) on and in a newly bought barrel of flour. It was one of several staples bought to supply the family for the winter. It was a real catastrophe, for all their savings were gone and they had to eat biscuits and bread and pancakes all winter with the ever-present taste and fumes of coal oil. That must have been pretty awful.

The army buildings were built right next to the jungle and whenever a soldier broke rules, got drunk, or went AWOL, his punishment was usually to be sent out to the jungle to cut down one or maybe three bamboo poles and bring them back to camp. Bamboos, there in the hot, humid climate, grew very thick, right next to each other, very tall, up to 100 ft. high and up to one foot in diameter. At each joint very sharp thorns grew out and inter-grew with the bamboos next to them. Cutting the trunks was bad enough but extracting the trunks and the rest of the stem from high in the top was difficult and murderous. My father watched men struggle all day to get only ONE plant out, their arms and legs getting scratched and torn until they were bleeding. They would jerk and twist and hack and struggle for hours and hours to the point of exhaustion. I will never forget his description of that kind of punishment.

All this and more came back to me because recently I saw bamboo growing on Bremerton Ave. in Rock Hill near Manchester. I saw it, glancing from the car, and went back with my trusty Polaroid camera and got a good picture of 1" to 1 1/4" stems. I know of another place in Brentwood and also heard of a stand in Kirkwood.

214

It probably grows in a number of places in the St. Louis area.

I reasoned, what do I really know about Bamboo? So I researched it. The Brentwood Library gave me much valuable information - from their *World Book Encyclopedia* and the 1980 *National Geographic* (October).

Bamboo is not a tree but a giant grass, even being related to our own blue grass. There are a least 700 kinds around the world. Some kinds grow 120 feet high and have stems a foot thick. The seeds at the top are often eaten by the natives when rice crops fail. People who live especially in Asian lands may live in bamboo houses, sit on bamboo chairs, eat food prepared in bamboo containers. Their beds and covers may be bamboo mats. They wear bamboo sandals, make bamboo cages and fences. Young bamboo sprouts are eaten as vegetables. Rafts, sails, tow rope, paper, and tools are also made from bamboo. It has more uses than any other substance in tropical countries.

The World Book says that construction engineers also use bamboo, and experts who compared the strength of laminated bamboo with soft steel found that the bamboo's breaking point equaled that of the steel and that the strong, light-weight bamboo makes an excellent reinforcement for concrete. The U.S. Government tests also show that the closely matted roots help control soil erosion and the high cellulose content of bamboo stems make excellent pulp for paper.

There are so many more things to say about bamboo. The *Pulse* gives me space every month to write about things that are interesting to me and I hope, you the readers.

I hope that you can get a hold of the Oct. 1980 issue of

215

National Geographic and read the article and look at the pictures of bamboo. As an old CCC boy who thought he knew a lot about trees, I certainly learned a lot of fascinating things about bamboo, that after all, is only grass. ✎

Runaway Car

One evening quite a few years ago, before I was married, and lived with my parents in Rock Hill, Missouri, we decided to see a movie at the Esquire Theatre on Clayton Road. The theatre was on the south side about 1/2 block east of Big Bend Boulevard. Both streets are always busy streets.

We got out of the show about 9:30 or 10:00. It was a nice summer evening and we were slowly walking to our car which was parked on the north side of Clayton Road across from the theatre. As we neared the curb I noticed a car, with its lights off, move out from the curb. I called out, "Pop, watch that car, his lights are out." Then I noticed the car had no driver or no one else in it. Someone had parked and hadn't set the brakes. Instantly I imagined the havoc a driverless car could make at the busy intersection west of me at Big Bend. The only thing to do was try to maneuver it across the street to a parking lot. As I remember, I couldn't get into the car quickly, but either the window was open or I opened the door and grabbed the steering wheel pulling it to the left, aiming it at the parking lot of the Town Hall Restaurant. The turning slowed the speed of the car so I was able to keep up as it was going, I guess, three to five miles an hour.

My father was out in front, waving off the cars coming from the west. The traffic wasn't heavy, but our runaway had no lights, so we were a definite hazard.

I was stepping pretty lively by now, almost running, as I neared the parking lot. That part of the lot was slightly upgrade, lucky for us, and between my father and I we managed to stop the car in time.

My father took the license plate number and the next day called the owner. He happened to be an army officer, as I remember. I don't remember any more details about the incident. I do know that if we hadn't stopped the car, the rest of this story could have been pretty horrible. At the angle that it was heading, and even if it managed to not hit a car, it could have run right on into Glaser's Pharmacy, which was on the southwest corner of the intersection. What a surprise they would have had!

I'm sure many of our readers have experienced incidents like this. Send in your experiences to the *Pulse*. We will be glad to publish it. ✍

Blue Jeans

The other afternoon, at Dynasty Donuts, I ran across Mal Hammack, a former Cardinal football player, with whom I've had a lot of enjoyable chats about birds, rocks, football, etc. He is only one of quite a few interesting people who come in for coffee, hot chocolate, chili, soup, etc. at different times of the day.

The conversation varies amongst the dozen or so people; profound at times, or what's wrong with the Cardinals, what stocks to buy, how to fix your car or air conditioner or plumbing, what's wrong with City Hall, and the weather.

This time I asked Mal where he'd been. I hadn't seen him for a few weeks and he said, "I've been to Colorado." Then he also remarked that he had stayed at Estes Park. It brought back a lot of memories about an unusual job situation in that city.

Our son had passed all his radio engineer exams and was working for KOA-Denver for the summer. One of his jobs was to go out to towns in the Denver area and do "remotes." A "remote" was when a radio engineer set up equipment to relay or record concerts that were sent back to the parent-station in Denver. For a young man, just out of high school, working during the summer, going on a "remote" was a serious, responsible job, besides being quite glamorous. So, when we went to Denver to see him that summer, he insisted we go to Estes Park and see him engineer a "remote." He explained that his "remote" this time was to record an unusual performance of a symphony orchestra. The peculiar thing about it was that it was called "The Blue Jeans Symphony Orchestra" and that it was composed mainly of young people; for-the-most-part, college types. It was a complete orchestra and the performance we heard was most enjoyable and professional. It took place in the big auditorium built especially for their use. We learned that these students came from states all over the union, took try-outs, etc. and rehearsed each afternoon or evening for a performance or performances held during the week, and when tourists and visitors from Denver would come out to hear them. Not only that, they performed for no pay! During their off-hours they worked at filling stations, cafes, general stores, even scrubbing and making beds in the numerous motels; just so they could further their musical experience by playing with a symphony. It was a marvelous expression of dedication to music. And, they all wore blue jeans while they performed!

Later, Steve introduced us to some of the players and they were charming. I don't know if the symphony still exists. I feel that some of your readers have probably heard of it, or even attended some of the performances. Steve did remotes at several places that summer for KOA-Denver, but finally came back to St. Louis to attend Washington University before being drafted. He now has a documentary film company in Washington, D.C. ✎

Airplanes Build a House

My son Steve was a babe-in-arms when I got my first job with an aircraft factory during World War II. Everyone advised me to quit my job at Gaskin Sign Company or I would surely be drafted. All of us married men didn't want to be drafted, especially since we had started establishing a home and family. Even then some of my unmarried or divorced friends, under age forty, were getting called to war. It was a bad time. Gas and tires were rationed along with meat and shoes and other things I can't remember.

When I applied for a job at Laister-Kauffmann, a plant that made glider airplanes on Oakland Avenue at the site of the Arena, I asked to get into the wood-working department. But when personnel found out from my application that I knew how to spray paint, I was put in that department. It was better than nothing.

I worked in an enormous spray booth. It was painted white inside with lots of lights and had two five foot wide exhaust fans and waterfalls that sent all the fumes outside after all the pigment was knocked out by the waterfalls. The fumes went up big two foot diameter stacks that were at least twenty feet high. We had to clean out the stacks periodically, a heck of a job, which I had to do at least twice while I worked there.

It was a new strange world. I soon learned to tell the difference between ailerons, elevators, vertical fins, fuselages, etc. These words were unfamiliar to me up to now.

I had spent about four years learning the sign and fixture business and I had progressed to the point when I could build signs and fixtures and install them, do gold leaf and window lettering, spray painting, lettering trucks, walls, etc. But aircraft was a whole new field.

I got $35.00 a week to start but when I left three years later I was making $94.00. I knuckled down and after nine months, I was made a lead man which really meant that you were dependable, did a good job, had no absenteeism but had to work harder and longer.

Occasionally I was called on to do a sign or letter N.C. numbers on a glider part. Sometimes there were promotional signs to do. I remember the movie "Winged Victory." The Laister-Kauffmann Company somehow managed to ship out and put their blue and yellow two man training glider together in various theatre lobbies around the country. I painted "WINGED VICTORY" in large blue letters on the wings. The idea was to sell War Bonds. Occasionally I'd see newspaper accounts or magazine articles with a picture of the glider in some theatre lobby. It is a nice feeling to see that.

After two years, I became foreman of the day crew. We had two shifts and for a short time, had three shifts. There was quite a production rivalry between us. The night crew always seemed to get more done than we did and I heard in a round-a-bout way that it was because management was always interfering in some way or another and slowed things down during the day, whereas the night crew didn't have management to contend with so they got more done. But we were all friends and management more than once said that the paint department was the hardest working section in the plant.

I can't remember when it was but there was a big shakeup at Curtiss-Wright Aircraft out at Lambert Field. A lot of personnel and engineers were laid off or didn't want to be transferred to other parts of the country so they came to our plant. They were hired, a lot of them, because they were valuable people and since our management anticipated getting a larger contract, building a new type of glider that carried many more soldiers.

That's how I met Bill Remmert. He had seen me working down at Starling Airport on Highways 61-67 near Arnold, Missouri. We were redoing about six or seven Stearman biplanes that had been used down in Texas for training pilots. We were going to use them for tow planes. The Army Air Force, as it was called then, insisted that every 10th glider we produced must be flight tested. Usually on Sundays, down at Starling, a crowd would gather to watch the yellow and blue training gliders get towed up. Many of the visitors would volunteer to ride up with the pilot, there being an extra seat behind him. It seemed to be great fun, although I never quite got around to volunteering.

Bill had seen me spraying and lettering numbers and signs, etc. so one day he came up to me "cold turkey" and introduced himself, saying, "I'm having a twin-engine Cessna plane coming in to Starling - I've got to repaint it - put new N.C. numbers and my name on it - Will you do it?"

Well, after I talked it over with my wife, Bobbie, we agreed to do it. We could use the money and after I got started, Steve would go with me occasionally although he was scarcely two years old. Bobbie was pregnant, and sort of glad to let him go. He was no trouble and many nights driving home, he would go asleep leaning against me, never crying or fussing.

I still remember Bill and Art, his first head mechanic, working on the engines, etc. And Betty, Bill's wife, who was always very busy doing all the refitting and sewing in the upholstered parts of the plane. They told me it was to be used in charter service. Bill and Betty sure worked hard, getting their start in a business that grew into a multi-million dollar business. I was fortunate to be drawn into it.

Somehow Bill got hangar space at Lambert Field and started doing charter flights so I had more planes to letter. The planes began to get bigger and Bill always insisted on painting a U.S. flag on the vertical fin near the tail, and of course on both sides, but he didn't want a stiff, flat, square flag and I must find a suitable flag design that showed the flag in a flowing, ripping fashion. I found one in my *World Book Encyclopedia* at home, enlarged it to an approximate size of 18"x24". I added a short flag pole to it, and put gold leaf on the knob at the top. The last touch overjoyed Bill, nowhere he said, had he ever seen a plane with a gold leafed knob on the top of its flag.

More and more work came in from Bill. He needed larger signs for the outside walls of his hangar, etc., etc. It was taking all my time on week-ends but we loved the checks when they came in. Bill never quibbled about prices.

Soon I was lettering other planes besides Bill's around Lambert, for flying schools that popped up after the war. Many of the ex-GI's wanted to learn to fly. The schools had planes to letter and needed signs to post around the hangars, too.

During this time, the glider plant closed at the arena and I was out of work but immediately I went to work at a sign shop in Brentwood. I told my employer there that I had lots of contacts at the airport but he didn't want to do any work there because it was ten miles out and ten miles back and the cost all added up to more than he thought the customer wanted to pay.

So I went along painting signs out at the airport, but now it was taking up a lot of my evenings besides weekends, too. Many evenings I would tumble into bed at midnight, but gradually the money was growing in the bank so in 1948 we built our home in Brentwood.

Bill had a partner, Robert Werner, an aircraft engineer so now the company was known as Remmert-Werner. Bill was an extrovert; Bob was more of an introvert. Bill made friends with everybody. He was an organizer and a planner with great foresight. Soon he was buying surplus C-46 planes from the government down south and hauling them back to St. Louis. Out at Lambert, he would strip the insides, repair everything that was necessary and convert them into luxury planes for corporate executives to use in their promotions.

During World War II, or even before, Bill had spent time in China assembling planes for sale, building air strips, and even supplying parts, etc. for the planes that "flew the Hump" from India. I'm not going to write too much on this part of Bill's life because I'm not too sure of it, but he really knew how to make things happen.

He would approach the biggest companies such as Dupont Celanese, Monsanto, Texaco, etc. selling them on his ideas and especially buying the big planes and refurbishing them. He always gave me the job of lettering the names or copying the companies' logos to put on the sides.

Once Edgar Queeny, who had written a book on wild ducks and geese, entitled Prairie Wings, bought a plane and had it refurbished in the American Airlines Hanger on the north side of Lambert. I had to copy the exact style of the lettering from the title page of the book, doing it in gold leaf and outlining it.

When Mr. Queeny went to Africa later to shoot films, Bill even took on the job of converting a station wagon into a safari car, cutting a hole in the roof for a turret-camera to be mounted there and putting special metal guards around the outside to protect the passengers from rough treatment by the wild animals.

Many nights I spent out at the Interstate Airmotive hangar at the northwest corner of the field, lettering and at the same time listening to the screaming of the jet engines being tested at McDonnell Aircraft. Lots of times, I had to move large work racks that were on wheels to get into position to letter on the higher parts of the planes especially on noses and vertical fins. I carried a long extension cord with a spotlight up to where I worked. Hangars weren't lit to accommodate the fine work of a sign painter. Sometimes getting to an area to be worked on took almost as much time as doing the job especially when you had to do both sides.

Once Bill called me at supper time and asked me to letter Arthur Godfrey's name on his plane that Bill had just finished redoing. Godfrey didn't want anything else on it, just "Captain Arthur Godfrey" in gold leaf outlined in red.

It was a warm summer evening, still very light but the plane was a way out on the field. The maintenance man at the hangar said there was no way he could tow the plane up to put it in the hangar so I took a tall stepladder out and climbed up to put my gold size paint on the area just below the pilot's window. The letters were maybe two inches high. When you do gold leaf work you use certain special paint that dries in a given time. You must put your leaf on just before it dries or the leaf won't stick.

Well, I put on the paint but the mosquitos were so bad out there in the grassy field that I went back to my car to put on my shirt. I was working in my Tee-shirt and I was getting eaten up. By the time I got back to the job, the paint had dried and it wouldn't hold the leaf.

I cursed inwardly but I commenced all over again. I got the job done finally and went home. Next day I came back and varnished it. I never did get a photo of it like I usually did but a few years later I saw a picture of Arthur in a trade magazine smiling away with his arm partially out the window hiding my sign. Little did he know.

One evening I had to do some work for Bill on a plane but he met me before I got started. He said, "Come on, get in. We'll letter this plane after we get in from our flight. We're checking out (something I can't remember). You ever been up?"

I said, "No," but he seemed to enjoy that and away we went.

It was much noisier than I thought it would be, like being in a big noisy box with the sound of the engines drowning out all conversation. I settled back but standing up as I remember. I was astounded to see how many ponds and lakes and streams - even the Missouri River showed up in the landscape below me. Years later in Europe, as our plane came in for a landing at Tempelhof (Germany) Airport near Berlin, I was again reminded of all the bodies of water that showed up underneath us.

I don't know how many planes I lettered for Remmert-Werner. I remember doing a lot of yellow Piper Cubs with the red Motorola radio logos on the sides. I did a lot of lettering in the Interstate Airmotive hangar and lettering the Gaylord Box Company's twin engine Cessna. It was quite a fancy logo to copy. I think I did two of them over the years.

It was then that I met a pilot who flew all the John Deere Implement Co. planes out of Moline, Illinois. He wanted me to copy in paint a green panel on the sides of their planes with a deer jumping over a log. I suggested doing the deer in gold leaf, the other lettering to be in yellow with black outline. It came out very nice and he and the company were so pleased that for three or four years I had to letter all their planes. They would call from Moline and make a date a week in advance. I enjoyed their work. I did it anytime I pleased, for now I was in business for myself.

For a while, in the beginning Remmert-Werner would fly sight-seeing trips over St. Louis and vicinity. Ed Wilson, an announcer for KWK then, was a certified pilot for some of the trips. I remember Ralph Piper, too, who did a lot of charter flights for Bill. He was Bill's No. 1 pilot.

I remember that they took a big charter to South and Central America and the plane came back with a lot of flags painted on the front of the plane, each from country that they had landed in. There were two, I think, that Bill wanted me to add that somehow hadn't got done. I think Mexico was one. When I looked at the beautiful work the sign artist had done down there, I was ashamed of my work. He had painted tiny stars (there are always lots of stars in flags) that were no more than 3/16 of an inch in width, with every point painted perfectly. I remember doing Mexico's flag which is red, white and green with an eagle in the center area, holding a snake in its beak.

Many times, on a Saturday, when I knew I wouldn't be working too long, I'd take Steve and we'd eat at the various restaurants on the west side of the air field. I think he enjoyed that. I know he did. Later, he'd sit in the cockpits of the various planes I worked on, never tinkering with anything or fussing or shaking the plane. I know he remembers all this.

Bill often asked me to come and work for him full time. I couldn't quite see driving twenty miles a day to work and maybe I'd have to do other kinds of work besides lettering. Bobbie couldn't see me doing it , either.

Anyway, recently when all these memories came back to me, I decided to call Bill and tell him about the story - if he minded, etc. His number was in the phone book so I called it. I got a recorded answer so I left my number.

Next day, Roy Lenck, one of Bill's best engineers for many years, called me to say Bill had passed on two years ago and that Betty was living down at Palm Beach. I must write her soon. This story will tell how I felt about all of our relationships through the years. She worked in the office all those years in the business and I imagine she had a hand in curbing his exuberance. He was an unforgettable person. I just had to write this.

March, 1991

A Cup of Good Coffee

A friend of mine, Wendel Chilton, during his high school days worked at a Walgreen Drug Store at the Corner of Kingsland Avenue and Delmar Boulevard in University City.

He had to get there early, probably at seven, so he could clean up the counter and floors, tables, etc. and prepare coffee especially for the early birds.

Of course, every morning the big coffee urn had to be cleaned meticulously inside and out from usage the night before. Wendel drained the urn and cleaned the inside very thoroughly, using a cleaning rag with cleanser and rinsing, etc. for the final cleanup. Next he polished the shiny exterior after putting in the proper amount of coffee and water.

He went ahead with all the other chores behind the counter. Finally his first customer came in and ordered a roll and a cup of coffee. He took a few bites of the roll and took a big swig of his coffee. Instantly he grabbed his throat with both hands and ran out the door. Wendel didn't think too much about it - he thought possibly the man had drank his coffee too soon and it was too hot.

But a few minutes later another customer came in, bought a roll and coffee and he, too, ran out, holding his throat.

When a third customer said to Wendel, "What's wrong with this coffee?" Wendel decided to do some investigating. He sipped some himself, too. It was terrible. He couldn't figure out why. He knew he had put in the right amount of water and coffee.

When the customer left, Wendel decided to drain the urn and start over. When the last of the mixture had drained out into the sink,

Wendel discovered the horrible truth. Somehow he had forgotten to take out the polishing rag and had left it in to percolate with the whole business.

When Wendel told me this, with all his gusto in telling a story, it made an impression that I'll never forget.

March 11, 1991

The Chalk Cliffs of Dover

I want this to be an enjoyable story - told in my own way, uncomplicated and ungrammatical as if I were talking to a small group in my home.

Perhaps twenty years ago, a mutual rock hound friend, Ed H., said he had answered an "ad" by a rock dealer from Dover, England that said they would send on order, one hundred pounds of black flint nodules that were found in the chalk cliffs there. When the rocks arrived we were greatly surprised to find them snowy white outside, and dark gray and black inside. They were called flint "nodules". The outside was chalky and dusty and rubbed off in your hand. Then there was a thin rind of white against the black of the flint, that was much harder. We have never heard the name for it. The nodules varied in shape and size - very irregular - some were as large as a football; some were grapefruit size.

A few years later my wife and I took our first trip to Europe, landing at Heathrow Airport near London. Later, we left for Dover by train, to cross by ferry to Calais, France. As we rolled along, the train went through a very white rock and soon I noticed layers of various sizes of black rocks between larger layers of white material. I reminded myself that since we were going to Dover for the ferry, this white substance must be the beginning of the layer of chalk that composed the great White Cliffs of Dover and the rocks that I saw were the Flint nodules that Ed had received years ago.

"Well," I said to myself, "when we get off at Dover, I'll run back from the beach and get some samples." But when we got off the train, the cliffs seemed blocks and blocks away and of course as luck would have it, there was no time - the ferry was leaving and all I got was a picture of the cliffs receding in the distance, but at least I had proof of the flint occurrence and that gave me a lot of satisfaction.

Ten years after this, (summer of '84), Betty and I went back to Europe on a Garden Tour, by bus, starting in Holland through Germany, Switzerland, France and finally winding up in England, our ferry to land at Dover. We saw a lot of beautiful gardens, castles, churches, lakes, cities, etc. in over two weeks.

I looked ahead on our map as we traveled through France and saw that we would be in the county of Kent, where we landed at Dover. We would leave our European bus at Calais and take the ferry to Dover, board an English bus driving to Canterbury for a one night stayover before going to London.

I thought to myself , "If I get a chance, maybe I could explore a little in Kent County and learn a little more about the flint nodules and chalk." But, as you know, a tour bus sticks to a tight schedule and hasn't time to cater to an individual's hobby like mine or anyone else's, and although in our group there were thirty women and fifteen men, we had little time for shopping either. By the time we got to Canterbury, the women were beginning to grumble audibly to our leader.

Anyway, while we were still in France, as we were leaving

Monet's garden, (he was the great painter) I picked up a plain white rock by the bus. Turning it over, I saw that the broken side was black. HA! A piece of black flint! I wasn't really surprised, for approaching Monet's garden the highway had cut through white rock, and I had even noticed the lumps of rocks in layers. This was the same flint layer and chalk that was occuring across the channel at Dover. But as we rode on to Calais, the white road cuts dwindled away and we were in the flat lands - farm country.

"Well, this time when we get to Dover, I'll scoot over to the cliffs and see for myself how they look first hand." Incidentally, the ferry was huge, carrying trucks, cars, cargo, and hundreds of people. The trip takes forty-five minutes. I read lately that the channel averages only one-hundred feet deep across this part.

We docked and almost immediately got to our English bus. I scarcely saw the tops of the cliffs through the haze. Imagine the cliffs around Alton and Grafton, Illinois, and you can visualize in a small way the view of Dover. They are so white and grand, it's no wonder the song written in World War II was so popular.

We drove along the bases of the bluffs. Homes and businesses and farms clustered almost all the way. If we strained our necks and looked out the windows we could barely see the tops flying by. The layers of nodules were very plain to see.

The distance between layers of chalk varied and were quite straight. No doubt of its sedimentary origin. In several places enterprising people had dug into the walls, making store rooms for cars, etc. in the cavity created.

About three-thirty or four o'clock in the afternoon, we arrived in Canterbury, the home of Canterbury Cathedral where Chaucer came as a pilgrim to worship and to write the Canterbury Tales. We took a guided tour and went to our hotel to unpack. Betty and I took a short walk down the main street, looking for stores that might be open. Most had closed, so there was no shopping as usual. I noticed a five or six foot wall across the street from where we were walking. We crossed over to the wall, which was of odd construction. I looked at it closely and discovered it to be composed completely of four to five inch squares of the black flint I was curious about.

We went back to the hotel, Betty settling down in our room for a rest. I went down to the lobby and, looking out the front entrance, saw that there was a museum on the opposite side. I crossed the narrow street, went in and discovered that it was only a book museum. What a blow! "Anyway," I said to myself, "got to make something happen." A rock hound never gives up. I went into the small office and took out my ESCOMO (Earth Science Club of Missouri) card and handed it to the small man at the desk. He listened to me attentively while I explained that I wanted to get directions to a material yard where stones and gravel and cement were sold. Maybe I would be able to get some chips, etc. to bring back to everyone in our club. (Little did I realize all that chipping and cutting was done in that area over 1,000 years ago.)

He called in another man who said I should go down a little street near by, to a small church called St. Mildred's. It was only fifteen minutes walking time and I would find some ruins in back, and maybe I would find some pieces. He said it was OK because every day he walked down there to eat his lunch and no one would bother me. What luck! I grabbed a small plastic bag and noting that I had at least one and a half hours 'til dinner, I took off.

235

As I walked down the shady, curving street, I noticed how quiet it was. There were no lawns, flowers, or trees. The front windows and doors were right on the sidewalk. I imagined everyone at their evening meals. I thought of Charles Dickens and how this little street would look at Christmas time, with colored lights and carol music escaping into the winter air.

I took another look at my watch and knew I had plenty of time. On my right I noticed another long building constructed of flint - walls twenty feet high or more. I noticed people hurrying through the doors of this place going to a travelogue. Some were carrying covered dishes, etc. I noticed a placard at the gate showing a charge of only seventy five pence. I thought maybe after dinner Betty and I would go there and get a real taste of English life and customs.

After a few more minutes, I saw a large building I guessed was St. Mildred's. As I walked around the front I saw the sign, St. Mildred's Episcopal Church, with leaning tombstones and mossy covered graves near the entrance. I walked around the church, but saw no ruins, no rocks, only a small parking lot, gravel, bushes, etc. That was all. I retraced my steps to the north side of the church, approaching another smaller building, probably a chapel, also made of squared off blocks of flint.

I walked down a grassy pathway, bushes and vines brushing me on the arms and shoulders. When I came to a small opening, I pushed through and saw a vegetable garden. Tomatoes, onions, etc. all in neat rows, looking very healthy and cared for. I took a left turn, staying on the edge, working my way to a five foot wall where maybe I might find ruins or fragments of rocks in between the rows of plants.

Out of the blue came a voice, "What are you doing here?" I

236

glanced back to the area where I first came in and walked directly and somewhat sheepishly to the stern-faced elderly man who was accompanied by a young boy. I pulled out my ESCOMO card again and talked like a Dutch Uncle, explaining I was from St. Louis on a bus tour, and interested in the geology of the country. At any rate, he seemed impressed and convinced of my sincerity and told me that if I would go through the front door of the chapel I would see remodeling going on, and I could help myself to whatever I would find. He walked only three or four steps when he noticed some full size blocks in the grass next to the wall of the chapel and told me to take them. Well, seven blocks of flint in my suitcase was too much and what would Betty say? I selected three of them, thanking him over and over again. I insisted on taking his picture near the wall by the chapel. I got his name and address and promised to write when I got home. He told me St. Mildred's dated back to 800 A.D. He remarked how much time it must have taken those early masons to "knap" the flint for all those buildings. He also said that building stone was very scarce there and a lot had been brought in from Italy. He reminded me that regular services were still held in the church after 1,184 years.

After I got home, I tried to research the flint and chalk geology. I learned that the area in that part of England and France was formed in the Cretaceous Period. "Creta" meaning chalk, remember your Latin lessons in school? The chalk was made from very tiny sea shells and laid in layers alternating with the flints which were formed from sponges, which have a high content of silica, thus giving the rock its hardness. This black flint was the same material that the colonists and armies used in their firearms in the early days of settling North America. And of course, everyone all over Europe used it. I found that during the "stone age" the early flint miners, who were a select group, were the first to use primitive tools such as deer antlers for picks and shoulder blades of large animals for spades. They even performed special ceremonies, praying to the Gods whenever flint was hard to find.

I hope in the future to make a contact in England that will send me pictures and more information about this interesting place, The Cliffs of Dover, and when I do you'll be the first to know. ❧

Naples, Italy

My wife, Bobbie, and I were in Munich, Germany visiting our son and his wife, mostly to see our new granddaughter, about six months old. Of course, while there, we visited the city; its churches, parks, beer halls, and the Isar river, where I found quite a few white quartz pebbles. I had a small rock shop at home and thought they would at least make nice conversation pieces. Determined not to leave them, I filled my pants pockets and took them back to our hotel and tucked them into my suitcase.

Steve, my son, was teaching high-school-age children of the Army personnel stationed there. He taught English, photography, and movie making. Paula, his wife, born in Poland, had lived in several countries because her family was always on the move trying to stay one step ahead of the Nazis or the Communists. She spoke four languages and was trying to get an Art degree at the University, plus having and caring for the new baby, Vanessa.

One evening Steve got a call from Ron Weise, a neighbor back home in Brentwood, Missouri, who was now living in Naples. Ron and Steve had kept in touch as long as they had both been in Europe.

Ron was doing well and had just bought a Porsche! Ron intended to drive north through Italy, through the Brenner Pass and into Germany. He planned to stay a few days, then sell the car, knowing he could get a lot more for it in Germany than he had paid in Italy.

Ron had the talent and good fortune to become a computer expert while in the Navy. In Naples he worked for a private company that was under contract to the United States Government, keeping surveillance on all submarine traffic in the Mediterranean. He picked up very little Italian, socialized mostly at the Officer's Club, went jogging regularly, and ate most of his meals out. His job paid well but he was becoming bored and had decided when his contract was up, he would return home.

He suddenly suggested we fly down to Naples, stay a week in his apartment, and see the sights. Our first impulse was "Wonderful!" But, I soon realized this would add another $400 to $500 to the trip which I didn't feel we had to spend at the time. My wife felt this was an opportunity we shouldn't pass up, and with some effort Steve managed to borrow and scrounge enough that we could indeed go, and pay him back later.

Ron made the drive north, sold his car, and flew back to Naples so that he was there in time to meet us at the airport.

On our flight over the Alps, we were at such a high altitude that I was somewhat disappointed. They were beautiful and snow covered but seemed so small, but as the plane started dropping down the southern slopes, I began to see very interesting things! There were the black rings left by extinct volcanos, and long black ridges standing out starkly against the dry arid ground. Suddenly, the realization dawned that we were going to be near Mt. Vesuvius, Pompeii, Herculaneum, the Isle of Capri, and much more. Having been an avid rock collector all my life, the enormous possibilities of the area began to flood my mind and I was so excited, I could hardly wait to land!

Ron met us at the airport, and we were soon climbing into the little car he had rented and heading for his apartment. Everything was quite new and spacious, and where at home the trim and moldings would have been done in wood, Ron explained that the Italian contractors preferred to use marble in beautiful combinations and colors. Looking south, we could see the Bay of Naples, but also noticed the heavy shutters on the windows. Ron explained they were needed as a defense against the awesome winds that sometimes came off the bay and screamed and tore at the windows. Everything was placid and warm now though, and remained so throughout our stay.

After lunch, Ron offered to show us the volcano he was living on! He explained that all of the apartments in this area were erected in a ring on the upper rim of a volcano called "Terre Solfa" or "Sulphur Land." We drove a few blocks to a kind of entrance gate, paid twenty-five cents each, and walked in perhaps 300 yards past family groups and picnickers enjoying the shade from the trees scattered about the area. We came to a clearing and to our left, behind a picket fence, we saw bubbling, soupy, grey lava. I was hoping to see some yellow sulphur crystals, but there were none. I was amazed to see all the three and four-story apartments up above me and wondered what kind of nerve it took for all these people to live in such a potentially dangerous area. But, Ron said there had never been any trouble, and pointed out an ancient arched shelter that the Romans had built for taking sulphur steam baths.

Ron had supplied me with an old screwdriver and paper bag from his kitchen, and I continued to look for sulphur crystals. Finally, pushing aside some tall grass and weeds, I actually saw some! They were very small, more of a yellow crust on the ground, but I carefully marked them into three-inch squares and proceeded to carefully loosen each one from the ground. To my surprise, when

I tried to pick one up, it was so hot I dropped it and had to turn each one over to let the bottom cool. The bottoms were not yellow, but looked more like a piece of toast. I had gathered about a dozen, when I noticed a lot of steam coming from where I had been digging. Becoming alarmed and thinking I might have started something, I hastened to find Ron. He didn't seem alarmed but thought it might be wise to leave, and we did. The pieces were quite fragile, and I remember using a lot of Kleenex to wrap them for the journey home. Later, we packed them in cardboard frozen food boxes as further protection.

We decided to go to Mt. Vesuvius for the day. El Vesuvio, as the Italians called it, lay east of the city. While driving, we came upon a man who seemed to be in distress. He was flailing his arms wildly and Ron stopped to see if we could help. He explained in broken English that he had missed his bus and was late for work, so Ron decided to give him a lift. No sooner were we underway than the man produced some intaglios of Tiger Eye. He explained they were produced where he worked and that he would be glad to escort us through the factory if we had time for a tour. If not, he would be glad to sell us what he had with him at a very special "wholesale" price. We declined his offer, and discovered a few days later that this was all he did, riding back and forth on this same stretch of road, propositioning unsuspecting tourists.

Shortly after this incident, we saw the little sign "El Vesuvio" and turned off on a dusty gravel road. It was wide and well worn, and off to the east we could see the volcano and the cable cars which would take us high over the lava flow to the summit.

Suddenly, I noticed the road was winding through black,

curling flows of lava very close to the car. I asked Ron to stop and I jumped out hoping to pick up a few fist-sized pieces to take home.

The lava had cooled into mostly large pieces about the size of a piano bench, interspersed with grass, and I found nothing small enough to pick up. It was a great thrill, however, to be able to feel the sharp roughness of the extrusions and think back through history of all the famous and infamous people who had passed along this same road before me.

We arrived at the base of the cable car ride, called a Funicula in Italy, bought our tickets and waited for our car.

We got off shortly, and walked a few hundred feet more to the rim of the crater. On the way I was able to pick up a few red cinders. Toward the north, back down the slope, lay a river of black lava cinders all the way back to the highway. Later, I learned this flow had burst through the side of the mountain and had covered the highway to a depth of forty feet.

Interspersed along the path to the summit we met enterprising natives hawking souvenirs. They were small boxes brightly lined with aluminum foil containing what looked like small samples of rocks and minerals. They sold for only two to three dollars. Closer inspection revealed not a single box contained any lava, (red or black), no basalt, no porphyry or any of the minerals readily available. What a shock! The boxes were filled with chunks of brightly colored glass and other junk!

Once on the rim, looking down into the crater, I could see the breach where the lava flow had gone to the highway. The crater itself did not seem very big, about the size of a football field, and yet I know distance can be deceiving out in the open. The sides were streaked black and grey with many holes and vents easily discernable.

Eventually, we all gathered around the guide, who said, "Ladeez and Gentlemens, paleez notice the extraordinary experiment I shall now show you!" He rolled up a newspaper, and lighting one end with a match, he plunged it into the nearest vent. Immediately, plumes of smoke came out of every vent in the entire circumference of the crater. Amazing! Everyone gasped, and as soon as he removed the paper it all ended. I've never understood what happened. Evidently all the vents were somehow interconnected, but I can't explain how or why. It was certainly something I'll never forget. It was the experience of a lifetime for a rockhound from Missouri.

Later, we went south for yet another thrill, Pompeii. We stopped for sandwiches and sodas near the entrance to the old city and paid a small amount to get in. Guided by a booklet and small map, we wandered around on our own. Many walls of the buildings were still standing but there were no roofs. Occasionally, if you peered under a partial roof you could see a wall painted in the famous Pompeiian red. This peculiar red paint has been revered by artists for centuries because of its unusual brilliance, and critics say modern pigments have never come up to its standards.

In my wanderings, I noticed a flat tube running along the buildings that looked like a slightly flattened pipe. In some areas it ran for quite a distance. I surmised it might be lead, and scratching it with my knife, I confirmed that it was. I wondered how the people of that far-gone day avoided being poisoned by it. Lately, I have read that that is indeed what happened.

As the afternoon wore on, I continued walking up and in a northerly direction and came upon a large underground cistern that had stored their water. It was dry now, and I marveled at the stone construction, knowing they didn't have concrete in those days. I suppose there were many such cisterns in these upper parts of the city and they depended on gravity to supply the individual homes. The homes were not huts or even small houses, but quite large and obviously belonged to the elite part of the population.

Eventually, I came to the edge of the part that had been excavated, in front of me was a natural wall of light buff-colored pumice. It was about twelve feet high, I found I could pick small pieces out of it quite easily. They were quite uniform in size and shape and resembled peanuts still in the shell. I picked around quietly, filling my pockets and trying not to disturb the wall.

These little pieces were instruments of death the few days they rained down on Pompeii, for they were flaming bits of sulphur when they fell. Have you ever had a strong whiff of sulphur? It almost knocks you down and I can imagine the terrible agony of the victims when that unexpected inexorable rain of sulphur hit them. The entire city was covered with twelve to twenty feet of flaming sulphurous pumice. It was hard to believe that here I was, from far off St. Louis, picking up these innocent looking pieces of pumice to take home to show my rockhound friends.

The next day, Ron dropped us off near the museum where most of the artifacts reclaimed from Pompeii were displayed. We had been cautioned that there was a separate room, open only to adults, and to view this exhibit you were required to pay seventy-five cents admission.

As we walked along the main street toward the museum, an affluent looking Italian gentleman spoke to us in English. He was

245

pleasant, and seemed concerned with our safety. He warned us to stay on the side of the street where we were and not to stray down any side streets. He said these people were very poor and desperate and might grab you and strip you of everything you had, including your clothes. He walked with us all the way to the museum and waved us a pleasant goodbye as he left.

The museum was fascinating and we finally came upon the "adults only" exhibit, paid our admission and went in. It was filled with sculptures, carvings, vases, paintings, etc., all depicting the most erotic scenes imaginable! Bobbie was embarrassed and said she thought perhaps women weren't allowed in. But I told her she should pretend to be a doctor or scientist, with only a professional interest in the Pompeiian culture. But it all proved too much for her and we left.

We thought we would enjoy seeing the Isle of Capri. As we left the museum, we came upon a line of busses with what we thought were the proper signs. Consulting my Italian language book I tried to convey to the bus driver where we wanted to go. He eventually agreed to get us to the dock where we could get a hydrofoil boat. Unfortunately, the bus wound all around the city of Naples for an hour or so before we reached the dock. We hastily boarded the boat and were informed that it was the last trip of the day. Disembarking, we asked a policeman for directions to the tour bus. He bowed, saluted, and in his best English told us explicitly where to go. We found the Italian police impeccably dressed and polite; more so than in any other place we visited in Europe.

We had to run for the bus, it was the last of the day also! Our bus wound its way down the narrow road, the rocky embankments were so close to the bus windows, I could have reached out and picked the wildflowers blooming on them. The bus flew along while we held our breaths. In about fifteen minutes we reached a small beach where we were allowed fifteen minutes to get out and explore. We gazed out toward the Blue Grotto which we had so hoped to see, but could not because of the lateness of the day. It was beginning to get dark and Bobbie and I searched in the dim light for a few interesting beach pebbles and then reboarded the bus. When we got back to Ron's and examined our specimens we found we had a broken blue cup handle, a piece of green glazed tile, and a tumbled piece of ordinary brick. Such glorious finds for a couple of rockhounds on the beach on the Isle of Capri. ✒

Chapter Nine - Life in the CCC

Author's note:

After the Great Depression, President Franklin D. Roosevelt called upon Congress to authorize a program which would recruit thousands of unemployed young men, enroll them in a peacetime army, and send them into battle against destruction and erosion of our natural resources. Before it was over, nearly three million young men engaged in a massive salvage operation, the Civilian Conservation Corps (CCC), the most popular experiment of the New Deal. (Excerpted from Roosevelt's Tree Army: A Brief History of the Civilian Conservation Corps. *Prepared and distributed by the National Association of Civilian Conservation Corps Alumni (NACCCA)).*

For two years I was one of those young men.

I joined the CCC in August, 1934 at the urging of a neighborhood schoolmate. We started at Reform, Arkansas, moved to Missouri and on to California before being discharged in August, 1936.

During those twenty-four months I learned carpentry; concrete bridge building; apprentice sign work; teaching art; building, manning, and supervising forest fire lookout towers; timber stand improvement; surveying; soil erosion control; map making; and many other auxiliary skills.

All of these occupations are explained in the chapters of this book. I owe the CCC for giving me a chance at all of this, besides feeding, clothing, and giving me work.

Howard F. York

July 21, 1991

How It Was In The CCC

Part One

It was a hot August afternoon when Phil, a friend of mine, rang the front doorbell and out of breath said, "Here's our chance to go to Arkansas! There's mountains, pine trees, etc., etc., and we get paid every month and get clothes, etc." He hit me when I was really low-no job-no prospects. I had caddied at a golf course one summer and fall, huckstered fruit and vegetables door to door to all my family, relatives, and friends, but nothing seemed permanent. To get away from it all seemed right at the time. I was soon to be twenty-one, and felt I could choose what to do. Phil said the Government had decided that the Midwest's drought was so bad that a few more boys could join the CCC. So we went downtown and signed up.

I don't remember how my parents felt, but I think my mother seemed to think I'd be OK and my father was so burdened with trying to keep a law practice from going under that I suspect he was relieved to have me out from under foot. He had coerced me into joining the National Guard in the summer of 1930, and I had spent three very exciting years there, but that is another story.

The day after we signed up we went downtown and met a few other fellows gathered about an army recruiting office. Our recruiter came out and said to Phil, "You're the tallest-you be the leader," and handed him some instructions. Phil told us the papers said to all meet at Union Station at 5:00 p.m., where we would get a box lunch and board our train. This was really getting exciting! No instructions on clothes, toothbrush, etc., just go!

We all, about fifteen of us, boarded a chair car, put our feet up, and settled down to a nice railroad trip to Arkansas. We talked a lot, but really didn't get too well acquainted. We slouched down in our seats and tried to sleep. We woke up in Memphis at 7:00 a.m. and had to change trains. We were a sleepy-eyed, wrinkled, dirty group, but we were still in good spirits and I took a couple of pictures with a miniature camera I had. Phil and I were wearing sailor hats. We bought them at Barney's Army Store before we left St. Louis. He said everyone looked up to the Navy, and we would look experienced. I wore mine mostly to keep my hair in place, and since we were together most of the time, the other fellows would say, "Hey sailor!" I never really got used to it.

Under way, Phil started telling me to watch for the mountains and rough, beautiful scenery. He said a month before he had joined the CCC but got sick and came home. He was always sort of a mother's boy, being thin and sickly 'til he was seventeen or eighteen. He was tall and thin like me, but we soon came out of it after a few months of eating plenty and regularly, and going to bed at 10:00 every night.

The train was not air-conditioned, and the hot August winds heated up our car. Our tempers were getting short. We were tired and the box lunches were gone. The train never stopped, so time just dragged on and on.

I think it was early afternoon when we got to Little Rock, and suddenly the scenery changed. All day we had traveled through flat, dry, burnt-out fields. The drought had hit here as hard as in Missouri, but now the train was going through deep cuts that were of a dark material that looked like shale or slate. Later on I did find out it was slate. We were getting into the foothills of the Petit Jean

250

Mountain Range of northwest Arkansas. Large pine trees shaded the tracks and we seemed to revive. Everyone crowded at the windows to see better. In the late afternoon Phil announced that our final stop was Perry, Arkansas. Part of our group was to go to Thornburg Camp, and we divided at Perry.

A large, canvas-topped Army truck met us and the driver told us to climb on. It was an all-metal truck; no seats, just sit on the floor and ride the best way you could. I don't remember if an officer was with the truck or not. Maybe there was a sergeant in charge. Anyway, I was tired and hungry and dirty. I didn't care what happened. The roads were gravel, and the dust rolled in the back of the truck until you could feel it in your teeth. We rode over forty miles in that dust to our new home, "Camp Reform." We fell out of the truck, looking like Arabs from the desert, and were immediately taken up the hill to a dispensary. We were told to line up and take the Oath of Allegiance, then take our shirts off and get shots. It was wearing us down, believe me, but we got our shots and were told to go to a supply building for all our gear. As we drove in, I had noticed probably a dozen men raking and sweeping around the barracks, stripped to the waist, and all had their heads shaved. They really looked horrible, and with the name "Camp Reform," I wondered what I was getting into.

Our Company number was 726, and we had army officers to supervise our shelter, food, and clothing. The camp was laid out on a slightly sloping hill as we were in rough mountain country where flat spaces were few. The main buildings consisted of four long barracks that would sleep sixty men using an upper and lower bunk arrangement, a large dining hall, dispensary, recreation hall, offic-

251

ers' quarters, Forest Service quarters, combined washroom and engine house, and a latrine that consisted of a metal trough urinal and squat, wooden cutout holes to sit on for toilets. Pretty crude bathroom facilities, but the men settled down to them. Later, in Missouri and California, we had toilets like at home. All the buildings were covered with heavy tar paper and were up off the ground on heavy oak timbers. We had electric lights down the middle of an aisle between our bunks, but the light was too weak to read by. If you wanted to read or write you went to the recreation room where there were tables, a piano, and a canteen that sold soda, stamps, tobacco, candy, etc. You had to buy a coupon book for two or three dollars to be able to buy at the canteen. That kept the canteen boys honest as they didn't get a chance to handle cash and keep some of it. Out of the $30 we were paid each month, we got only $5, as $25 was automatically sent home to our parents. Some boys were lucky and had money sent back to them, but it was frowned on and always hush hush. Immediately after receiving their pay, a lot of the fellows would buy their tobacco, matches, and stamps for the month out of the $5, so they wouldn't run out before the end of the month. I never seemed to need money. If I was short, I did without. We had plenty of food and no place to go where we needed money. Gradually the spenders would find out who saved his money and would try to borrow, but I only loaned to a very select few, as you never got it back. I minded my own business, obeyed orders, tried to get along with everyone, and things seemed to go along smoothly.

Every morning before we walked to the mess hall, the first sergeant would give out announcements as we lined up in front of our barracks. For instance, there would be ball practice after supper, or an Army truck would take a lot of boys to roller skate at a rink forty miles away. Imagine taking a group that far for skating, and they would not get back 'til midnight! Anyway, you had to sign up before supper, and sometimes they would take two trucks. Of course the attraction was seeing the town of Morrilton and girls, but you had to catch the truck going back to camp or it was a long way back. ❧

Part Two

At the supply house, the first evening in Camp, after we had our shots, etc., we were issued a mattress, sheets, blankets, heavy army shoes and socks, 1918 BVD's for underwear with slit-type opening in the rear, blue denim pants and work coat, and wool pants and wool shirt, black tie for dress up, blue denim cap, wool overseas cap, and toilet box that had safety razor, metal soap box, trench mirror, a hand brush, etc., also, a canteen and canteen cup that had a heavy canvas cover holder that you could hook onto your heavy canvas belt. Believe me, we used all of it. Also issued were two large bath towels and a small hand towel. We had to launder our own clothes, but after two or three weeks we learned of a farmer who came to camp and picked up laundry, doing it very cheaply, but satisfactorily. He never lost anything and was always on time, hauling the clothes on a wooden sledge that was pulled by a mule. I forget the man's name; seems like it was Luke. He was blind in one eye that should have been closed but wasn't, and it shocked me greatly at first, but after a few transactions with him I soon forgot his affliction

253

and we got along nicely. Some of the fellows never washed their clothes, and I can still see them going to the washroom with their muddy, dirty towels. How they could stand them, I'll never know.

The Forest Service handed out the work projects. The supervisors were mostly career men who were experienced in their line. Some were timber oriented, some were construction engineers, road builders, etc. We had about six or seven stake trucks and several dump trucks.

My first job was in camp, working on top of the mess hall, building a large ventilator for over the officers' mess. A young fellow approached me and told me I was to help him at carpentry work. We got acquainted and I found out he was an assistant leader, who earned $36 a month, and was a darned good carpenter. He had come down with a group from Kansas City and the Army found out he knew his stuff and promoted him right away. His name was Eddie Reid and he asked me to pick out a helper, so I picked one of the boys that had come to camp on the train with me. Norman Brown was his name, and he was from Overland, Missouri, but he soon got the nickname of "Butts," because he was always cadging cigarettes from his buddies.

When we finished the ventilator I asked Eddie why he picked me for the job, and he said he had looked up my questionnaire in the Army headquarters and saw that I had put down that I was handy with a saw and hammer and had been an acting Corporal in the National Guard. When I was discharged from the National Guard they wanted me to reenlist and promised me a corporal's job that eventually could lead to being a sergeant. I had turned them down; I had had enough military life, it looked like war was in the near future, and I was wanting no part of it.

Eddie came up one evening after supper and told me that the next day we would become a bridge building crew of about fifteen men. He and I would build wooden forms for a low-water bridge about eight or ten miles from camp. Mr. Parker, our Forest Service supervisor, was to go with us and get the job started. Now the Forest Service people knew that a certain amount of local people would be invaluable for advice and know-how in their particular area, and they were paid just like us CCC boys, and were called Local Experienced Men, or LEM's. All of them were older men, some married, and they could live on camp or not. We had one attached to our crew called Andy. Andy was stout, wore overalls and a larger farmer-type straw hat. He lumbered along in a quiet manner, and offered advice, and helped out in his own way. Occasionally he would help us building forms, and I learned quite a bit from him.

The bridges we built were really not bridges, in the sense that they were elevated so that water could run under them. Although, our last one (we built three) was about two feet above the flow of water. We would simply build concrete walls, rectangular in shape, in the middle of a stream bed, put a cap on top of them, and in the time of spring or fall rains a vehicle could cross without getting stuck in the rocks and boulders. The rocks were all sizes; hard, flinty, basaltic, and granite types. We had a crew that excavated the holes for the concrete, but it was slow work. There was no digging...all pick and mattock-type work. The rocks would be all sizes from two inches to twelve inches, all round or oval, and after they were loosened had to be picked up and thrown out of the hole. Parker, our superintendent, had instructions to go down deep enough to hit the slate before we laid our concrete footings. It was tough going in the hot, humid August weather. Usually we went down to four, five or six feet before hitting the slate. Even the slate had to be excavated somewhat, to give the concrete a chance to level out, and it had to be chipped out carefully because it was on a slant. I never had to work in those holes but I can see those boys yet, stripped to the waist, sweating and getting red in the sun. Usually we dug out two or three sections per bridge.

We would pour concrete footings, making sure they were level, and Parker himself would get down in the hole and set large, tall stones in the fresh concrete, making keys for the final walls of the bridge to fasten to. The walls of the bridge would never shift, being keyed into the footings. It was always a big day when we poured concrete...a sort of mission accomplished. We had a gasoline operated mixer in which we shoveled in the mix, and Phil was in his glory, for Parker, seeing Phil was the largest on the crew and a sort of gold-brick, gave him a big hatchet and told him he was permanently in charge of the cement that went into the mixer. He had to keep track of the wheelbarrows of gravel and sand that went in, too. I can still see Phil with his hatchet, chopping the bags in two, throwing them in the mixer, each half weighing over forty pounds, cement dust over his whole body, sweating, but living it up. Phil was getting to be a big man, over six feet tall, and prided himself on being macho, although we didn't call it that then. ◢

Part Three

Building the forms was particular work as they had to be perfectly square. We used ship-lap lumber that overlapped each successive piece, thereby making it leakproof. Usually the forms were at least five to six feet high and sixteen feet or more long. Some of our lumber was warped and it took a lot of coaxing and ingenuity to get a good square form built. Our saws were not sharp sometimes and we sweated out a lot of muscular sawing. Gradually our crew settled into a team, either group doing the same job and getting better every day doing it. After setting our forms in the excavation and getting them plumb and square, we had to put spacers and wires in them to keep everything in place, keeping the walls the same thickness throughout the bridge. We had a roughneck crew of wheelbarrow pushers. There were four of them, and they were reckless, strong, and wouldn't surrender their job to anyone. One day, during the middle of a big pour of concrete, some spacers came loose between the forms. My job was to get down between them and put the spacers, which were 2"x12" pieces of wood, back in and tighten up the wires. This wheelbarrow crew pretended they didn't know I was down in the forms and poured a whole wheelbarrow load of concrete down my neck and back. I came out of there swearing and ready to take them all on. I've often thought about it, and I guess they did it to get even, because they thought I had the easy job, building forms, etc., using my head while they were using their backs. There were really no hard feelings as later on I lettered their names on their foot lockers and blue denims when they where on the tower crew when we built fire towers in Missouri. Their names were Grubbs,

Coons, Brown, and Kegler, and they were tough. The CCC did them some good. They worked hard, played hard, ate good food, and got tanned and healthy. We built three bridges during the months of August, September, and October.

There is one incident I remember about our food at noontimes on the job. Parker, our superintendent, didn't like the hot food brought out to the job, and we always had bag lunches, but one day our bag lunches were so bad he put us all in the truck and we went back into camp. We didn't work the rest of the day. He was a tough, flinty-faced man, who rarely praised your work, but took pride in what we did. Once when we poured a large top that was about two feet thick, he called the crew together and said, "This concrete will take 100 years to dry, and while it's wet let's all throw some coins in it for good luck." I had never heard of such a thing, but we did it. These are experiences I'll never forget. At that same bridge, I was one of the workers underneath knocking out props. One of the other guys swung his sledge hammer and missed, smacking me in the middle of my neck sideways. Strangely, it didn't hurt, and Parker said, "York, you sure have a tough neck." Phrases like that you never forget.

Years later, in 1940, my wife and I, on our honeymoon, tried to find the low-water bridges and discovered that a dam had been built in the valley east of our camp area and everything had been covered with up to thirty feet of water, forming Lake Winona, a lake for the water supply of Little Rock. The camp site was covered, roads, bridges, quartz crystal mines, all gone.

During the three months of August, September, and October, there were many interesting things that happened besides work.

Every week one of the barracks (there were four of them) was on fire call. That meant that day or night a crew had to be alert to a siren that was fixed to a pole near the truck workshop. I had to go only once and that was to a burning pine tree snag that had been hit by lightning. The fire tower at Oak Mountain spotted it the morning after a rain-storm, and since we were the closest, we had to go. It was after supper, and about twelve miles away, but the fire hadn't spread; only confined to the top of the tree about twenty feet up where it had broken off. We had to saw the tree up into about two-foot pieces, and split it into smaller pieces, almost as small as matchsticks, dousing everything with plenty of water which we carried on our backs from the truck to the site. In the Ouachita Forest pine trees were the protected tree, although, some years the white oaks were. The Forest Service had figured, to a very fine point, the value of the pine crop and the oak crop for each and every year. If there were too many pines, or there was more money in oaks, the order would go out to thin one crop or the other. We had a large crew that were called "girdlers" and their job was to "girdle" the white oaks by stripping with axes a six-inch to nine-inch section of bark all around the tree about waist high. They cut to the solid wood so the sap could not reach the upper part of the tree, causing it to die. It was quite a sight to see from a high point, all the oaks turning yellow and pale orange prematurely in the late summer sunshine. Of course, the green pines made them show up all the more. The oaks, you see, would lose their leaves and not shade the young pines near them, giving the pines a better chance to grow. And grow they did, for the short leaf Southern Yellow Pine grows faster in the norther Arkansas and southern Missouri areas than any other tree. Later the Oak tree would decay and fall to the

259

forest floor. The girdlers, hiking miles every day, slashing the trees and breathing the fresh air, soon became tanned and strong, and proud of their job. They carried their canteens from the belt on their hips, and actually became the envy of all the men in camp. Everyone wanted to be a girdler. They sometimes became arrogant and obnoxious. On one occasion they found a small barrel of home made whiskey stashed away by a moonshiner, and all of them sampled it a little too freely and had to be brought in early off the job by their foreman for fear of their own safety. On another occasion, one of the boys caught a rattlesnake and carried it into the truck, holding it by the back of the head, but it got loose and bit him on the thumb. He had to be taken to Little Rock for medical attention. He was gone about a week, and his thumb was quite a mess when he came back to camp. When they gave him first aid in the field, they sliced his thumb pretty bad. Incidentally, we heard the moonshiner, whose keg the boys stole was mighty mad, and vowed to get the crew if they came back to work in that section of the forest. So the girdlers changed, and we didn't hear much more about it. Of course, on weekends the fellows were free to leave camp, after signing up at the Company office. A few knew where to buy moonshine and they brought it back to camp in one-quart fruit jars. It was very cheap, and although it was forbidden in camp, the fellows would sneak it around, but never really caused any trouble and always showed up sober for work on Monday morning. ⋆

Part Four

The Forest Service had a really good system going in the work program for the men. Their purposes were timber improvement, road building so that trucks and men could put out fires quickly, and bridge building to expedite movement of trucks, etc. We surveyed through virgin timber, usually following the tops of ridges for road building, thereby keeping down the cost of fills in building bridges and in digging cuts. An experienced Forest Service foreman would hike the ridges, blaze trees, and mark the path of the road. Phil helped blaze trees like this for a short time, until he cut his leg badly and had to be taken to camp for thirty or more stitches. He had hit a hidden knot in a tree and the blade glanced off to his leg. As a result, he liked hospital care and after his injury became an assistant in the dispensary until he asked for a discharge. A timber cutting crew went in after the trees that were blazed, cutting off trees about waist high with long cross-cut saws. The chain saw had not been invented in 1936. The logs were stacked along the right-of-way and all brush-tops, etc., had to be dragged at least 300 feet back from the edges. This brush dragging was a hard job. The countryside was rough and up hill and down. Rocks were everywhere. Sometimes the boys would literally crawl with their load. There were ticks and chiggers and flies, and the hot humid weather, on top of it all. Many did it, and didn't murmur, but some hated it and always begged to get off of the crew. If you laid back and goldbricked, the leaders would find out and the work was loaded up even more. It was tough.

After the tree clearance crew came the dynamite crew, who blew up the stumps so that the bulldozers could come in. Bulldozers were new then, with their big pusher blade in front. Jarring the stumps loose first with several sticks of dynamite made it easier for a bulldozer to push the stump out later, although some of the larger stumps were very stubborn and sometimes twenty to thirty sticks of dynamite were needed to blow them out. One of my buddies in our barracks said one pine tree he worked on was seven feet across when they sawed it off waist high. After the stumps were cleared, more "dozers", as we called them, and road graders, pulled by ordinary tractors, began scraping off the rock and dirt and putting it where the roadbed should be. In various places along the road, ditches had to be gouged down and into the woods for drainage. They were called "tail ditches," which were left in a pretty rough condition. There were roots and boulders to be moved out so water could run off and keep the roads and ditches clear. After the graders, dump trucks would bring gravel and spread it on the surface. All the Forest Service wanted was room for a truck to get in and out of the area quickly. One width of a truck was all that was needed although generally two trucks could pass safely. We had to crush all our own rock for surfacing, and it usually had to be hauled miles and miles, but when the call went out for the gravel trucks to move, they really did. There were six, or maybe ten, gravel trucks available, and the drivers would literally fly to the loading and unloading sites. The roads were dusty and vision wasn't too good, so it took an alert driver to do the job. They got to be a breed like the girdlers, very proud of the job they were doing. I remember one incident where a loaded truck met an unloaded truck, flying along much faster than he should have. One of them took off the road to avoid an accident and turned over four times, not hitting a tree or rock, and the driver got out without a scratch. Later on in camp, one of the supervisors interrogating a new recruit, knowing that most of them would like to drive a truck, would ask them if they could drive a Fairbanks, and they would always say yes and he would hand them a slip of paper sending them to the supply house for a wheelbarrow. What a blow! ❧

Part Five

Making our gravel was quite a chore. Sometimes a CCC camp didn't need gravel, and the rock crushers would be idle. When the word got out that the crusher was coming to our area, the men would groan, and pray they wouldn't be drafted to work with it. Sometimes the crusher, which was self-propelled, or driven, would move slowly along the gravel roads and the crews would walk along side it throwing in boulders of all sizes. I never had a good look at one, but it had large iron weights that revolved in it, somehow crushing the rock until a certain size came out the rear. Almost all the roads in our area were boulder lined, and all you had to do was pick them up and toss them in the jaws of this monster, but the racket was deafening. All the crew stuffed cotton in their ears and dragged along in the dust, throwing in rock in a never ending day. We could hear it three quarters of a mile away, and always felt sorry for the boys on that crew. At other times the machine would park near a creek that had plenty of rocks and it would stockpile until they had enough.

In my off hours, maybe after supper, I would go off, usually by myself, with my pastel chalks, and try to do some sketching. I had learned a little about doing this kind of artwork a year ago from a friend back home, and seeing the beautiful fall colors appearing among the big pine trees, along with vistas of roads, etc., I couldn't resist trying to do something worthwhile. I used brown paper from the inside of cement sacks, not having any good kraft paper to work on. In pastel sketching, the chalk areas that you didn't fill in as you worked would show up glaringly if you worked on white paper, but if you worked on light brown, or kraft, the background was not so obvious and gave a nice mellow flavor to the completed sketch. My friend, Mrs. Queal, showed me other tricks as well, in the short time she taught me. I had some water colors at home before I joined the CCC, and made a lot of the tree trunks black. She soon showed me that was wrong, and showed me that there were blues, purples, and browns, and even light colors where there was direct sunlight on the bark, etc.

Anyway, I made two or three sketches and thumbtacked them to the slanted roof over my bunk. One of the officers on an inspection saw them and I was called to headquarters one evening. I wish I could remember his name, it was something like McLean. Anyway, he asked me if I would teach sketching to a class twice a week in the evenings. I was dumbfounded. Here I am, the rankest of learners, being asked to teach. Anyway, I figured I'd try, and the first thing we did was portraits, profile style. We picked out a few macho-type guys that had good faces, and about six or seven others started in drawing. Well, they were using my pastels, and one Italian, who was pretty good, really dug into them. Our supervisor promised to get more supplies at Hot Springs, so we went ahead using mine. This started late in the fall, and sort of fell apart when we heard that the camp was going to move; no more information than that—big question! Rumors like Alaska, or California, or even Minnesota, where they had a lot of zero weather. I hated to think about it.

While I was doing my sketching during off hours, one of my original buddies that signed up in St Louis, Bill Mays, came up to me after supper and approached me about painting his name on his homemade wooden footlocker. He'd built it out of scrap lumber he had scrounged somewhere. He even showed me how he had built it, with top and folding tray, and with hinges, etc. He'd seen that I had a small red sable 1/4-inch brush in my belongings and wanted his name on the locker. I found some white house paint, laid out his name in Roman-type letters on the top, and did it. I'd taken drafting in high school one year, and the final plate was a complete alphabet in Roman letters and numerals. I really had them memorized, so his job came out quite well, considering the wood was rough and the paint thick and oily.

That proved to be a turning point in my whole life, for another fellow had a box he wanted lettered, and another, and another. I charged them ten cents a letter, and if they wanted their whole name and city, etc., it would amount to several dollars. We started getting new army metal foot lockers later—those of us who could afford them. I had to send home for some better brushes and paint. Most of the lockers were light olive-drab color, so black letters showed up nicely on them. If a fellow wanted white, I said no, I didn't have white, and if I did it would take two coats and cost double. Anyway, most of this work was done on a credit basis, a promise to pay on payday. The barber and photographer tipped me off and told me to wait at the end of the line where the officers handed us our $5.00, and collect there and then. So it worked, everyone paid off. They were embarrassed in front of all their buddies not to pay, so they did.

It wasn't very long until every night before lights went out I was painting foot lockers in all the barracks. When the lights blinked before they finally went out, I'd clean my brushes and pack everything in my box and leave. My box was stored away under my bunk and no one ever bothered it. 🐾

Part Six

One evening our company truck mechanic, Brigham, came to me and said there was an emergency. We had to haul some dynamite from Hot Springs, and needed a bunch of sideboard signs for the sides of some stake trucks that had to be lettered in orange and black reading "Explosives." I told him all I had was a small lettering brush and black paint. He said he'd get the boards, and we'd use red lead powder mixed with light linseed oil. (They painted dynamited stumps with red lead.)

There were no large brushes in camp, so we painted these raw boards with wooden tongue depressors we got from the dispensary. We just spread the paint and by the next day they were dry. I guess there were about six boards, four feet long, and I lettered them with six-inch letters on bright orange backgrounds, using my old reliable Roman-type letters, only I slanted them; it was easier to letter and faster, too.

I had heard a lot of bickering amongst the fellows in the camp, even from the first evenings. Seems like a lot of them didn't like the Captain, whose name was McQueen. He never seemed to say much when he stood near the lineups for breakfast or supper; always had his campaign hat pulled down in front over his eyebrows. In the late evenings, when a lot of us would sit on the steps of the porch of our barracks, the loud-mouths would voice all their grievances. I can't remember what they were, but some said the food was bad, or they didn't get to go to town enough, or something. McQueen had trouble enough, so bad that the big offenders were banished to work after they came in at 4:00 off their regular jobs. This extra work was called "B" class. It consisted of sawing and splitting wood for the camp stoves, mostly the boiler room for showers and washing, and for the cooking in the mess hall. This made matters worse, and rumblings increased 'til there were several boys every week that would go A.W.O.L.; just walked out of camp and went home or somewhere. This didn't look good for the management at camp, especially the Captain, and after a five or six week span of A.W.O.L.'s, the Captain was replaced by a new Captain by the name of Stinsman.

The first night at supper he got up in the Mess Hall and spoke. He was trim, with a small narrow mustache, starting-to-grey hair, and matter-of-fact manner. He said, "I hear you boys have had a bad time the last few months. This Saturday evening we're going to have a big chili supper—beer for everybody, and cigars will be passed out." He did that, and one Saturday every month after that. The A.W.O.L.'s ceased immediately.

About two or three weeks before we moved to Greenville, Captain Stinsman met me at the entrance to the Mess Hall after supper and asked if I'd letter his footlocker. I said I'd be glad to, and

he said I was to charge him like everyone else. I remember the job
so well. His locker was maroon, and I had to do it in white, but by
the time I had a good working white enamel, the job came to $3.00.
"Captain Stinsman, Salina, Kansas." 🖎

Part Seven

    I'll never forget my first time in a lookout tower. One of the
LEM's told us about a lookout tower at North Fork, about seven miles
north on a truck trail that went north out of camp. I was all for going
to see it on a Friday evening after we were off duty until Monday
morning. I got three others to go with me. It was dark by the time
we signed out at headquarters. It was really dark on that road, and
I don't remember anyone having a flashlight; we just went by the light
of the stars. We hadn't been in camp but a few weeks, and were in
puny shape, but we finally got to the tower about midnight. The men
there were really surprised to see us. They slept in a small wood
cabin at the base of the tower and told us we'd have to sleep on the
porch; no beds, no blankets, nothing. They said don't sleep out in
the grass or rocks, for the rattlesnakes were out in that area. I tried
to sleep, using a canteen for a pillow, but it was miserable. I slept out
of sheer exhaustion. We had been told we'd get a place to sleep and
good food, etc. At breakfast, the leader of the tower crew (they seemed
to be older men, like LEM's) told me that their food was rationed, but
they would share some scrambled eggs and coffee with us. Well, that
was better than nothing. We filled our canteens and left, but before

that I went up in the tower. There I saw my first *Alidade (Fire Finder). The tower had glass windows on all four sides, and in the middle was a post with a map of the area on it.

The routine of work for us started early in the morning, get-up time about 6:30. We'd hustle to the washroom, trying to get there before the hot water ran out, and to get space to shave, etc. Sometimes the men were two deep, washing teeth, shaving, and combing hair. Once, one of our leaders, a $45.00 man, reached over my shoulder and rubbed his toothbrush on my orange Lifebuoy soap, apologizing, saying he ran out of dental powder. Imagine, he almost seemed to relish it! I think I'd do without until I could buy some powder or paste.

If we had some time before mess call, we'd straighten our beds and grab a broom, sweeping everything out to the aisle. Certain men were assigned to clean the aisle each week, and there was a lot of hullabaloo about broom possession. The barracks had to be neat when we left for work. In fact, we were inspected and graded each day, and the barracks that was the best would get the "E" award hung outside their door; "E" standing for excellence, and you'd be surprised how we worked for it. I think our barracks, Number 4, won it two to one over the others. When we returned from work each afternoon, we could see from the road that circled the camp which barracks had the "E", and a big cheer always came up from the truck as the boys saw it. We got two clean sheets and a pillow-slip each week, although we had to go to the supply house to get them. Of course we turned in our soiled ones. The Army wanted to be sure we were clean and didn't get sick. Incidentally, I had a bad tooth, and the doctor making a close inspection each month, sent several of us to Hot Springs for attention. That was when I lost my first molar. We came back the same day. The trip was only forty miles or so. I'd been to Hot Springs before, on a trip in the evening after supper. Eddie Reid asked me to go and see the sights, although another buddy and I had to load in 100 pound sacks of cement for bridge building jobs we were doing. Hot Springs was very beautiful, with lots of new Government buildings around the Springs. It was a National Park, and very well kept. The City was nestled in the valley, and the tall pines grew everywhere. I told myself, I'll come back here some day and see the sights leisurely and thoroughly; and I did—on my honeymoon and again with my family, including my son, Steve, and my daughter, Carolyn. ❧

Part Eight

Somehow, everywhere in my life there has been singing, mostly with groups. On our train ride coming to camp during the first days and weeks we sang and I harmonized, encouraged to a large degree by the fact that one of our group had a guitar. He was a novice, and strummed chords in a light off-hand manner, but it got us going in the evenings on our front steps. We'd sing old tunes like "Ain't She Sweet," "Brown Eyes," "It Ain't Gonna Rain No More," etc. We got quite a reputation in the camp, and we finally settled down to a small group of four or five. We sang sort of barber-shop, but not really. We did have harmony, and we would have an audience every evening. One of the local men said some people down the road wanted to hear us and invited us for an evening. We dressed in our good uniforms and hiked down about a mile I guess. We stood below a high porch where maybe five or six people sat in the kerosene lamplight, listening. We did five or six numbers, and waited—there was no applause; no talking or anything. The lady of the group got up, went inside the cabin, and in a few minutes came out with ice cream and cake. No talking, sociability, or nothing. We ate in silence, thanked them, and walked back in the dark to camp. I'll never understand what happened. The only guess I ever made was that they were disappointed because we didn't sing hillbilly songs like "Red River Valley" or "Clementine."

Lots of evenings, when it began to get cooler, about in October, a dozen of us or so would play basketball. Our court was pretty awful. It was on a slight slant besides being up hill. In other words, one basket was downhill at least a foot, and it was mounted crooked on the post. The floor was hard dirt, but small sharp rocks were always coming out of the ground and you could take a bad spill or lose the ball when you dribbled and it hit loose pebbles. But we loved it, and every evening would rush to get chosen for the first ten players. We'd get pretty hot playing in blue jeans and heavy G.I. shoes, but it was great. After I got to painting foot lockers, I gradually quit playing. One evening, shortly after getting into camp, a call went out for baseball tryouts, so I went up to try out, for I had been a catcher when I was in high school. I hadn't caught twenty balls before I caught one on a finger nail and it hurt so bad I had to quit. I worked all next day but it got worse, and the second evening Andy, our helper on the bridge crew, asked me how my hand was. I showed him and he said the blood has collected under the nail and the

271

pressure was what hurt. He took out his knife and using the point, slowly drilled a hole near the base of the nail. The blackish blood came out and I got instant relief. I thought of the mouse that had taken the thorn from the lion's paw in the old Aesop fable. I think of Andy still when I get that kind of injury.

Lots of times on off-hours we'd walk the roads (we called them trails, for the Forest Service calls them truck trails) looking for adventure; not exciting adventure, but just to get away from camp, enjoying the smell of the pines and talking, "shooting the breeze" we'd call it. Once, one of the older boys showed how we could find tarantulas. He'd lift up large rocks in certain areas off the road until he'd find a den. The creature would jump out at us for disturbing it, and we learned that the brown ones were females and the black and white ones were males. We heard all kinds of stories, how they could leap six feet or more, and how deadly their poison was. Once, we left camp with a quart mason jar and lid and went to holes we'd find in the rocks. We'd put the jar down, open end to the hole, and then bang on the other side, hoping the tarantula would come out. If it did, we'd clamp the lid on and we had it trapped. On one of those trips we caught a female and two males. We had only one jar, so they were all together. The two males immediately began fighting, jabbing at each other with their fangs, which were 1/8 to 3/16-inch long. They circled 'round and 'round and finally wore themselves out. When we looked closer at the bottom of the jar, we could see venom on the bottom 1/16-inch deep all over. We let them go before we got back to camp, but that was an exciting experience.

Another time in the evening, we hiked along the road, Phil and I and another boy, Bob Sharpe, who was big and tall and rangy.

We had a hard time keeping up with his stride. He worked on the surveying crew, and that crew covered lots of mileage in their work every day. Anyway, we were talking quietly in the early shadows after sunset, when Sharpe said to stop, there was a tarantula ahead, and he'd show us how tame they were. We crept up, and Sharpe went ahead while we watched. He went right up to the creature and laid his hand down in front of it very quietly. Darned if the thing didn't walk right up onto his hand and sat there. After at least a minute, it withdrew and went down the side of the road. Bob said he thought the thing liked the warmth of his hand, and as long as he stayed quiet, it wouldn't bite him. We managed to get a picture, but I can't remember what became of it. There were scorpions and centipedes in that country, too, but they were pretty wary and we didn't see many.

Once when I was sketching a beautiful spot in the woods, I decided to back up a few feet to get a better spot to sit down, and if I'd gone another fifteen or twenty feet I'd have sat on a skunk. I just happened to glance back as I was backing up, and I stopped right then. I didn't ever try to finish my drawing; I just made tracks back to camp. ᴥ

Part Nine

We had an Army truck, painted olive drab, (the Forest Service trucks were forest green), that went to Hot Springs every day to get the mail and supplies. The driver, George Williams, was a likeable, happy guy who always had stories to tell, and especially about how he'd catch rattlesnakes. He'd leave camp early, and on his route over the dusty roads sometimes he'd see the winding tracks of rattlers that had crossed earlier in the morning. He would stop his truck and cautiously look on both sides of the road for a specimen. He had a specially built wire cage in the truck, and he always said he could get good money for a live snake. If a rattlesnake was in the area where George was poking around, it would make a loud rattle with its tail you'd never forget. I've got a picture of George with a snake he accidently ran over on one of his trips.

A couple of times we had entertainment brought out from Little Rock. It mostly consisted of a group of girls chaperoned by a reserve Army Captain and his wife. There wasn't much to their entertainment, except we had a juke box in our Rec Hall and the boys would pick out a girl and dance with her. The girls weren't supposed to leave the Rec Hall, but gradually they did, although most seemed to sit outside and drink soda and be friendly. It was usually a Saturday night, and everyone seemed to have a good time. A lot of the boys didn't have any money to spend, and a lot of them didn't dance, so sometimes it was awkward. One of our boys asked his dancing partner if she ever did the "rubber leg," which, believe it or not, was a current dance at home in St. Louis. However, it infuriated the girl and she slapped him and stomped off, saying, "I'm not that kind of girl!" The Army Officer's wife and I somehow got acquainted, and we tried a few dances. We seemed to move together quite nicely, and I started to hum quietly. She remarked she bet I could sing louder if I wanted, so I did, and sang a lot of the old ballads that were current in those years. We really had a good time. There was no hanky-panky, no kissing or anything, just pure, close human enjoyment. Near the end of the evening the Captain separated us, saying something like I ought to have a few dances with my own wife. They came back another weekend, and we did the same thing, although we never exchanged names, or made anything of it. Of course the boys razzed me, but it didn't bother me.

Finally, a week before Halloween, the last day of October, the news came that we all had been waiting for. We weren't going to move to Minnesota or Alaska, but to Greenville, Missouri. What a letdown! But, a bunch of us in the barracks realized we'd be only 150 miles from home, and we could get leaves a lot easier. We went to Perry and boarded our train in the late afternoon. It seemed like it was the slowest train I'd ever ridden, but a 7:00 or 8:00 in the morning we pulled into a little town called Taskee, Missouri. Hardly fifty people there, and it was bitter cold. We hadn't been issued heavy wool coats, and we shivered standing there waiting for trucks to show up. They finally did, but they were open stake trucks, with no seats, and no covers. We had about a fifteen mile ride, and really froze.

When we got to camp, which was a brand new camp, we found there was no water supply. The well drillers hadn't hit water, and all of the drinking and cooking water had to be hauled in by tank truck.

The barracks were new and smelled good. We were in a different type of forest, mostly oak, although later we found there was a lot of short-leaf pine, too. We had a hard time washing and bathing. We'd get a canteen cup of water to shave, etc. with and then someone discovered a small pond down the road from camp, and the boys started to bathe in it. After a week or so of that, the water began to look soapy blue, and no one wanted any part of it. The weather had really gotten cold, and we were in bad shape. I took one bath about a mile from camp on the edge of a creek that had a few small pools of ice cold water to wash in. I remember wearing my raincoat for warmth and bathing half my body at a time, putting on clothing as I went. Almost turned blue doing it, but what a relief hiking back to camp, all clean and smelling good. We finally got water, but it was quite an experience.

Gradually, I got to do more signs for the camp, lettering signs like "Engine Room," "Mess Hall," "Barrack No. __." We had about six or eight in this camp, and several of the fellows would come up and say confidentially, "York, I'll bet you get a rating," which meant I'd be moved up in rank to be an assistant leader, drawing $36.00 a month, and wear two gold stripes on my dress shirt. I secretly hoped it would happen, 'tho I never felt like a leader. I just did my job and kept my mouth shut, but the rumors persisted, and one evening the Captain and I crossed paths and he stopped and said, "You think you could handle an assistant leader's job?" I really don't remember what I said. Anyway, he said he was turning me in for the job, and so it happened. I got No. 1 bunk by the door of No. 8 barracks. ❧

Letter From A Tower Man, Howard York

April 5, 1935
Saturday Evening

Dear folks-

Should have written sooner but wanted to send money with this letter. I may and may not. You see, being out here at the tower caused us boys not to sign the payroll when it was sent to Leavenworth, the 15th of March. That makes us get paid a week or 10 days late. Well two of the boys went into camp, last night and were paid, but tho they insisted, the captain would not give them my "dough." So I have to go in to-morrow and get it. Even then I may not. For the captain is in town usually on Sunday. So what?

I may send home just $5 or maybe more. You see my black shoes are pretty old and I can get some pretty good ones for about $3 in Poplar Bluff. I owe $2.00 for cleaners bills, laundry, canteen card (stamps, films, gun, etc.) and a couple of shows. That leaves me a dollar for this month to run on. I may figure out a different plan tho.

Well, we are working hard here, the four of us. We've a long hard job ahead of us and its pretty hard being the boss here. But we have finally become adjusted and are getting along fairly smoothly. One of us works as a cook K.P., housemaid and wood-cutter. The other one takes a half a day in the tower while the 2 remaining work in the field on different projects outlined by the Honorable H.F. York. Ahem!!

We have built a fence around the tower, a good, heavy, strong one made of oak, exactly like ours at home.

Also have mounded the dirt around the tower thus: and built gravel walks.

Flower beds, sod, etc. are to be added. We have good black dirt to work with, lots of timber, rocks, gravel and muscle.

Also have to almost rebuild a solid mile of road, or trail. We will fill ruts, dig tail ditches, trim trees 10 feet high for 20 feet on both sides of trail, pile rocks, rake leaves back, grub out obnoxious stumps, drag brush and cut unsightly diseased trees. That's a real job! Will take us a month of absolutely steady labor to do it, but it will be worth it. The road is level, winding, and leads thru pines, oaks and ash. The trimming of trees will open up lots of pleasing vistas. The only trouble is getting the rest of this gang out here to see the artistic effect that will result when the end is reached. All they can see is sweat and dirt and work and rocks and mud. It isn't so beautiful when it comes to that but I'm working along with them so there's no room to kick.

Our food is fair, occasionally being excellent. We sometimes have cherry cobbler, chicken, good pancakes and cornbread. I will say Fox and Brown are darn, good, hustling cooks. We cook on an old battered rusty stove that we borrowed from a farmer's wife a month ago. We cook biscuits, gravy, coffee, everything on it! I don't see how Fox or Brown manages. Believe me if all 4 of us wasn't as resourceful as we are, we would have an awful time. But as it is we have tables, closets, cupboards, lamps, pantry, "ice box" and even a 1st class "privy", York design. 20th Century pattern.

Now about my nurse friend. She is OK. That fits her and nothing else does. Of course, I could say, beautiful, wonderful, sensible, economical et cetera but that's a lot of hooey. I don't see her much for this job is more or less confining except when it rains but even then you can't get out. I see her maybe once every week and a half. She is a nurse for a doctor Burton in Williamsville, 23 miles by road away. He is the only doc. there but even so has it fairly tough. I have driven his V8 Ford which has a radio and do we have fun-She & I and the radio riding along about 20 miles an hour thru these pine covered hills. Ho! Ho! Ho! I'm quite a Romeo if someone furnishes everything-girl, car, radio, road, moonlight, etc. Hurray for life in the CCC.

Seriously, tho, I know "you all" would like her, tho its not as bad as all that. O no - for $36.00 a month is a nice ball and chain to a fellow who lets himself think about "a dame."

The 3 boys have gone to Poplar Bluff to-nite. I didn't want to go for I hadn't taken a bath and had no money. But next week I'll have some, I hope and will get my shoes. I need a light half sweater for spring and I may manage for it, too but it can wait. We are all drinking that old favorite, sassafras tea and we all keep a certain "path" hot, too. Fox keeps us on a good diet and we all more or less exercise in the morning.

The first time, yesterday, I got a little homesick. I got to thinking of church and all the things I used to do, scout work, parties, etc. And about high school and the old long halls where I used to carry my books and hope for the day to end. Things have certainly changed. So quick, too. Just think, last year, at this time, no one could have told me I would be manning a fire tower in a National Forest, right here in Missouri. Who knows, next year I may be in Peru or China or the South Pole. Years are short, that is true, but they are long when you think of the things that can happen to you.

279

Last week was a pretty dry one and on one day we turned in 3 fires. 2 crews were sent out on each, making a total of 6 crews out. The 6th crew was a scraping-up of all the men in camp that were necessary for its running, blacksmith, K.P.'s, cooks not on duty, orderlies, Hospital orderlies, dog robber, etc. Boy we get a kick when we get the whole cock-eyed camp out on fires.

This week however it has rained and rained. Fires won't bob up for another week even if it does stop raining and its raining now. Incidently our tent leaks in spots. One night I was awakened by rain in my ear and Fox discovered he was sleeping with his feet in 3 inches of water. Oh - we have a "melodious" time as Dewey Brown says. He has a vocabulary like "Amos and Andy"! Honest - he makes me laugh so much I hurt. He had his 2 small boys 10 & 12 yrs. out here for a couple of days and they romped and played so much and had such a good time. I almost wished I had some. That's some confession, I must admit.

Our tent is on a platform now, with its sides touching the platform but soon we are going to change it, if we can get permission to cut some pine logs. We plan to raise the tent for Summer for it will be so hot. Here's the idea. We can roll the tent sides for ventilation.

I hope we get a bungalow as is planned, this summer. When they build that tho, they are liable to take us off. I don't know how that's going to work.

Kerosene lamp is failing me and out of kerosene-
Write in the morning.
Well here I am. Am sending some pictures.

Will have more soon.

Sun isn't out yet this morning.

Howard.

P.S. This is called Flatwoods Tower. It's about 10 miles north of Poplar Bluff.

Flatwoods

Early in the fall of 1935 I was working in the Civilian Conservation Corps (CCC) out of Camp Greenville, Company 726, about six miles south of Greenville, Missouri.

We were building a lookout tower in an area called Flatwoods, about ten miles north of Poplar Bluff. I was the carpenter that made the forms for the big concrete blocks at the base. There were four of them and they had to be perfectly placed, level and square. They went into the ground at least six feet deep and were about four feet by four feet on the sides. We were constantly checking the forms with surveyor's instruments, and the final placement of the big iron hooks in the form was quite a task. These hooks were about 1 1/4" diameter and were threaded at the top where they stuck out of the forms. The hook was at the bottom, anchored in the concrete. Of course, we hand-mixed the concrete.

Our barracks was selected to be the tower crew. This crew had to learn the art of putting up the steel legs, cross braces, etc. They learned to use "gin poles," a wooden pole with block and tackle equipment to hoist the heavy legs. The whole tower went up to a few inches short of being one hundred feet tall, including the seven feet square watch cabin on top. The cabin had windows on four sides and a wooden floor. The steps from the ground were wooden and zigzagged up to the top.

Towards the end of the construction I was asked back to cut and fit the wooden steps with a fellow named Butler Fox. Fox was an unforgettable character. He came into camp with a bunch of new enrollees in October. He was one quarter Indian and seemed to excel at everything. He never refused a challenge and would take on men almost twice his size in boxing, wrestling, or plain fighting. He was educated and you could talk hours with him on serious subjects.

Anyway, after the tower was finished he came up to me out of the blue and said, "Howard, they're looking for a crew of four to man the tower we've just built. Let's you and I go - you're assistant leader and with two other guys I think we can do it. We won't have to hang around this camp and we can cook our food the way we want it and after doing our time on the tower we'll have free time to do anything we want."

Well, the idea appealed to me so we put in for the job and got it. Of course, the other two men we knew fairly well. Dewey Brown, the older man, was a Local Experienced Man who was called an LEM. His nephew was the fourth man, whose last name was Inman. He was a quiet fellow who wasn't much more than a good working hand.

All of us went down to the lumber shed and tool room and picked out an eight man tent, lumber for a floor, all kinds of tools such as saws and hammers, shovels, mattocks, axes, etc. We really "gorged" ourselves on equipment, some of which we never used, really.

Dewey lived about fifteen miles away at Rombauer and got some stove pipe from a friend and we put up the tent after we built the floor, cut a hole in the top off to one side, put a two foot square piece of tin to hold the smoke pipe, and settled down. Of course, we had good steel cots and plenty of blankets, etc.

We went out in January, about a week after all of us had spent a week at home for the Christmas Holiday. It was quite a transition from home to living in a tent in January.

One of our first jobs was to maintain a temporary phone line that ran from the phone in the tower, down the steel leg, and off into the woods towards the highway, about three miles, I guess. We had to trace it every day or two because falling branches, etc. might disrupt our reporting of conditions in the pine forest all about us. A telephone crew was building a permanent line from the highway, using heavy wire and poles. It was slow work and I remember one worker digging a hole for a solid week. He had run into a shelf of rock and had to beat his way through it. The hole went down about six feet and it had to be in line with the rest of the poles and line coming through.

Fox and I went into camp one weekend and the Captain had arranged for a dance in the canteen for the boys, complete with a small five piece orchestra from Greenville. During the dances, we got acquainted with the girl playing the piano and she asked what we did, so we told her we were the tower men out at Flatwoods. Little did we know she would come out for a visit later in the spring.

So this is when I wrote the following letter home. My mother had saved it out of the many I sent home the three years I was in the CCC.

November 13, 1990

The Tower Man's Lament

The tower crew at old Flatwoods,
I'll tell you men, they produce the goods.
Get up at Six, turn in at nine.

Tower life, now, is not so fine.

You may ask what we do for water
Well men, - we carry it a mile and a quarter.
We cook our meals - police our tent
One good thing - we don't pay rent.

One man goes up the tower to stay
The others work ten hours a day.
When it's time to knock off - time for repose -
There's a new job done with each day's close.

Grubbing out stumps,
Fixing roads
Hauling off junk, by wheelbarrow loads -
Raking leaves in piles to burn
A new job to do wherever you turn.

Building log fences, dragging brush,
No-one to boss us, no-one to push -
We just keep doing a little each hour
To improve the looks of the Old Fire Tower.

We get most of our food - out of tin cans,
When fixed, we eat from granite pans.
We sleep in a tent that leaks like a sieve
On rainy days, it's a hard life to live.

Go to bed at night, all tired out -
Fall asleep - then - just about,
The time you're dreaming of Home Sweet Home,
You discover a leak - right over your dome.

Drips in your ear -
                    Drips on your nose -
Beds soaking wet - also our clothes.
Get up in the dark to move your cot -
Tower life then is not so hot.

But everything has its sunny side, too,
And that's how it was with the tower crew.
We work along till day is done
When night comes - we have our fun.

And I believe we are justified.
If we view each day's work with a little pride,
For after all, our efforts will be -
Another project for the CCC.

The last thing - and I think it best.
When our time is up - our stay here ends.
We will emerge four, staunch, strong friends.
And - one thing we agree, that is not denied,
It's no Bed of Roses - but we're satisfied. ❧

Christmas Eve

It was about midnight on Christmas Eve in our CCC barracks when I heard the wind pick up and start blowing around our building. It was rattling the big doors at both entrances, shaking the windows over our bunks and tree branches brushed back and forth over the roof and walls. We could feel cold air coming up through the cracks in the floor, too.

We pulled our sheets and blankets closer around our shoulders. We had good spring beds with clean sheets and covers so we were warm. Down the center aisle of the barracks were two wood-burning stoves that the night watchman refueled every hour as he passed through, checking everything in the camp.

It was my second Christmas in the CCC but we didn't dwell on thoughts of home or of what they might be doing there. We were glad we had work to do and a place to eat and sleep. All of our wants were being taken care of by the government. I personally didn't think of my future, I realize now.

Some of us spoke to Shorty, the night watchman, about the weather. He said that it was snowing - we'd have a white Christmas! We slid back into our covers, some of us I knew thinking we'd enjoy a big Christmas dinner at noon. I don't remember any gift-giving or presents or cards from home, it was too grim a time to do things like that. Everyone was just getting by on necessities.

We had a great Mess Sergeant in "Pop" Emerson. He was an unforgettable personality. He was easily 6'6" and had a commanding presence with his hawk-like eyes and erect stature. He hadn't always been the mess sergeant. He was older than most of us and admitted to being over 40. He had some gray sprinkled through his hair. He hadn't been in camp long before he began complaining about the food and the way it was served.

All of us, "Pop" included, were axemen who daily rode out in open stake trucks to various locations in the mixed pine and oak forest to do timber stand improvement, called (TSI) on the charts in the Forest Service Office. We took out diseased trees, thinned out too thick stands, (mostly pines), and cut large, dead, dry snags. Where a tree had been cut down for use as a railroad tie (usually only one from a tree) a large top was always left, maybe twenty feet high. We would have to cut it down to a level of no more than 18" high. We had to scatter the brush out because, being dry, it would burn a long time if it caught fire. Being cut down to the 18" level, it would rot and become part of the forest floor.

Timber thieves often would take ties illegally and they were very clever at it. Illegal or not, an experienced man could get a tie out of a tree in a few minutes. Down in the forest country they were called "tie-hackers." They would saw the tree down, measure the eight feet, and saw the other end of the tree off. Then, using a broadaxe, they would hack the log in four or five or six places pretty deep and then proceed to one end or the other, prying off the whole notched section in one deft, twisting movement. Then, turning the load a quarter turn, do it again, prying off the notched section in one twisting movement and so on until the log was square. He finished with a good four-sided tie which was acceptable to the railroads and the mines in the area. These tie-hackers became famous for their craft and it was quite a sight to see after the tie was gone. The hacked pieces were laying in place where the log had been, almost like a nest.

It was a work of art and skill.

In the woods, at noon our lunch was brought out to us and while we ate, we'd sharpen our axes. "Pop" always had a stone that he loaned around. He said dull axes could cause more accidents than sharp ones. Many times in the morning after riding ten to twenty miles to our work site in open stake trucks, we would practically fall off half frozen in the December weather. We would swing our axes like crazy to get our circulation back. After warming up, you could coast all day. It was enjoyable work and no one complained. At lunch our food would get cold in our mess kits before we could get it eaten, so we wolfed it down.

We usually quit in the woods about 4 o'clock, depending how far we were from camp. We washed up and rested until chow time. During these times "Pop's" conversation was quite stimulating and downright provocative. His pet peeve was that people, that is the average person, shouldn't have cars; that they were luxury and most people should use streetcars. He complained that everyone was saddling themselves with debts, paying for cars they really didn't need. He could prove a lot of his points, too. We were most of us in our 20's and he being over 40, had a worldly knowledge that had us in awe.

Our meals in the mess hall were so-so to sometimes bad and every once in a while we'd see "Pop" Emerson go up to the mess sergeant with a bowl or a platter in his hand. He'd complain and say that these men in the mess hall deserved better after working hard all day in the woods.

Finally, one day, "Pop" met us at the door as we went into supper. He had been made the new Mess Sergeant! Things changed right away. I can still see him, standing erect with his hawk-eyes taking in everything, daring anyone to complain about his food!

As I lay in my bunk thinking about Christmas dinner, the fire bell rang and rang and rang. The whole camp was ordered out to fight a wood's fire. Three or four trucks loaded up with about twenty-five men each and took off.

It seemed that "PeeWee," our lookout tower man, hadn't gone up to look around at his usual time that morning, thinking because of the snow there was no danger of fires. Now as he looked to the northwest he saw a huge black hole in the timber, burning furiously. The winds had really whipped up some 400 acres into flames.

We sat on wooden boards that rested on the stakes of the truck and rode facing rear, away from the cold. There was a large box up behind the cab that carried all our tools.

As we got near the fire we could see that it was mostly a leaf-ground fire and our fire-rakes could take care of it. But it still wasn't easy, for the wind was still strong and you had to be careful. Besides that, the forest floor was stony and rough, with lots of 18" to 24" high wild huckleberry bushes.

The Forest Service fire rake was a peculiar looking tool. It was not like a garden rake at all. It had triangular teeth that had very sharp edges that chopped and raked at the same time. That cut the bushes fine but the rocks were tough to work around.

We worked for hours and finally about dark we had the fire licked. As we rode back to camp, there wasn't much conversation except as to why "PeeWee" hadn't gone up to his place in the tower at the regular time. There was poor supervision somewhere.

As we pulled into camp, we saw "Pop" Emerson waving. He

shouted, "Come on boys, we saved your Christmas dinner till now!" Everything! We couldn't believe it! And it was good.

Later we found the cause of the fire. Some coon hunters had treed a raccoon in a large, dead, white oak and being unable to get him down, set fire to the tree. He was either holed up or had moved to another tree. So they sat around drinking and celebrating. We found the whiskey bottles lying around the area. After a while they got tired and cold and left. The tree was still burning and caught the woods on fire.

That was an unforgettable Christmas.

May 22, 1991

Fried Chicken

Back in 1935, while doing Forest Service work in the CCC (Civilian Conservation Corps). I worked on a forest fire lookout tower in Missouri. There was a crew of us, four in number, that took turns up in the tower during the day, watching for any smoke that might show the start of a fire in the forest. Besides our time in the tower, we cooked meals, kept our cabin straight and did various things to keep the area neat around the tower, like cutting weeds and grass, raking leaves, removing unsightly trees and brush, etc.

Gradually we made an acquaintance with the local people, most of whom lived down off of our tower site in the valleys maybe a mile or so away.

Our tower, called Julian Tower, was very close to a country wagon-truck trail where a few local people came by - maybe once a day or several times a week. These people went to Piedmont for various supplies, fuel, food, etc. Some of them were very friendly and visited our cabin, sometimes eating cookies or having a cup of coffee.

The Grahams, who lived southeast in the valley, were good neighbors. Oscar, a man about my age - 24 perhaps, his father, Oscar's sister Lossie, Oscar's wife Polly, and a baby made up a total of five Grahams.

Oscar worked hard, cultivating a small plot of ground, planting all sorts of staple vegetables such as potatoes, beans, berries, peanuts, corn, etc. none of which he sold. He and his wife canned and stored all they raised.

Oscar cut timber, mostly pine trees that had grown to a size that would make at least a 4"x4" piece of lumber. This was pretty small but most of this country had been cut over back in the 1920's and wasn't really recovering until the Forest Service and the CCC moved in.

Periodically the Forest Service would offer tracts of pine and oak to be cut. People like Oscar would offer so much to cut out the surplus trees. He had to be a pretty sharp estimator, for he had to sell his logs to a local saw mill where they would be cut into lumber.

Oscar would come by the tower occasionally with a load of logs, mostly pine, and if we needed something from town, he would pick it up. Sometimes we would ride in the cab with him or if his father or wife already occupied the cab, we would ride on the logs. It was a nice feeling. Sometimes we needed film or kerosene or a radio tube or even a hair cut so we really appreciated his coming by.

The road sometimes was muddy and soft, with ruts full of water. Several times Oscar's truck would get stuck but he always carried an extra log chain about twenty feet long that he would fasten to a tree a short distance in front of the truck when this happened. Next he would fasten the chain to the rear driving wheel of the truck and put the truck into gear and the chain would wind around the axle and pull the truck slowly out of the mud. I helped to do this operation several times with Oscar. It was always a great experience.

One evening Oscar came by going home and asked me to come down to visit after we had eaten our supper. Since our tower duties and hours during the non-fire season were only 7am to 7pm, I felt that my responsibilities were nil. Besides, there were three other men to call in to the ranger at Williamsville every hour. We did that every hour, even during the off-fire season, which was when all the trees, etc. were in full leaf.

293

After supper, I walked down the trail to Oscar's house. Most of the trail or road was natural hard packed gravel that led thru the pines and oaks most of the way. On all sides were patches of Korean Lespedeza, a yellow clover whose seeds had been planted by the Forest Service from the air by low flying aircraft. The seeds really took off in the Ozark woods, adding nutrition to the soil because of the nodules of nitrogen that grew on the roots of the plants. The plants are hardy, grew fast and stopped erosion, besides being good food for the animal life. I can't say enough about the benefits of Korean Lespedeza.

When I got to Oscar's, it was not quite dark but they met me and showed me around the outside. Oscar and his father, whom I always called Mr. Graham, had built a log cabin a few years before our tower was built and it was quite finished and settled in. It had a kitchen, small living room, and two bedrooms.

We sat in one corner of the living room and played cards and after a while Oscar roasted some of the peanuts he had raised and we ate them. About ten o'clock, I felt I should get back to my bunk at the tower, but Oscar and his wife, Polly, insisted I stay all night. They had the extra bedroom, so I stayed.

I undressed by kerosene light and soon I was asleep in the soft, comfortable bed.

Next morning, I woke and looked around at my room. I reached over from the bed and felt the wall had been plastered over the logs fairly smooth, but you could still feel the shape of the logs slightly. What was so delightful to me was how these industrious people had papered the wall. They had used only the heavily printed pages of magazines like the *Saturday Evening Post* and *Colliers.* They hadn't used any heavy advertising copy pages. It was all done so neatly and evenly. I'll never forget that room.

Oscar showed me where to wash up, and while his wife prepared breakfast, he took me outside. He showed me his bee hives, which were made from hollow gum logs. I think there were three or four of them standing upright and as I stood looking at them, he got his equipment ready to get some honey. First he got a small bellows and a used worn out piece of cloth. He lit the cloth and after it was burning pretty well, he put it out. The scorched material made a lot of smoke which he pumped with the bellows into the bottom of the hollow log. This put the bees out of commission temporarily so that Oscar could scoop out a small bowl of honey, beeswax and all.

He went back into the house where all kinds of good smells were coming from the kitchen. Polly was frying chicken, making milk gravy, and had a lot of biscuits baking in the oven.

Imagine fried chicken for breakfast. We soon grouped around the table to a wonderful feast, complete with honey just drawn from the hive. Eating the honeycomb wax which hadn't been taken out was a new experience and it was delightful. You can see it wasn't a breakfast I'd soon forget.

May, 1991

Fleas

The more stories I write convince me that I've had a lot of interesting experiences. At least they are to me and I want to tell them to someone. Writing them seems to be more satisfying than telling them.

During the depression years I was fortunate to join the Civilian Conservation Corps. After a year of doing all kinds of outdoor work such as building low-water bridges, road work, thinning timber, painting signs, etc., I volunteered to do lookout tower duty after helping to build our company's first lookout tower. It was called Flatwoods Tower and located on a hill near Wappapello, Mo., where of course, in 1935, the dam hadn't been built.

I was an assistant leader and had 3 men assigned to me. We moved out from camp in January and lived in an 8-man pyramid tent. We did regular 2 hour shifts up in the tower, watching for fires. Sometimes in the dry season we'd be up all night.

After about 5 months the Forest Service supervisor moved me up to another tower near Piedmont, Mo. He said the boys were floundering around and couldn't get organized: Cooking their food, getting their work done, etc.

The first thing I did was to go to town and buy a coffee pot. Imagine! They were making their coffee in a No. 10 tin can set on rocks! Next, I built a stove by piling large rocks on top of each other, forming 4 walls and cementing them with clay to a height of about 2 feet. Somewhere I found a piece of sheet metal to use as a top and that made cooking a lot easier.

We cut down pine trees and peeled them. Then we built walls

four logs high to put the tent on. That gave us a lot more head room and ventilation. We built shelving for our food such as dry beans, dry spaghetti, and dry cereal, out of small logs. It was rough living but we managed.

As usual, we took our 2 hour shifts in the tower, watching for smoke. I learned to tell the different kinds and colors of smoke, whether it was train smoke, oil smoke, grass smoke, or timber burning. We could always tell where a train went through the tiny town of Taskee, about 10 miles north of us, for it gave off black smoke.

Every Saturday in Piedmont, Sweazey's Saw Mill would burn up its surplus wood slabs, that couldn't be used for building purposes. It was a kind of blue smoke. Grass smoke was yellow. If we saw serious burning, we'd call our camp and they would send out crews to put out the fire. Once I sent a crew to put out a fire that we had pinpointed in the middle of the Black River towards Poplar Bluff. It turned out to be moonshiners cooking up a batch right at evening time, when they thought the revenue agents weren't watching.

Another time I called camp so many times that on the last call I made the dispatcher said, "York, everybody is out so don't call in any more fires - all we have left are cooks and we have to keep them in to feed the boys on the line."

Our tower, which was about 6 miles from Piedmont, had been built on old logging roads and gradually we became acquainted with the local people who lived back in the valleys.

One man that I shall never forget was Oscar Graham. A lean, honest, openfaced woods man who lived down the hill from where our tower was perched. He lived in a log cabin with his wife and new baby.

297

He had a very tiny garden and had his own chickens and bee hives. He raised vegetables and even peanuts. He often came to visit us on Sundays when the country people would come for miles around to visit this strange thing called a lookout tower. They would sign our register and climb the 100 steps up to the top to view "their" countryside. And it wasn't always the local people who signed our register, we had a couple sign in from Hong Kong China (real climbers, too).

Oscar would come by the tower maybe twice a week in his truck which was pretty battered and worn. It had no body on the back, but he sometimes fastened a 2 wheel extension to the rear that he piled logs on to take to the saw mill in Piedmont.

He would always stop and ask if he could get something from town for us. And he often did, like Kerosene for our lamps (we had no electricity), Kodak film (I have always taken pictures of my adventures all my life), various kitchen utensils and even radio tubes. We had a small AC-DC battery radio that someone had given me back home in St. Louis when I had a 2 day leave. Believe me, that was a luxury! And sometimes Oscar would take us to town to get haircuts.

Oscar occasionally got contracts to cut pine from the Forest Service tracts in our area. Lots of times he hauled the logs past the tower to Piedmont. I would ride the logs only if he had his wife and baby in the cab.

I noticed one day while in the saw mill yard that a lot of slabs cut from the outside of the logs were pitched to the slab pile for burning. Quite a few had nice square sides. I thought that with a little ingenuity I could build a cabin to house our crew instead of sleeping in a tent.

Oscar agreed to haul all the slabs we needed at no cost because he was coming back empty anyway. So I proposed the plan to our camp superintendent to build a 3 room house with the slabs. He agreed and sent out a good local man, a carpenter, who supervised the job.

In about 2 weeks we had it built with even a tar-paper roof. We had lots of slabs to work with so I designed bunk beds for the four of us, built living room furniture and tables for the kitchen and living room, kitchen shelving, and even a front and back porch. Everything built out of discarded slabs.

I got a Rumford cook book from my folks at home and we started cooking exotic foods like tomatoes and dumplings, ginger bread cookies, and doughnuts. But it wasn't easy, all our rations came from camp every 10 days and a lot of it came in No. 10 cans. That's a big can and even 4 husky eaters couldn't eat a can of corn or sweet potatoes at one meal. We had a lot of food left over but camp sent out to us a double walled (filled with saw dust for insulation) box about 3x3x3 feet that we buried in the ground and with a 100 lb. chunk of ice our food kept very well.

We each took a turn cooking for every meal in a day and the cook also didn't have to do tower duty. He had his hands full preparing meals and starting fires and cleaning up.

Our No. 10 cans of peaches and black berries caused us a little trouble, but that trouble was soon solved, for Oscar had a sister named Lossie who made us a couple of peach or berry pies and she got to keep the rest. It was a great day when Oscar would show up with pies in his truck. We even got a watermelon in town and stored it in our new ice box.

Forest Service personnel eventually came by, checking our work and I gave them homemade cookies, cool drinks, and other delicacies as they sat in our living room in our lawn-type slab chairs. Word gradually got out that Piedmont Tower was the place to visit.

We were even adopted by a big old coon dog, whom we fed table scraps. He slept under our cabin on hot days and nights. And there was where the trouble started.

As our cabin slabs that were green when we installed them began to shrink on the sides and floors, 1/4" cracks began to appear. Later in October on some of the colder nights we could feel the breezes whistling thru the cracks. But at present we didn't mind the ventilation, it was summer time!

I noticed a couple of the other boys scratching one day and I had started too. We began to feel pretty miserable and Hank, one of the country boys on the crew said, "I think we've got fleas in this cabin and I'll bet they're off that dog who sleeps under our cabin. See how big the cracks are in the floor." We put up with it a few days more and then one day when I was on duty in the tower, I could feel a persistent biting so bad that I took off every bit of my clothes, hoping I'd find that flea. But I didn't, and as I found out later, it is impossible, for they hop and jump constantly, as much as 2 feet in the air or more. You literally never see them. You just know you got 'em.

I mentioned it to Oscar, our friend from the valley. He laughed and said, "Oh, that's easy - go out in the woods and pick some walnut leaves - get plenty and put them under your sheets and on your floor and the fleas will leave!"

With some misgivings, I did what he said and in one night

300

they were gone! Another farmer's remedy that worked. Since then I always listen to old remedies like that. It helped get rid of the dog, too. I don't know what happened to him.

A few months after this episode, I was put in charge of 4 towers, driving my own Forest Service pickup truck going from tower to tower, keeping the towermen supplied with food, water, and whatever else they needed.

That job only lasted a month, for all the camps in Southern Missouri were moved to California and Oregon - that's another story.

Finally, the reason I wrote this was because a few weeks ago, my daughter complained that their cat, who lives outdoors and explores outdoors too, had brought fleas into the house. She had the exterminator come in and give the place a good fumigating , but it wasn't entirely successful!

So, I told her my flea experience and to be sure she took it seriously, I went out to my own back yard and picked a big box of walnut leaves and mailed it to her - along with 2 walnuts. Will she be surprised when she opens it. I'm waiting for a response. ✖